Praise for

HURT

"Joe (…), your story is like no other (…); this book is unique, compelling, beautiful, happy, and sad. (…) The story never left me."
—Susan Konig, *Author, Executive Editor, Willow Street Press - New York, USA.*

"What a book you have written! What a privilege it is to work on it! Thank you. I'm really impressed by *HURT*. It's a poignant, (…) heartbreaking, intelligent, and profound memoir (…).
—Alice Peck, *Editor, Alice Peck Editorial - New York, USA.*

"(…) So compelling! … Some people are never able to overcome what you've been through! This is one of those books that you just won't be able to put down. (…) It keeps better and better. I just can't figure out what is going to happen next (…). The hardest part for me is to have to stop reading it."
—J. Ecargsid, *Independent Reviewer*

"I stayed up late last night because I could not put it down (…). WOW!!! What a great read! Seeing you before, I could never think of you as a writer; but knowing you now, I cannot imagine you not being a writer. Very impressive (…)."
—Bree Hangloose, *Reviewer*

HURT

Fears, Tears, and My Crusade Against Destiny

*memoirs of a boy shackled, shattered,
and reaching up to life, love, and forgiveness*

Joe Fotso

Shackled, Shattered, and Reaching up to Life, Love, and Forgiveness

NeverDown
PUBLISHING

Libertyville IL, USA

HURT

Fears, Tears, and My Crusade Against Destiny

Library of Congress, United States Copyright Registration #:
TXu 1-611-646

ISBN 978-0-9889114-9-9 (Paperback)
ISBN 978-0-9889114-0-6 (Hardcover)
ISBN 978-0-9889114-8-2 (eBook)

Cover Design & Interior Layout by Book-Covers-That-Sell.com

www.joefotso.com

NeverDown
PUBLISHING
Libertyville IL, USA

Dedication

To the Tens of Millions of Abused Children Worldwide

My heartbreaking experiences pale in comparison to the gruesome misfortunes some of you endure each day. May *HURT* add my shallow voice to your loud and untold fears and tears, for us—Humanity—to listen, hear, and lend a hand.

To my Adorable Children, Milly and Chris

I wouldn't be whole without the both of you and the ever-flowing stream of joy and love you infuse into our home. Over the years, I chose to share only age-appropriate episodes of my odyssey. You will now meet the vulnerable little boy I used to be, and get to know me—all of me—the *strong* man I have become. Each of my profuse tears was a building block to the man and father I now am. Likewise, each good or bad day of your journey is a cornerstone of the great man and woman you aspire to be and will be. As you plaster each stone of your existence, **1)** be without fear; **2)** always ask yourself, "Others, Why Not Us?!", and **3)** never forget that "forever" is my unconditional word for "loving" (you).

To Angel

To say the very least, THANK YOU!

Acknowledgments

Dr. Esaïe D. Tamboue

I would like to express my sincere gratitude to you for helping me escape social injustice, political turmoil, professional uncertainty, and financial cul-de-sac in Cameroon, into *the Land of the Free* and of opportunity. My life would have taken a different course— probably not for better—had it not been for the hand you lent. I am forever grateful.

Bree Hangloose

The best of my words and myself owes it in part to your closeness and encouragement. With my voice now being heard, it's obvious that "never" is truly my word for "quitting." Thank you!

For Their Support and Encouragement

I am deeply indebted to many more people who have positively impacted my life through the years in many ways.

- ANDRÉ MARIE TALA (Legendary Cameroonian singer, and mentor - Paris, France)
- ARMAND AND JANICE PAGANELLI, AND FAMILY (Family friends - New York, USA)
- JACQUELINE DURHAM, GWEN DAVENPORT, AND SHARON HILTON (Family friends – Chicago area, USA)
- SUSAN KONIG (Author, Executive Editor at Willow Street Press - New York, USA)
- DR. SCOTT SMITH, MRS. KATHY SMITH, AND FAMILY (Former supervisor, Family friends, Kansas State University, USA)
- RICHARD PITTS (Friend, Wonder Workshop Children's Museum - Manhattan, KS, USA)

For everything you have done for me and a lot more, thank you!

HURT 's Readers

Please accept these words as my modest token of appreciation to you for not turning your back to the famished, teary little boy I was decades ago, and the evolving man I have become. I am profoundly honored and humbled that you have decided to stop and listen to him through *HURT*. Because you care, you have made or will make a difference in many lives, now including mine. We, Humanity, need each of the providential step tools you embody, to help all of us in our unsettled ascension toward compassion, care, and love.

The United States of America

In addition to wiping out most of my fears and tears, you restored my dignity. I am truly blessed to be sheltered by you, *the Home of the Brave*. Looking up to the glory of your banner's stripes and stars, I pledge—with my right-hand palm on my beholden heart—to always make you proud, from the dawn's early light of my children's existence till my twilight's last gleaming ray.

Contents

The Road Chosen

On this cold January day, as I carry my burgundy canvas bag through the crowded Air France jet that is about to take me back to Africa, I know it is too late to change my mind. I hustle down the aisle to avoid contact with the other passengers, certain that my exhaustion is apparent, given my sweaty forehead and red eyes. I have spent many sleepless nights trying to comprehend and fully embrace the surreal event that is about to redefine my life.

After squeezing my carry-on bag into the overhead bin, I claim my assigned seat. Though disturbed by a restless toddler kicking the back of my seat, I start catching my breath as the flight attendants busily prepare for takeoff. I distract myself by admiring the various airplanes circling the JFK International Airport, but I know I won't be able to hide in daydreams for long. This plane is taking me back to an inescapable reality.

As eager as I am to see my family, I become hesitant and extremely nervous when I think about the main reason for my visit: I am an over forty-year-old man on my way to wed a total stranger. In embarrassment and dissatisfaction with my shameful status—single at my age—my elderly mother has chosen a bride for me. In Cameroon in general, and within my tribe, the Bamiléké, especially, a mature man must be married! It is a matter of pride, and Mom does not want my family to be made fun of any longer.

I was married before, but my union with the woman I thought I knew well quickly turned into a nightmare. I discovered that my new wife was a psychopath ready to plant a knife into my heart, judging by her unpredictable and explosive temper, the constant fury in her red, highly vascularized eyes, and the violence of her actions. On this day, I am launching myself into the unknown once more, and there is no guarantee this time will be different.

Months ago, while I was still indecisive about the arranged marriage, I phoned my mother in search of some reassurance.

"I will die happy if you marry her. She can cook everything you like, and very well." She argued.

"What else, Mom?"

"Stop asking so many questions! What is the date of your arrival?"

"I'll be there in a few months. Soon I will tell you exactly when."

My commitment to travel back to my birthplace is a commitment to marry a girl based only on the information that she can cook everything I like, and very well. However, because I believe in true love, I am conflicted. I have often fantasized about meeting the beautiful girl of my dreams. I would get to know all of her qualities, both her perfections and imperfections, go on dates with her, fall completely in love, and eventually marry her. Never in my wildest dreams have I ever imagined walking my ancestors' traditional path, straight to a prearranged marriage.

Over the years, I have tried very hard to find love. But as patient as I have been, romantic love has been uncertain, erosive and evasive, flying away like a wild bird whenever I approached. So what am I losing by marrying my mom's dream girl? Probably nothing. At least it will be my way of having a convenient companion, an adult to talk to, and a woman to satisfy my manly needs.

After a layover in Paris, I board a direct flight to Cameroon. Each minute that passes is accompanied by fear, confusion, and apprehension. On the one hand, I feel as though I am living the life of a stranger by embracing a custom that seems so archaic and out of place to me. But on the other hand, it seems like I am slipping into an old skin of mine, revisiting my roots. My confident, successful self, who lives in the Western world, is wrestling with my much younger self, the one who was lucky to survive his childhood in Africa. The commitment I made to my mother has ignited a conflict between the culture that has been hibernating inside of me, and the values I have acquired in the United States—a ferocious battle between my dormant essence and my true existence. But I am tired of living by myself; I am traveling to find a solution to my loneliness, since I have yet to find love on my own. *Perhaps this is my destiny, as chosen by my ancestors,* I wonder as I doze off.

I jolt awake when the plane rumbles, landing on the rough, modest runway of the Nsimalen International Airport; in a few weeks, when I lift off from this soil, I will be a husband.

I drag my bags through the raucous, happy crowd, looking for my friend and my sister. After a short while, I hear, "Welcome, Joe!"

"Oh, there you are!" I exclaim, happy and relieved to see Louis and Irene emerge from the crowd.

They are excited for me, and I try to share their enthusiasm.

After spending a few days in Yaoundé, the captial city, adjusting to the new time zone and climate, I depart for my family's village, Bandjoun. Because it's early in the morning, buses are less crowded. But the unbearable heat, unrelenting smoke, and nauseating smell of burning rubber grow overwhelming. A this moment, I can't help but dream about the rusty, white 1994 Mitsubishi Galant I drive in the United States; as shabby as it is, it seems brand-new compared to my current ride.

After six excruciating hours, we finally arrive in Bandjoun, the land of my ancestors. The time to meet my fiancée is approaching. My emotions are high and mixed, but I hide them well as I know that all eyes are on me. I have arrived from the United States of America, and nobody ignores my status. After being welcomed at the main road by brothers, sisters, and cousins, I jovially greet everyone else I meet—neighbors, friends, and strangers—as I walk the mile up the dusty and hilly road that leads to my family home.

It seems incredibly tiny compared to what I'm used to in America. The effect of the smoke seeping from my mom's house over the years is evident on the walls and around the only door to the kitchen—some of the bricks' edges have turned from bright red to a shiny black.

As I arrive, I can tell that my mom has been waiting for me. It has been only a little over a year since I last saw her, but a year is a very long time for a ninety-year-old. Nervously stepping into her house, I hear Mom start praising God loudly, in gratitude that He has kept me safe as I journeyed back to the land of my roots.

"Welcome, son," she finally says, after completing her praises.

"Thank you, Mom. How are you?"

"Just okay… You must be very hungry."

"Not really, just exhausted."

"That means that you are hungry. Here, start with this before I call your wife over."

She emphasizes the words as if to remind me that I am not here for a holiday. As much as I want to tell my mom that the girl is not my wife, at least not yet, the fact that she is the main reason I have traveled all this way keeps my mouth shut.

The gray smoke from the blazing fire is so thick I can taste it. My mom gives me a bowl of well-seasoned plantains and pork, which, surprisingly, I don't feel like eating.

Despite my doubts, I feel certain that my ancestors are guiding me. Decades ago, a man in the Bamiléké tribe wouldn't have thought twice before marrying a woman who could cook everything, and very well. I am doing all I can to hide my reluctance from my mom. She would be heartbroken if she knew how strong my doubts really were about allowing her dream girl into my family.

After watching me force down a few bites of the plantains, Mom sends my sister Irene to get the girl. We then spend about thirty minutes not saying much to one another but certainly thinking a lot about the same thing; then she announces, "I know you will like her… The wedding is this Saturday." Shocked by this declaration, I say nothing.

Although the girl and I are complete strangers, it is only a matter of time before we alter the course of our lives by uttering two tiny words—I do—for a lifelong commitment.

My sister arrives, followed by the shadow of a girl, whom I cannot see clearly from my position. I decide to stand for a better view of my soon-to-be wife.

"Come on in, please," I say politely.

Without a word, our guest comes forward, visibly unsure of what to do. I can tell she has worn her best clothes for the event: a denim skirt, a red-and-white T-shirt, and a pair of black open-toed sandals. She has smoothed her hair with some kind of styling gel, which is above the norm here. Taking another furtive look at her, I realize that her eyebrows are full, almost meeting between her eyes. As resolute as I am to accept my fiancée with all her qualities and flaws, I know that this unattractive uni-brow will be the first feature I will change.

After an awkward moment, we finally shake hands. I invite her to have a seat next to me on the half-century-old bamboo bed that serves as a chair in my mom's kitchen. I am hesitant to look this girl in the eye, afraid of my reaction. Aware that Mom is scrutinizing my body language and demeanor, I look in her direction, and she smiles. Knowing my mother, I am certain this is her way of asking me, "What do you think about this wonderful girl I have brought you? She is wonderful, isn't she?"

Deciding to break the ice, I start a conversation. "How are you?" I ask.

"I am doing well," she replies, with a hint of a smile.

The voice that has delivered such a concise answer is a little deeper than I have imagined it to be. To get it over with, I tilt my head up and look straight at her, ignoring the sudden silence in the smoky room. She lifts her head and looks back at me. As our eyes finally meet, I understand that she will never be the girl I had hoped for—my love at first sight. My heartbeat has slowed, and I feel overwhelmed, as if I'm sinking. *What have I done?*

I also realize how young this girl really is—only in her late teens.

How can I go through with this? Neither my mom, nor my sister, nor my fiancée can possibly imagine the turmoil of my thoughts.

"What's your name?" I ask with some discomfort, as Irene has already told me her name.

"Gina," she replies nervously.

Never in my life have I had such a hard time making conversation.

"Would you like some food?" I offer.

After another glimpse of a smile, she gives another concise answer. "Yes."

Her smile is really bright, but not enough to affect me. As she starts eating the rest of my plantains, my mom and sister glance at one another; although they don't say a word, I know they are pleased with the progression of the planned events. I am digging deep within my heart to find the motivation to pursue Gina, something deeper than the cooking and the convenience of a companionship.

Fortunately, the visit does not last long. Gina announces her departure. As she stands to leave, my mom asks me to lead her outside. A little embarrassed, I step outside the kitchen and proceed to walk with her toward the upper east corner of our yard.

"I have been waiting for you," Gina declares.

"Really?" I ask, a little flattered, almost disgusted, and surely surprised at the same time.

"Yes. I am very excited about being your wife."

"Why? You don't even know me."

"I don't have to know you. I have always prayed to God for a good man. I think you are one, and I love you."

Did she really fall in love at first sight or is she like so many others in Cameroon who would kiss the devil for a visa to the United States?

After reaching the edge of our property, I declare, "Okay. I must return now. I don't want to go too far from the house."

"I understand," she says, in a disappointing voice.

"I really need some rest… Have a good night."

As I walk into the house, I dodge the conversation I know my mom and my sister are dying to have. I grab my PDA and try to escape to the tiny guest room, but Mom is quick to call me back.

"You can't go yet. You haven't told us anything. What do you think about her?"

"She seems to be a really nice girl. But surely she is too young for me," I reply, still conflicted.

"That is a very good thing, believe me," my mom interjects; "do you know how young I was when I married your father? Over forty years younger! Son, it just means you will mold her to obey you, to do everything you want her to do. I don't want you to wander around alone in life. I want you to have someone, like Gina, who will take good care of you. Trust me, she will."

My mom has never appeared more sincere. So I decide to trust her and take what is being offered to me. Surely they would not insist if this girl was not wonderful. Why not try?

Before heading to my room, I whisper to my mom, "She is wonderful; thank you."

Later, as I fall asleep, I know my decision is controversial; it is one with which most people would never agree. Despite my apprehension, I will certainly marry a girl I don't love. Will I be able to slide the ring onto her finger as we each vow to forever belong to one another? Will I take her hands into mine and promise to stand by her in sickness and in health? Will I put my lips over hers and *kiss the bride* in front of all of Bandjoun? Will I be able to carry on with this arranged marriage and ultimately be sexually intimate with this girl who is almost as young as my own daughter? And what does Gina know of me? All she has heard has been told through the filter of my mother, who probably shared only the shiniest parts of my journey. If Gina were to learn of my life story—of all that I endured and did before I met her—would she still think that I am a good man sent by God?

Chapter 1

Why At All?

(1970s)

As I approached our rundown mud house in Yaoundé's Mvog-Ada valley, my heart beat fast and hard. As always, I tried not to let my eyes release their tears. I hated it when they dried on my cheeks, leaving tiny white lines that revealed my emotions. With no strength to look up, I walked head down, unable to face my friends and neighbors. I knew they were staring at me, but I did not want them to read the fear and sorrow in my eyes. It would hurt more than what I was about to endure.

I must have been eight, nine, or ten—I did not know my real age and only guessed it by comparing my height, strength, and grade to that of my friends. The day had started as usual. I had slept relatively well and continued to rest in my little room as I did not want to hear knocks on my dilapidated door. They always felt like lashes of a whip to my soul. I never liked who or what was on the other side of that door waiting for me: most often one of my parents holding a torture tool and ready to lash out, ready to squash my frail body and hear my screams until I had no energy left to continue. But soon enough the smack of approaching flip-flops hustled me out of my bed.

"What are you still doing in there?"

"Nothing," I shouted.

I stumbled into the living room and found the Sunday load of bananas waiting for me. As I grew older and stronger, it grew bigger and heavier.

For a fraction of a second, I stood silent. I then put a little cushion on my head, and with my mom's help, set the load of bananas on top. They were big, healthy, and bright yellow. I opened the front door and proceeded to head out. It was time for work, time for me to bring money home and most of all, time for me to be free for a while. I would be free from feeling hated, free from being hurt by my parents, free to smile, far from my mother's terrifying eyes. Selling bananas was my door to freedom; so as always, I did not mind at all. I was free for the time.

The day was sunny, hot, and horrifically smelly. As I crossed the small makeshift bridge battling flies buzzing around me, I tried not to look down at the sordid stream of human sewage on beneath.

The Bridge

As I rounded the corner and passed my sweaty friends playing soccer in the tiny courtyard, my big toe began to throb, reminding me of how I had hurt it a week earlier, running away from bullies. Speed was my best defense, but I needed shoes.

I was limping and still about five miles away from Bastos—the wealthiest quarter of Yaoundé—but it was worth the pain. In that part of town, I had loyal and more generous customers, from Europe for the most part, who would buy a banana for the price of two. I never knew whether they purchased my bananas because they wanted to help a miserable-looking little kid or because they liked my merchandise. Who cared? Either way, it worked for me. I would ring the bell when I got there, and they would come out of their fancy houses with their children sometimes.

So I started my barefooted journey as usual, focusing on my final destination, and hoping to make some sale on the way.

I had forged a secret friendship with one lady and her son. They were everything I wanted to be, and had everything I wanted to have. Seeing them gave me a taste of hope. I would picture myself dressed in the nice clean clothes they wore, smiling, and playing just as they did. They were the only people who called me by my first name, Joseph. It was a big deal in the Bamiléké culture to call a child by his or her first name. Doing so meant the child was appreciated and loved. It was like giving that child a hug or a kiss. I never heard my first name until I got to *my friends'* home.

I was very excited as I arrived at their gate. The smile on my face hid my exhaustion and hunger. That home was my dreamland. I breathed the rosy smell of the pink and red flowers they grew inside the tall white fence and around the porch. This aroma, spread by the soft breeze, was in complete contrast to the stench I had left under the bridge in my neighborhood.

I rang the door bell. Soon, I heard footsteps approaching. The lady opened the gate. Even though she was a white, European woman, she wore a traditional African dress and her long hair was tied up in a ponytail. One of her sons held her hand. Her smile instantly sprinkled some glitter onto my somber day and caused me to grin.

"Oh, Joseph! How are you?"

"I am well, madam."

"Are you tired?"

"No, I am not, madam."

I looked her in the eyes for the first time and was amazed. Her eyes were green, not the usual brown or black color of all the eyes I'd seen. The color was so captivating that I couldn't stop staring. I might have noticed them weeks or months before, had I had enough confidence to look up. This woman was radiant, with an unforgettable expression of warmth on her face, an affectionate voice, a gracious walk, and a gentle touch. I had grown to trust her and was very slowly coming out of my shell.

Why couldn't I tell her that I was miserable, hungry, and exhausted? Looking into her eyes seemed to show me her thoughts. I could tell she was worried about me. But being only a stranger in her front yard, I was uncertain and nervous about how to handle my emotions. I expected her to buy some bananas and close her gate behind me as I left. Instead, she invited me into her house. It was strange but wonderful, unusual but idyllic.

Her son, Henry, stared openly at me with the same curious look I secretly gave him. In contrast to Henry, I felt like the poorest and unluckiest child on earth. I was nervous but eager to play with him, to let some of his good fortune rub off on me. Henry and I were about the same age and could be friends.

As his mom sorted through the bananas on the paved walkway of her front yard, Henry walked right up to me. I had never been this close to him. I gathered all of my courage and forced my eyes to meet his. He held a little silver car so close to my fingers that I was sure he wanted me to touch it. Ignoring my pounding heart, I reached out with my right hand and finally held it! Though Henry looked pleased, I was confused. What now? As if he understood me, he pushed a little button between the two front wheels and shouted, "Joseph, put it on the ground," excited.

As I bent down, Henry slipped his hand into the pocket of his khaki jacket and took out a little rectangular device, from which he pulled an antenna before handing to me. It then occurred to me that maybe he wanted me as a friend—too. But it seemed unbelievable, surreal. He was everything I wanted to be and had everything I wanted to have. He was clean, while I was filthy and had forded a stream of human waste to get there. He had a smiling mother who cared about him and I was the very last thing on my mom's mind. He owned toys, the likes of which I could only dream about. His life was certain and whole, and mine was a puzzle with many pieces missing. *How could he ever want me as a friend?*

Keeping my focus on the toy, I used my thumb to press a button on the rectangular device. To my surprise, the little car sped away! I felt my eyes grow wide with excitement. I was having a blast and was never going to stop playing with that car! I forgot about my throbbing toe and my hunger. Bananas? Who cared?!

Henry's mom called out, "Joseph, please come here." I wasn't sure what she wanted. Maybe she wanted me to leave; but why did I have to go back to my home? I wish I never had to.

"Yes, madam."

The sun was high in the sky, and the temperature had risen since my arrival. Wet with sweat, my thin, torn shorts stuck to my skin. As I walked toward the lady, her eyes took me in from head to toe. I concealed the pain from my toe and held my head up to show that I was just fine. I would lose my little boy's dignity if I let my true emotions out.

Though I did not want her to inquire about my injury, she asked, "What happened to your foot?"

I wanted to find an acceptable answer so I could get back to my car. I just wanted to play, play, play, and just be a little boy with Henry. The joy of pure play had overtaken my craving for care and affection.

I decided to concoct and tell a little story but surprisingly, my chapped lips wouldn't allow a single word out. Maybe something inside me had wanted her to ask that question after all. Maybe the answer was as important as driving the car. As I struggled to speak, the lady continued looking at me. At home, a long stare usually meant big trouble. But the compassion I saw in her eyes was something new. It conquered my tough-boy act, and my eyes welled up. Steamy tears ran down my cheeks. I wanted her to see the feelings floating in them, my years of fear and pain. I wanted her to see me drowning in this ocean, one hand slightly above the turbulent surface, ready to grasp anything—maybe her—to survive.

Without another word, she wrapped her hands around my wet and warm little body and hugged me hard, rubbing my head softly. Many long seconds went by, during which I could hear the rhythmic beating of her heart. I wished the moment would never end. I heard a reassurance of safety in her soft chest. Then she let go, kneeled, and we came face to face. Realizing she was crying cut me open. She put her lips to my sweaty forehead, gave me a reassuring kiss, and then left the yard and went into her house.

Henry and I got back to playing. This time, I drove the little car with less enthusiasm. Not that I didn't care about it, but I was very confused. *Why was the lady crying?* I couldn't find one reason other than that she felt empathy for the dirty, scrawny little boy wearing ripped and soiled clothes. I suddenly heard my name from Henry's mom, now sitting on the porch.

"Did you call me, madam?" I asked.

"Yes, Joseph. Would you please come here?"

"Yes, madam."

I walked cautiously to minimize the risk of further injuring my toe. The lady asked me to have a seat in front of her. She then opened a little white box and began removing some materials from it. She set a bucket full of water in front of me, moved closer, and took my foot in her hands. After a very close look at my injured toe, she said, "Please, wash it very well in here."

As I dunked my foot in the water, I started to shiver, not because it was cold, but because I was not used to cleaning any part of myself. Even worse, I was afraid. What was Henry's mom going to do to my toe? I wanted to yell, "Please do not touch it!" Instead, I anxiously said, "Madam, it does not hurt anymore."

She looked at me, certainly a little amused. Then she bent down to dry my foot with a white towel. I had never seen my toe so clean. It had emerged from thick layers of dried brown mud, dirt, and debris. She started clipping my overgrown toenail with a tiny pair of scissors. The pain was overwhelming and I was scared to death. I was squeezing my chair so hard that I thought I heard it crack. My usual reaction to extreme fear or pain was wetting my pants when I could not take it anymore. I felt the warm sensation trickling down. The fear and pain had, once again, gotten the best of me and forced me to pee, lavishing me with deep shame. How could I ever look Henry in the eye again?

After Henry's mom clipped deep under my blackened toenail, a sudden and steady flow of dark fluid stained the white cloth she held. As she applied gentle pressure to empty my toe of its poison, I held my breath to avoid inhaling the foul odors emanating from the wound. Fortunately, the good smell from the white box gradually predominated, as she cleansed my toe several times with alcohol. She wrapped my shrunken toe with a light brown bandage and I felt immediate relief. Enduring the pain had been immensely difficult, but worth it. Had I not urinated, I would have said I felt great.

The lady shook her head and gave me a reassuring smile. "Joseph, you should go now."

I knew that moment would come. It had been too long since I'd arrived and I still had to sell the rest of my bananas. I reluctantly said my good-byes and Henry's mom helped me load the tray of bananas back on my head. She had bought about a third of my load; so I was delighted for the good sale and the fun I had. It would take a painful walk throughout the city to get the remainder sold. As Henry opened the steel security gate, I heard his mother calling me again. I looked back and saw her waving. She wanted me to come back! In a fraction of a second, I stood in front of her, praying she would invite me to stay as long as I wanted. I saw her eyes focus on my toe. Her raspy voice revealed her concern as she said, "Your parents should take you to the hospital."

My eyes then followed her movements as she reached into the box she was holding. She pulled out a pair of brand-new sneakers, white with red stripes and laces! My heart raced and I wanted to snatch them out of her hands and kiss them. I tried them on and they felt marvelous. As I took a few test steps, I pictured myself looking like the other kids—with shoes! For once, my toes would not be exposed. For once, I would fit in and not be an outcast. I would play soccer uninhibited, without fear of injuries.

But she had just mentioned my parents. I did not want to think about them. Doing so always brought back memories of my fears and tears. This was *my* moment. Knowing that they would never let me keep these beautiful shoes, I began taking them off, trying hard to hide my sadness.

"No, Joseph, don't… they are yours. Keep them on."

"Thank you, madam. But I cannot keep them."

"Why?"

"I cannot, madam. I want to go now."

She certainly understood that it was useless to argue, and once again helped me transfer the bananas back to my head. As the gate closed behind me, I felt terrible for having turned her gift down; but I had no choice. I could not have brought those shoes home. My parents would have been furious. I thought about taking the shoes and hiding them somewhere between my home and my school. I could wear them on my way to school and hide them on my way home. But it would never work. My entire neighborhood would talk about me and my parents would surely get the news. That wasn't a price worth paying.

And yet, I didn't mind. I had been transformed. I had experienced compassion and something much stronger. I had received the very first hug of my life.

Chapter 2

With My Hands

As I walked through the city, I was confused; after experiencing such kindness from Henry's mother, I wondered how my parents could be so cruel to me.

I never remembered feeling like a normal kid. I had always been teased and shunned—for my Bamiléké origin, my banana business, and my filth. Being a Bamiléké—Bami—seemed to be a sin. "Bami!" was an insult I often heard ten to twenty times a day. Each time, I felt shame. We, the Bami kids, grew up feeling crushed by others. That everlasting discrimination forced many of us to adapt by rejecting our identity, and adopting that of other tribes, be they Douala, Béti, Bassa, or another. A stereotypical Bamiléké had a lower standard of living, a strong French accent, and was a pragmatic businessman, more concerned with money and ownership of land and houses than with education.

I was relieved after selling my remaining bananas. They were the last of my parents' current stock; so it would be at least three weeks until I would have to sell more. I could finally rest. In my exuberance as I walked home, I injured my foot again. I needed shoes. My parents wouldn't let me keep the white lady's fancy new shoes, but maybe if I found something humble.

As I sniffled and limped down the road, I spotted a dumpster, about a quarter of a mile from my home. Several skinny dogs circled it in search of a way to get in, one of them hairless on most of its body and covered with pimples. I brushed off my fear, relinquished what was left of my dignity, put my empty banana tray on the ground, and climbed in.

The heat smoldered. Fumes rose from the warm trash pile, as if from a long-dormant volcano only seconds away from eruption. The stench became unbearable with each elapsing second. Even *I* didn't stink that bad. I gagged several times but my empty stomach had nothing to release. Those odors must have originated from putrefied dogs, cats, or rats.

While I dug through the dumpster, I thought of the tender moments with Henry's mom and the nice shoes I had foolishly refused. The task of moving irrecoverable waste around was arduous and I was sweating heavily. I finally pulled up a cardboard box, which I opened. Inside, I found layers of old and filthy underwear, bras, and artificial hair. As I reached the bottom, I hit the jackpot

My Parents

and began to shake with excitement. In my lucky hands were flip-flops, one approximately size 7, and the other 10.5. Although they were old, crappy, and mismatched (left foot blue, right foot pink), they were destined to my feet! I prayed that my parents would let me keep them. With all the money I had been making selling their bananas and helping in their little shop, they could certainly afford to buy me a pair of shoes, some clothes, a soccer ball, or even a little action figure. They could afford to feed me every day, maybe more than once a day. There was no reason I should go to bed hungry.

I climbed out of the dumpster and put my sandals on. They felt okay, not exactly like the beautiful shoes I turned down a few hours earlier. I guessed they would not last very long because they appeared as if they'd already had several owners. But all I needed was one hour at a time, one day at a time.

As I crossed the wobbly bridge that led me home, I could tell by how our family dog, Jealousy, was shaking her tail that she was happy to see me. She seemed to be encouraging her offspring to share her joy. She had given birth to seven puppies about three months earlier. They were happy and healthy, and I loved playing with them; but I knew I should not get attached to those little, adorable creatures. It would not be long before I would be sent to the city to sell them.

The sound of my mother's voice filled me with terror. She probably had a friend visiting. I just hoped and prayed that she was in a good mood. I hesitated, and then walked up the three stairsteps and opened the door. My mother looked at me with her fierce eyes, so unlike Henry's mom, and returned to the conversation she was having with our neighbor. I was not sure whether she had noticed my flip-flops. I greeted her and wished she would stand up, give me a hug, and acknowledge my throbbing toe. But as expected, she totally ignored me and kept on talking. I put the empty banana tray on the table and handed over the money. While she was counting it, I went to my room and sat on my bed. I was exhausted—having walked over ten miles, carrying many pounds of bananas—and my day was not over.

I heard her walk toward her room, certainly to hide the money. When she returned to the living room she yelled, "Come here!"

I obeyed.

"What are you wearing?"

I looked down and back but I didn't dare voice my thoughts. I knew the tone of her voice too well. I watched as the rage built in her steely eyes, not understanding why she was angry. I had sold all her bananas and not one franc was missing. I was a good boy!

"Who did that?" She asked, looking at my bandaged toe with fury.

Before I had the time to say anything, she ordered, "Go choose one!"

This was routine. I had to choose between a thick electrical cord and a strip of rubber from an automobile tire. It was time to be beaten. It was time to scream and cry. I hated it when my friends and neighbors heard my pleas for mercy or saw my tears.

I was confused about which whip to pick. The electrical wire took its pain to my soul, but the tire piece reached a greater surface area. Choosing between the two was like picking sudden or slow death.

My mother told me to lie on the floor, and even though I dreaded it, I did not hesitate to obey. She yanked my shorts down and wet my butt with the bottle of water she had been drinking. I knew better than to move—that would only make things worse. Over the years, I had learned to absorb and tolerate the beating. I saw her lift the tire tread and closed my eyes. The same questions echoed in mind: *"Why? Why me? Why at all?"*

Each stroke erased the hope and dreams Henry's mother had seeded in me that morning. I knew then, without a doubt, that my mom hated me. Only hatred could dictate that kind of unjustified assault on a child. Only hatred could lift the hand that delivered that much abuse. The punishment was so harsh that I wet my pants and defecated.

As I lay still on the floor, smelly and trembling with pain, seizure-like spasms shook my bleeding body. I lost my voice. I lost my strength. I lost my desire to live. At that moment, I remembered Henry. What if I went back and told his mom everything? But what if my mom found out? I was a little boy, totally confused. I pulled together my scattered bits of courage and dignity, and stood up. I used my shirt to wipe my tear-stained face clean. I knew my neighborhood friends had heard everything, but I wanted them to see me smiling as if nothing had happened.

"Fotso! Come back and clean this!"

My mom had just ordered me to clean up my mess on the floor.

After a moment of hesitation I stammered, "Mother, let me get some paper to clean it."

"Do it now!" she shouted, moving toward me.

I managed to avoid her fist as I read the message in her eyes—I had to clean it right away. She would enjoy watching me pick up feces with my bare hands.

I bent over and reached for the disgusting pile. Having noticed my hesitation, she smacked me, forcing me to use my hands to mop the floor. With the burning sensation of my beating still traveling back and forth over my bloody skin, I ran directly into the bathroom and got rid of the pasty excrement I was holding. How would I ever be able to use my hands to eat again? I could endure the torturous spankings and the tears, but somehow this was worse.

Holding my head down, I ran as fast as possible to the close-by Ewé River. None of the neighbors dared stop me, make eye contact, or even say a word. Nobody was surprised to see me like that; they were used to it.

I used a small stick from the riverbank to scrape my infested fingernails. Though my hands seemed cleaner after several washes and rinses, I wanted to peel the skin off of them and leave it right there beside the polluted river where I believed it belonged.

As I headed home, I knew our neighbors were already dining. The clink of forks and knives on plates was torture to my starved stomach. I could tell exactly what was on each table by the delicious aromas: exquisite *bitter leaf* soup (*ndolé*) and yams; dark, spicy hot catfish soup (*bongó tchobi*) and rice or plantains; or well-seasoned, thick and meaty tomato or peanut butter sauce and rice. Of course, they were all my favorites.

Ambling back, I felt dizzy. Murderous hunger twisted my internal organs. I had not eaten since the previous night, so I decided to ask Sita Fidèle, a caring neighbor and my good friend Nicholas' aunt, for leftovers. She had told me to knock discreetly at her window in times of need. Because my parents had ordered me never to visit her, I had to sneak at my own risk.

I slipped through the front gate of Sita's house and stretched up under her living room window, too short to reach the glass pane. I had already reached out to her many times before, so I knew the discreet and effective how-to.

Sita Fidèle's house, showing the providential window

I was in danger of being heard by my mom, but I had no choice. I was hungry. Soon the panels opened. Sita looked at me and disappeared without a word. I started salivating; I could not wait. Soon, she returned and handed me a plate, which I grabbed and dug into with my filthy hands. It was one of the best sensations I ever had. I prayed to the Lord to please let me finish this exquisite fish soup and cassava meal.

But this was not meant to be. I smelled my mother's characteristic body odor. She'd appeared as if out of nowhere and stood behind me. I heard her breathing heavily from fury and the short climb up the hill to Sita's house. I hurried to stuff my mouth.

"What are you doing here?" she asked. "Again."

Her voice was shallow but firm. I sensed her underlying rage, but knew she would not alert Sita by yelling or spanking me right there. Realizing that for a moment I had control, I decided not to stop. I had to empty that plate or go down trying. I ignored her and continued cramming my mouth full of food. I felt her move closer. "If she touches me, I will scream my lungs out," I thought. But she did not touch me. Instead, she snatched away my plate in a swift movement.

"You will finish this at home."

My mother disappeared into the darkness, humming. I continued to chew the leftovers in my mouth. I did not want to swallow them yet. I wanted to savor them, make the taste last as long as possible, because I did not know if or when I would have food again.

I got up to go home, surprisingly calm. No matter what happened, at least I had food in my stomach and nothing could take it away. When I reached our doorstep, I saw that my mother had given Sita's plate to Jealousy, who was licking it clean with unsolicited help from her puppies. I had an urge to kick those puppies that I loved so much one by one and send them all to Hell. Better yet, I would have started with my mother. I wouldn't have minded getting beaten for the rest of the night if it had meant eating all of Sita's fish soup, and my mother knew it. She knew how to break me down, how to win.

Chapter 3

The Eyes I Knew

It was Monday, a school day. I woke up earlier than usual because I had soaked my bed. Before going to sleep, I had drunk a lot of water to deceive my empty stomach. On weekends or holidays, I could hide until my shorts dried out. But that day, I had no time, and I was very worried.

There would be a school assembly that day, and I ran a high chance of being called out. The first time I was forced to stand in front of every single person at my school, I was horribly made fun of. For a very long time afterward, I continued hearing and seeing everyone laughing and pointing at me mercilessly. With my eyes closed, it seemed like all those heartless little voices merged into one monstrous tone.

I would not allow them to make me stand away from everyone else at recess and watch all of my friends and schoolmates have fun. I would not give them the chance to torture me because of my tribe, my filth, and my shabby clothes. I would not let anyone trample what was left of my dignity and crumbled pride. I was not going to school that day!

First, I had to wash the dishes before school. Doing so increased my chances of getting something to eat from my mom. When it came to that, I did not fool around. I always did whatever it took for a food reward.

The weather had been calm the previous few days, but now it was cloudy and windy. It seemed like the air was suddenly visible, as it carried around dust and other particles. In the sky, only a few adventurous birds defied what nature certainly had in store for us. A major thunderstorm was, without a doubt, in the works. I had to hurry and get out of there.

As I finished washing the last pot, my mom stood at the door, inspecting my work. I hoped she noticed the marvelous job I had done.

Time to go to school came and I had to get around her to get my schoolbag. I walked toward her without lifting my head, hoping she would let me pass. She did not move an inch. I stopped in front of her, my terrified heart beating very hard. Knowing she was staring straight at me, I couldn't meet her eyes, for I would only see rage and hatred. Why try facing that? I had seen enough.

She finally took a step forward, which gave me enough space to get through. As I entered my room, I heard the front door closing and perceived my mom's heavy breathing and pounding footsteps as she approached me.

"Fotso!" she yelled.

"Yes, Mother."

Within seconds, I stood in front of her. Instant tears started to flow and I silently begged for her mercy. She pointed to order me closer. Closer, closer, and closer! Once I got within her reach, she suddenly gripped me by the left ear and started pulling me toward her. I knew where she was heading, so I started getting ready to endure it. She reached for the electrical cord and immediately lashed out furiously, inflicting deep pain across my upper body, and forcing me to start screaming.

"You do not urinate in your bed! You understand that?" she asked.

"Yes. I do. I will never do it again... please, please..." I pleaded.

As she continued, I could not help it. I wet my shorts again.

"Get up and get out of here," she ordered.

Sniffling and shivering, I got my schoolbag, which was made out of a white flour sack, put its strap over my right shoulder, and started walking out of the house.

I courageously stepped outside and started walking toward my school. It was rush hour, so everybody was in a hurry, trying to get to their destination before it started raining. It was getting darker by the minute, and I didn't think the storm would wait long.

As I approached an abandoned piece of land about a mile from my home, I wrestled again with the idea of skipping school. I had everything to gain by not going. No one would tease me, laugh at me, or reject me. I could stay hidden in those bushes and connect with my stranded, wounded self.

The narrow alley I followed was used as a shortcut to school. The surrounding bushes also served as public toilets. This hideous place was about to become my safe haven for the day. Nobody would ever imagine someone in the tall trees of the central area. I looked back and forth to make sure no one was coming. Then, with the agility of a monkey, the determination of a predatory lion, and the speed of a cheetah, I jumped into the bushes. Under a tree, I spotted a small suitcase, perhaps abandoned by some thieves. I dragged it to the nicest area to use as a seat. That was how I would spend my day. If I needed to take a nap, I would just lie on it.

From the depth of my hideout, I saw my school on top of the mountain. It killed me not to be there like everyone else. Even though I sometimes dreaded being at school facing isolation, I enjoyed learning. I heard the echo of students repeating after their teachers and momentarily tried to follow along. But I had bigger issues to think about, and the biggest of all was myself. Life had not treated me well at all. I didn't understand why. What was I doing wrong? What did I need to change?

My thoughts led me as far back as I could remember, though not too far, in reality. I sought to uncover something that had gone wrong at a given time in my short life; but I could not. It seemed as if being hammered for years by unforgiving parents had wiped out some of my memory.

The sky started to clear up. Not a single raindrop fell despite all threatening appearances. The winds slowed, and the birds sang once again. I decided to wash my filthy clothes in the tiny effluent from the Ewé River. I was there alone, so no one would see my naked body.

With my clothes in hand, I navigated through the muddy path. I suddenly realized how my friends, schoolmates, and teachers saw me, for even I could not stand my own disgusting smell. I gave some of them credit for having, at times, tried hard to accept me; from then on, I would not force myself in. I would hide my shame and stay away.

Suddenly, I had a strange impression that the outfit I was washing wasn't mine and had never been. My shorts looked nothing like shorts. It appeared to me that I had been walking around in a little *skirt* for about two months. During a soccer game, the seam between the two legs of my shorts had ripped. It had not really hit home until that very moment just how much the nickname *Skirty Fotso* actually fit me. I realized how awkward and different I looked in my skirt. With no underwear, people saw *all* of me all the time. In fact, I did everything without a second thought, just like boys were supposed to do. I guessed I now had to sit or bend like a girl. Although I was deeply saddened and embarrassed by what I had finally come to realize, I understood that this clothing was all I had, and that I needed to take good care of it.

After about half an hour of rubbing, scrubbing, and soaking my clothes in the light brown river water, I hung them on the lowest branch of an adjacent tree, low enough not to be seen from the muddy path. Exhausted, terribly hungry, and sad, I lied back down on the abandoned suitcase. By the time the school bell rang at the end of the day, everything would be dry.

I closed my eyes in an attempt to take a nap, but I could not escape my own thoughts. I felt as if surrounded by a brick wall, with no way to escape. How could I stay up? How could I keep going? That day was peaceful and a part of me wanted to have more like it. But it was probably not a good idea. With internal shame lavishing punishment on me for having skipped school, with my body, mind, and spirit in disarray, my unbreakable inner voice whispered, "*There is a way—a better way—and you must find it.*" It spoke to me when

I was about to give up. That day, it delivered its strongest message. The joy and happiness—or just normalcy—I so longed for would never be handed to me. I had to seek it out in the moment and for the rest of my life.

I looked up to the trees, hoping to find edible fruits, but there was nothing. I had to deal with my hunger alone, for at least a few more hours before heading home with everybody else. To keep my mind off food, I started thinking about finding the way, my way for survival. A number of ideas came to mind, including stealing food and money, and digging in dumpsters. As stealing could pay off big, it did not take long for me to understand that this would be *my way*.

The loud singing of birds awakened me. Gazing up, I realized they were bunched on one branch, looking down as if teasing me. Some spread their wings, others vigorously shook their tails, and all were very vocal. Brushing off my growing curiosity, I stood up to get my clothes, as I was sure the bell would ring soon.

As I went to retrieve my skirt and shirt, the noise got louder. Those birds were flying unusually close to the ground. I felt the wind trails following them and crisscrossing one another. In close proximity to my clothes, a sudden spitting and whistling sound forced me to jump backward. Landing on my backside, I was chilled to the bone as I spotted a huge cobra coiled up with its head raised, hissing. The hooded part of its body shifted from left to right, as its red eyes stared at me, its V-shaped tongue stretching in and out of its angry mouth.

Every single hair on my head raised up. I stayed motionless. Although I hadn't even blinked, I felt tears easing down my face, as the giant snake moved its flattened upper body back and forth, coming closer to me. As it moved, I saw something very familiar in its expression. I had seen such eyes before—full of rage, anger, and hatred. They were transplants from my mom. Those were eyes I knew!

With that connection made, I instantly jumped back and sped away. My heart pounding, I stopped. My eyes and my ears became living radars, calibrated to hear that snake glide in the bushes.

I could not go any further, or I would have to cross the road, naked. I was forced to stay right there. The bell rang, marking the end of the school day. It was time for me to head home. But first, I had to get my clothes back. I found the courage to tiptoe toward the danger zone, only because I had no choice.

Under the tree canopy, the animal frenzy had stopped. My eyes found the smooth spot where the big snake had been... but no snake. Because I did not know where it went, I was even more worried. It could attack me from anywhere. Refusing to let fear win over my needs, I snatched my outfit and my schoolbag, and flew toward the road. By the time I appeared in public, I was completely dressed.

Chapter 4

My Way

After joining the late afternoon crowd on my way home, I felt like one of the boys. I still had a skirt on, but a clean one. People would not halt their breath when I passed by. But probably more than any of the boys, I was praying for some food.

Home was not too far away, and I would be there in no time. I hoped none of my classmates had already stopped by to betray me. If any had, who knew what would happen? Maybe nothing at all, as I did not think my parents thought as much about my education as they did of the money I brought home from banana sales.

I usually slowed down as I got closer to our house. Not that day. I didn't feel scared. I walked cautiously because only a tiny, rusted steel wire was holding my sandals together. In the immense crowd going and coming, I tried hard but in vain to locate my friends. Walking with them would prevent suspicion. I would appear as one of the kids after a typical day at school.

After about ten minutes of a jovial walk, I spotted a treasure on the side of the dusty road. Looking around, I realized that nobody seemed to have noticed it. They were unbelievably missing a fortune, making it mine. As I came closer to that priceless piece of bread lying on the ground, I started to salivate profusely. I first gave it a furtive look because I did not want to attract any competitors. I did not want to ruin my chances of having a dinner of my own. I had to have it! I felt everybody's attention on me. Looking around, I grasped how wrong I was. Nobody cared! But I still proceeded with caution. I kicked the bread as if I was playing soccer, hoping not to crumble it. My subsequent soft kicks lovingly tortured my meal on the dusty road, while they carelessly disturbed tiny creatures inside. An army of panicking, angry ants came rushing out. If they could, they certainly would eat me alive. Not disturbed by these unfortunate competitors, I dropped my schoolbag over *my* feast and scooped it up all together in one smooth movement. No one seemed to have noticed my ploy. The food was mine!

Overwhelmed by my luck, I clutched my folded bag and followed the unsuspicious crowd, regularly blowing off the last few persistent ants escaping from the tight grip on the disputed possession. After a short while, I sneaked into an abandoned house and devoured the bread in the scary semi-darkness. I did not have time to even consider the few ants still feasting deep within. As the last mouthful slid down my throat, I began to engrave in my mind the unforgettable sweet taste. The mixture of chocolate and salty butter in my floury meal turned garbage into cake.

I emerged from my hideout, vigorous and ready to take the trapping brick walls down. Although I saw our house from a distance, I was, for once, unmoved. I would look straight in the eyes of my friends and neighbors that day. Their sorrow and pity would only illuminate my *way* in the darkness of my overdue quest for happiness. It was my lucky day and I was determined to enjoy myself. The jovial little boy buried inside me for so long had been reborn. As I walked, I alternately whistled and sang various popular Makossa and Bikutsi songs. Whistling was a sign of my maturity and singing, one of confidence.

From a distance, I saw a crowd on the vacant lot adjacent to our house. As I approached, sharp cries from behind a firefighter's house got my attention. He was beating up his wife again, and to me there was nothing unusual about it.

Disappointed, I turned around to head down to our house. Then I saw Nicholas' excitement as he ran to me and said, "Did you see it?"

"See what?" I asked, confused.

"Don't tell me you did not see it!"

The screaming became louder, as the firefighter's wife headed out in front of everybody. She was naked, as naked as I had been in the bushes. I grasped what Nicholas emphatically talked about: I saw *it*. Her husband chased her down and blasted her with the belt from his uniform, yelling "*If I want it, you give it, anytime and anywhere!*" whatever *it* was. If there was one person among us feeling her pain, it was I. As her husband lashed at her, I closed my eyes. The cruel sound of that belt on the naked, wet skin of the defenseless woman ripped me open. Desperately hoping that she could somehow hear me, I whispered, "*There is a way... you must find it!*"

Out of nowhere, someone pinched my right ear from behind. The pain was such that I could not even turn around to see who it was. But the characteristic smell—a mixture of sweat from a hard day of work and beer—could not lie. It was my father. That day, he certainly had a lot more beers than he should have. As he dragged me by the earlobe, my shoulder bumped into his distended stomach. I decided not to scream. Not that day! It was a blessed day for me, and whatever happened, I would keep my spirits up.

"What were you looking at?" he asked as we arrived at our doorstep.

I looked at him, but did not answer. He got irritated and his red eyes betrayed his fury. As he bent over to get closer to my face and roar, a loud burp escaped. In that nasty smell, I detected a mixture of hot pepper and roasted pork. But with the wonderful taste of *my* exquisite bread still in my mouth, I had no reason to envy my father's lavish meal. After he finally let go of my earlobe, I spotted my mother, seated inside their little corner shop, and opening a package she had in her hands.

"Fotso, here!" she called, without even looking at me.

As my father entered the house, I wondered why my mother called me. Had someone betrayed me? Maybe she wanted me to fetch some drinking water. Hopefully not! Going back and forth between our home and the public fountain was exhausting. If she asked me to do it, I would say "no!" Not this time!

She opened her package and reached in. It was *soya*—seasoned and freshly roasted beef jerky, which everybody loved. I tried hard not to look, but my eyes came right back to it each time I attempted to force them away. As she ate her first mouthful, she started humming a song she knew I liked, even though it was in Douala, a language she could neither speak nor understand. She uttered a few inaudible words between singing and swallowing.

"I did not hear you." I said, puzzled.

I saw her oily lips move again, and I moved closer to hear the words. She whispered once more, and this time I understood what she wanted of me. How was I going to chase down and capture every single louse hiding in that nappy hair? How in the world was I going to dig up every single gray strand out of all that? Disgusted by her orders, I was torn between standing up to her and pulling my skirt down myself for a beating, or doing what she wanted and losing my appetite for a long time. The little voice of the obedient boy inside me muttered to me that she was my mother after all, and that I had to do it.

As my hesitant hands reached her scalp, the amount of dandruff I saw was shocking. She pulled a small wooden chair over and put a piece of paper on top of it.

"Crush them there," she said, while noisily cracking a chunk of edible bones.

Because I had never eaten *soya*, I didn't know what it tasted like. But judging by how determined she was to shatter and chew those bones, I guessed it was delicious.

Some of my friends went back to playing. I heard Nicholas singing, and imagined him dancing. As for me, I was reduced to going from one ashy hair follicle to the next. I crushed captured creatures with my thumb nail, and a considerable area of paper was already covered with the dark brown liquid erupted from the swollen stomachs of the giant lice. Some seemed determined to keep moving to escape the death row, but none were able to, as they all bathed in that thick frothy blood. I had also plucked a handful of gray hair, and the nappy hair on her big head already appeared significantly darker than before.

After standing up for almost three hours, I was dizzy and didn't know how long I could continue. Fortunately, the invading darkness seemed to be coming to my rescue. Even the weak luminosity from our kerosene lamp did not make it any easier to differentiate gray from black, or a piece of dandruff from a live louse. As I continue to struggle, my father entered the shop, finally walking straight after some rest. He pulled the cash drawer out, examined it, and pushed it back in. After furtively looking at us, he pulled the drawer out again and started counting its contents. I loved the sound of the coins clanking against one another. To me, it was the sound of power. I could eat what I wanted, when I wanted.

Oh, my father loved money! One could tell just by the idolatrous way he held and looked at coins and bills. It was no secret in our nation that the *Bamiléké* tribe loved money. I was teased so much about being a *"Bami"* that I had to adapt by learning three different native languages other than mine—Éwondo, Bassa, and Douala—in addition to French. So, submerged by my aspiration for being accepted by everyone and my reality of being repulsed by all, I felt like I was everything I never wanted to be: my parents' son and a *Bamiléké*.

My father finished counting and stacked the coins and bills in his century-old black leather moneybag. As he zipped it up, he called, "Marie."

"Yes?" my mother replied.

As she stood up, I heard her bones crack in a loud noise that could only correlate with my endurance. As they whispered, I guessed it was time for another round of bananas, and they were strategizing about when and how much to buy and stock. I didn't care. I was just glad my disgusting catch-and-crush was over. I could now wash the layer of dried filth off my fingernails; but after my mother left the shop, I first started cleaning up the lice graveyard. As I did so, I spied my father hiding the moneybag on a shelf. He had no idea I had discovered his hiding place, the Fort Knox of the house.

I announced my presence with a loud cough and he began

deceitfully moving some cans of condensed milk, butter, and Moroccan sardines on various shelves. Disturbed by this rearrangement, giant cockroaches flew, ran up and down, or just came out and stood on the edge of almost everything, exploring the environment with their long antennas.

"Have you eaten?" my father asked.

"No, I haven't, Papa," I hurried to answer.

That day, I had some food waiting for me. On the table was a yellow bowl covered with a plastic plate. My mother had cooked some cassava meal and okra soup. I was not very hungry, but it was always good to store some food in my stomach for the days to come.

That night, I went to sleep with the biggest smile on my face. A wonderful night was definitely ahead. I promised myself to get my smelly grass-filled mattress out in the hot sun for a day whenever possible. The heat would burn out those lingering urine odors.

I had the strength to think about God. Not sure whether or not He was listening, I said my prayers. Before falling asleep, thoughts of my need to pursue *my way* brought me back to my father's money stash. But a part of me did not want to steal; that was not who I was; however, the other part was calling me "stupid" for hesitating. Who I was inside—in my entirety—was not going to survive much longer. Wouldn't it make sense to take a little bit, just a little bit of money? God would surely understand and forgive, unless He was not God.

I would no longer have to beg my schoolmates for food. I would be able to buy my own doughnuts and fried, spicy beans, like they did. Picturing what I could do with that money was really a faraway dream, rather so close to me that it became scary and mind-boggling.

In the darkness of my room, only my ears kept me connected to the rest of the world. The distant noise from old vehicles and motorcycles struggling to climb the Mvog-Ada and Nkol-Ndongo hills seemed to be coming from next door. A few owls seemed to be talking to each other, hidden in the mango and avocado trees that constituted our neighborhood's greenery. Errant dogs barked from all directions. I also heard some men singing incoherently and as loudly as they could. I knew they were drunk and aimlessly walking around. Those who managed to get home would certainly wake up their wives and children, make a big deal out of nothing, and beat them. Because I had witnessed many families being dismantled by beer drinking, I had declared beer my enemy about a year before, pledging never to have a single one in my life.

In my room, mice relentlessly searched for something to eat. They chewed on everything they stumbled on, generating a steady, annoying noise. Regularly, I gently clapped to claim my space. Each time, they stopped, uncertain. But those that ran away came right back and continued as if nothing had ever happened. In that cacophonic orchestra, even if I had closed my eyes, I would never have gone to sleep.

Outside, roosters began to claim their masculinity. Dawn was near. But somehow, I hadn't slept, as I kept thinking about my father's bank. Imagining the moneybag in my hands became asphyxiating, irresistible. I was tired of living my despicable life. I was fed up! The rage inside me propelled me up from my bed and, very slowly, I tiptoed through the living room, being careful not to stumble on our old furniture. My heart pounded, and every single hair on my head became a sensor, in addition to both of my ears, ready to perceive any noise from my parents' room.

Outside, the sound of footsteps on the bumpy path adjacent to our house became more frequent. I hoped they didn't disturb my parents. After reaching the door that opened to the shop from the living room—my door to normalcy—I proceeded to open it, holding my breath. My shaky hands turned the knob as I pushed it inward, just enough to crack it open. My sensors detected a noise coming from within the house. Unsure if it came from my rodent roommates or from my parents, I sneaked behind our brown couch, where I folded my body to fit in the tiny space, with my eyes wide open with terror.

After the reassurance that my parents were still sleeping, I was back at the door. And that was it! I was following my way. I pushed the door by increments of just a few millimeters, stopping after each segment to listen. Estimating I had enough space between the door-frame and the panel, I slipped in and rushed straight to the money-bag, climbing on a wooden support to reach it on the fourth shelf up. I squeezed my right hand in between boxes. Barely reaching the bag with the tips of my fingers, I tried to force it out so I could grab some of its contents and run. A few puzzled cockroaches tickled my arm. But I was determined and finally held it!

I was shaking like a leaf stranded in a windstorm in the autumn of its life. My hands were sweaty, and I had to pay attention so as to not let the bag drop from my nervous grip. I unzipped it. At that moment, every little sound was deafening. I was, without a doubt, in the enemy's camp, and that could be fatal. With my right hand in the bag, I joyfully felt the money. In just moments, some of it would be mine. Lunch breaks would never be the same. Originally, I had vowed to take as much as I could, but then I got confused. If I did so, my father would notice right away, and I would be in the deepest trouble I had ever been. If I took just a little, it would not go as far and before long, I would be back in the swamp. Also, I couldn't decide between bills and coins. Though bills were worth a lot more than coins, a bill in children's hands meant that either their family was wealthy—unlike mine, or they were thieves—unlike me.

Because I had to make the hard choice in only a fraction of a second, I let my instinct guide me and, without really knowing how, I was holding some coins in my wet palm. I put the bag back where it belonged, and started sliding down. Just as my trembling feet touched the floor, I heard, "Who is in here?"

It was my father's sleepy voice. He was standing at the doorstep.

"Nobody, Papa," I anxiously replied.

I didn't know what I was thinking, but it was too late to take my stupid words back. Had I kept quiet, his sleepiness would have saved me—probably. I instinctively crammed the three one-hundred franc coins I was clutching into my mouth as my father stormed in, pointing a flashlight straight into my eyes.

"What are you doing in here?" he asked, perplexed.

He furtively took a look at the money shelf where nothing seemed out of ordinary. I did not say a word. The sound of the coins in my dry mouth would have betrayed me.

"I asked you a question!" he shouted.

With the light beaming into my eyes, I could barely see him. But it was not hard at all to hear the growing rage in his croaky voice. I had to come up with something.

"Nothing, Papa," I mumbled.

"Why can't you speak?"

The intensity of the light increased, and I knew he was approaching. I felt paralyzed and wished I could vanish from the face of the earth. If that man put his strong hands on my tiny body, I would die. Before I could make an excuse, I heard, "Fotso, do you have something in your mouth?"

"No, I don't," I struggled to say.

"Yes, you do... open it now!" he ordered.

I prayed to God to save me, to come to my rescue. At that moment, no human could. Only Him. I did not remember ever praying that hard. My now-awakened mother had joined her husband and, knowing I was in a deep swamp, I was not sure how long I would be successful in holding my urine of fear.

I felt my father's hand forcing my jaws open. But I was not going to let him. As he slipped his fingers into my mouth, I clenched my mandibles tightly together. It was the first time I had ever heard my father scream. I hoped he would let go, but my silly defense just enraged him. After wrestling with me, he started breathing like a wounded bull.

As if biting was not the last thing I tried, I began to execute my sudden idea of swallowing the coins, but choked. A reflexive cough spewed them out, and my father beamed his silver flashlight on the coruscating coins strewn across the unfinished cement floor.

All of my senses seemed to be lost, and I was torn between staying there to face my punishment, and running away forever. The train station was less than two miles away and would be perfect as my new home, where picking pockets would become my job. I had never robbed anyone but I would learn fast. I would just have to befriend some kids that worked there, and they would teach me how to not get caught. Then I would fit in with other kids. It would be great to experience that brotherhood, to live in a world where no one would tease me. Most likely, I would be beaten up, or even killed after being caught stealing. If I died there, like many had in the past, I would go down with no regrets at all, because I had to follow my way or die trying.

"Why did you steal the money?" my father demanded, irritated, while gently rubbing his hurt fingers.

Not seeing any blood from his fingers was a little disappointing. I wanted to watch him bleed. My mother stared at me without blinking. Her steely eyes were undisputable reminders of the cobra. Although I was not as frightened as I usually was, I didn't dare look straight at either of them at that moment. Even a brief eye contact could ignite the switch and they would be all over me. I felt as if I had been there for hours. Seconds dragged by, and minutes were static. I started to weep and sensed I would not be standing there much longer. I wanted to be out of that infernal house forever.

I desperately tried to jump through the small gap between my parents, but in vain. My father caught my skirt, which he used to pull me. My life instantly flashed right before my eyes.

"Why did you steal?" he yelled.

"I was hungry," I whispered, terrified by his grave voice. "I also wanted to buy a soccer ball," I sincerely added.

My feet barely touched the floor as he dragged me to the living room. I resisted as much as I could, but was no match for his brutality. He reached for the top of the living room's rustic armoire, and pulled out a new electrical cord, upgraded with knots. My mother took it and as he held me down, she started delivering punishing blows to my body. I had promised myself not to scream. I had promised myself not to cry. I had pledged to stay strong, not to give them the pleasure of seeing me hurt and sad. But I couldn't hold any of my promises. The pain was indescribable, as my punishment went on, and on, and on. I collapsed on the floor face down, defenseless; but they did not stop.

A crowd had gathered by our front door. In between the relentless blows, I heard some of them talk. When the strokes finally ended, both of my parents were breathing hard from rage and exhaustion. They walked away, but my shivering body did not have the strength to stand up.

The door opened and the voices became louder. Some expressed their sorrow while others just tried to understand what had happened so early in the morning. As usual, a few seemed to enjoy the scene. I adjusted my skirt to retain what little dignity I had left. Hearing Bébé yell, "Hang in there, Fotso!" was what I wanted to hear. Not pity! Not sorrow! Bébé was my friend Nicholas' cousin—Sita's daughter—just a little older than me.

My father started cutting something with a knife. I looked over and realized he was holding a piece of cardboard in which he had punched two holes. He then threaded each end of a short rope through the holes, and began writing something with a piece of white chalk from the shop. I could not read it from where I lied. He came back near me and said, "Up now!"

I did not want to give my father an additional reason to slaughter me in front of my friends. So I stood up instantly. He held me by the neck and started directing me toward the door. The crowd became silent. Everyone followed us to the veranda, where my father finally let me read what he had written.

"This is what you are," he said, hanging the horrible cardboard sign around my neck.

The word "THIEF" had never been as crushing and cruel. I was now wearing it as a pendant to the humiliating necklace my father had crafted. I wondered if he would order me to go to school with that thing around my neck. I would have preferred to spend another day with the cobra. Everyone in the crowd was astonished. I heard some people say to my father, "No… that's just too much!" But was he listening? I guessed not.

He pulled two ropes from the pocket of his stained gray trench coat. Then, he pushed me against the wooden column in the middle of the veranda. He tied my wrists firmly together; I did not even try to fight it. I let him do whatever he wanted. I was up with my back against the pillar. He pulled my shackled hands above my head and tied them to the vertical support. He then double-checked to make sure it had no chance of coming loose, before proceeding to my legs and doing the same unbelievable thing.

One by one, people started to leave, shocked. Some of them surely wanted to help me, but couldn't. I was my father's property. I belonged to him. Several women did their best to conceal their tears. Those tears meant a lot to me. They meant that someone cared. Some left silently, but a few spoke. "Tino, how can you do that to your child!" they said. Those words were ignored. My parents had already gone back inside and had closed the door.

Because I was facing the main path in my neighborhood, I didn't know how I was going to handle the looks from people passing by, just yards away from me. I could be there all day long. But how could that be? I had to go to school. Had they forgotten that?

After a while, adults and students started their journey to work and school. I did not want to look at anybody and I did not want anybody to look at me. *"Just go!"* I shouted to a few teenagers who stopped and tried to lift my skirt, realizing I was defenseless. We knew each other well, so I was surprised just how cruel they were to me. The biggest one came close and pinched my nose. As I reacted to the pain, he shamelessly spit in my wide-open mouth and started laughing out loud. I immediately rejected all of his filth and began to scrape my oral cavity with my tongue and my teeth. I was disgusted. Monsters!

In my suffering, I could not stop thinking about Henry and his mother. They were exactly what I needed at that moment. The feeling of her hugging me was as vivid as ever. I would have given almost everything to have that moment back. The look on her face was never that of pity, always one of concern; I had never read sorrow in her eyes, only unscripted love and compassion. She had certainly understood how lost and miserable I was, and tried to rescue me. She had made me realize what I was missing all of my life. Not shoes or nice outfits, not toy cars, snacks, or even lunch money, but the warmth from a caring heart. She had helped me retrieve some of the shattered, scattered, and eroding puzzle pieces of my vanishing childhood.

My father came out and walked past me without even looking at me. I wished he would make a U-turn and come untie me. But with his head up and the moneybag in his hands, he disappeared between the houses. I knew he was en route to purchase another round of bananas, which I would be more than happy to sell at that point. Bananas were my passport to the outside world, and my visa to Henry's planet.

Hours went by and I became unable to feel my arms and my legs. They were tired and shaky from supporting my body mass. I wanted to give up, but could not. Jealousy came over with her puppies, shaking her tail, and jumping up and down. The little ones wrestled against one another, playing hide-and-seek in the open. The presence of the dogs attracted flies, some of which landed and walked on my face and limbs. I was too weak and disabled to chase them away; no matter how hard I tried with facial movements, they always came back, seemingly in greater numbers.

The heat became unbearable and I began to sweat profusely. I was being cooked alive and desperately needed to be freed. Being on that post reminded me of Jesus. But I didn't want to entertain the comparison because I was not Him; I was suffering for myself, not for humanity. I was just *Skirty Fotso*, not Jesus Christ, legs and arms securely tied to a column, and fighting for my own survival, no one else's.

Increasingly, my connection with my surroundings blurred as time passed. What I was hearing was not as clear as it had been; and suddenly, I was hearing even less. Any effort to open my eyelids failed and I hoped not to die.

After a few more hours, Hervé, one of our neighbors, stopped in front of me on his way home from work and scanned me from head to toe, avoiding eye contact. He then reached up and began to untie my wrists and hands. My mother came out and silently watched him, chewing a piece of buttery bread. Without paying any attention to her, he untied my legs, too. Finally free, I had to get away from the place where I had been humiliated all day long. In an attempt to walk, I crumbled. My legs were too weak, but my arms were strong enough to take that horrible necklace off and tear it up in a million pieces. I was enraged and not hiding it. More than ever, it was obvious that I had to find my way, a way to get a real life, one with dignity. I had tried and failed. But I was not giving up. I would keep on trying, until I found it.

Hervé looked at my mother and said, "Tell him *I* did it!"

His voice was the true expression of disgust. Even though I was unable to take a step, I was grateful for what he had done. As he went away, my mother stood there, staring at me. I knew she wanted to put me right back on the column. I would not let her. I had had enough.

Chapter 5

The Bone

(1973)

Deep within, I felt bitter and revengeful, and constantly dreamed of getting even with my parents. Turning my obsessive delusions into reality soon appeared possible. All I needed was a horse bone! Word had spread around town that sucking one granted the miraculous power of invisibility. Fascinating anecdotes from all corners of Yaoundé were regular and I couldn't wait to be invisible at will. No one would see me unless I wanted to be seen; and I wasn't sure even God would have such a privilege.

About three days before, I had come across two runaway horses strolling alone down a less-traveled, secondary road of the city. I had instantly thought of catching one of them, slicing off one of its legs, and vanishing with a mystical bone. But after following them for about twenty minutes, I realized how ridiculous my plan was. Instead, I negotiated with a local bone dealer, and obtained my precious piece of bone after handing him the 125 francs I had saved from overpricing some of my parents' bananas to Europeans. I would get the 375-franc balance with the help of my invisibility.

I would experience the God-given virtue of my tiny fortune. From the next day on, I would never be the same. That night would be long, but the following day would be mine.

As the morning approached, I woke to the crowing of roosters and sat up on the edge of my bed. I heard the usual early morning footsteps and distant voices of women waking their children up. It was time for me to get outside and see the world like never before.

After cautiously opening the main door, I stood on the stairs leading to the side yard. Hesitating for a brief moment about what to do first, I decided to relieve myself in the bathroom. Stepping into that filthy little room, especially first thing in the morning, was never pleasant. As I aimed at the hole in the middle of the cracked floor to urinate, I couldn't escape the nauseating odors from the exposed, horrendous, and fuming black sewage. Through it all, I possessively held onto my precious little bone. Had it fallen into the hole, I would not have thought twice before sifting with my bare hands through the maggot-filled waste to retrieve it.

As I prepared to leave, I heard the enchanting voice of a woman singing from behind our house. Listening to her melody seeded an ingenious idea in my mind. Gently closing the shabby door behind me, I hurried around our house. The bathroom she was singing from belonged to our neighbors, and I could only access it by going through the main entrance of their wooden house. As I started trotting down the small hill that led there, I placed the bone in my mouth and frantically sucked it to ensure my invisibility. With each decisive step, I felt as if I was vanishing and within a few seconds, I would embody the power that only God and a few other human beings around there claimed.

Convinced that I was now invisible, I passed by the neighbors' front door, furtively peeking inside. With an overwhelming confidence, I approached the bathroom entrance. Only a grungy curtain from a brown fabric stood between the woman and me. Just as I had expected, she was taking a shower. I saw her through the multiple holes of the rundown drape, and her blurred body took a more distinct shape with each of my steps. That was the day I was going to see *it* without fear. That day, my curiosity would be satisfied.

Finally standing at the doorstep, I stretched up and pulled the curtain open. With that movement, I shattered the last remaining barrier between us. I stared in amazement as she bent to get water from a large metallic bucket with the palms of her hands. Soapy water ran down each curve of her body. As I re-adjusted my position to make sure I didn't miss anything, she poured half the contents of the bucket over her head. I was stunned to finally see *it* only a few feet away. My eyes were wide open, and my breath halted. The world was mine! Unlike the firefighter's wife, she was not attempting to hide *it*. Why should she? She could never imagine not being alone at that moment. Now I would have as much to talk about as some of my friends. Never again would I just listen.

Inwardly celebrating my newfound self, I peered up at her, only to realize that her eyes were locked onto mine as if she was seeing me.

"Who is this?"

She was looking at me, but surely there was no way she could be seeing me. I had sucked that bone really hard. In fact, I recognized doubt in her voice. She knew me and would not have asked that question if she were actually seeing me. Therefore, convinced of my invincibility, I did not hesitate to answer with confidence, disguising my voice.

"It's me!"

"You, who?" she asked, trying but failing to shield all of her wet body with just her small hands.

"Me!" I shouted.

She looked stupefied. In an abrupt movement, she grabbed the bucket from the floor and vehemently poured the remaining bath water in my face. With my confidence unexpectedly shattered, I ran away, taking giant uphill leaps. I was now certain she had seen me. I had to understand what had gone wrong right away.

Safe at home, I started brainstorming as I washed the dishes. Perhaps it was how I had handled the bone? I should never have stopped sucking it. That certainly was the secret!

Halfway through my daily chore, the shadow of someone approached me and stopped. The woman from the shower stood beside me. She did not look happy at all. There was no doubt that I was in trouble. I knew she was seeing me this time, and there was nowhere to hide. I was paralyzed by fear and ready to express it by instantly emptying my bladder on the spot if she took another step toward me; but to my surprise, she turned back and walked away without saying a word.

Immediately after her departure, I started thinking about what to do next to ascertain the power of my bone. What crossed my mind first was to put that bone in my mouth and walk straight to my mother or father—whoever I found—grab them by the ear and spank them in public. But I put this tempting thought on a temporary hold and decided to go on a short walk to see what I could find that would allow me to exercise my newfound power. It had to work right this time.

As I walked along a narrow path between rundown houses in a poor neighborhood of the city, I noticed one larger shack that stood out from the ruin. Surrounded by a high plank fence, it seemed to be home to a wealthier family. I glanced through the green portal to the front yard and thought I was dreaming. A large black-and-white soccer ball and a yellow sports car laid unattended in the yard. My legs shook with excitement. I put my bone in my mouth and started sucking. This time, I remembered not to take it out.

Outside the fence where I stood, nobody was approaching. I had to act fast. Having sucked the bone enough, I opened the pedestrian gate and stepped into the yard. As I strode toward my two coveted items, I glanced inside the house and saw a shirtless man sitting in the dining room. Looking closer, I noticed more people around the table, most likely the entire family sharing a meal together. The man looked up, but immediately turned back to his plate. I grabbed the ball and proceeded toward the yellow car. I imagined myself turning the black plastic steering wheel, and pictured my friends bombarding me with admiration and envy. Unfortunately, the shirtless man now running toward me interrupted my short daydream.

"Hey! Hey! What are you doing? Get out of here!" he yelled angrily.

Each of his giant steps brought him dangerously closer to me. Two boys followed behind him, the smallest with a loaded slingshot, and the other with rage in his eyes. As I exited the fence, I was afraid they would shout one fatal word: "Thief!" If that were heard, the entire neighborhood would certainly track me down and stone me to death. But, they did not say it. Perhaps they understood I was just a child, not a thief.

Back home, winded and panting, I realized how close I had come to vigilante justice. Moreover, I would not get even with my parents! Irreversibly disappointed, I headed straight to our horrid toilets and threw my now scorned possession into the maggot-filled human waste. It was useless, completely worthless. I understood that my invisibility and invincibility had never been anything other than a fantasy, and my vulnerability was reality as usual.

Chapter 6

Lost and Found

A very sad day arrived—one I wanted to postpone forever. This Sunday was the day I was being forced to go sell our puppies. The very idea was already haunting me. Over the years, our dog and her offspring had proven to be always there by my side, even as my human family rebuked me.

The puppies were already stuffed in a big cardboard box. My father mercilessly yanked their heads through the tiny holes he had cut on each side. They cried and Jealousy frantically barked, getting a strong, cruel boot each time she came too close. Her world was crumbling. She was losing everything.

Each puppy was finally body-in, head-out, and my father secured the top of the box. Through the gloomy look on their face, they each seemed to be saying, *"Don't worry, Mom, we will be fine."* They seemed to behave as if they wanted their mom to stay strong. I had never known Jealousy to express her disagreement so violently. My father recognized her threat and chained her down. All she could do now was powerlessly watch *me* steal her offspring!

I was enraged. I did not want to be the other half of the iron fist. How would I face her afterwards and play with her again? Moreover, I was humiliated. I imagined my friends and neighbors saying, *"Shame on you, Bami! You would do anything for money."* No, not again! I was not going to walk through that city with a box full of her sad-looking puppies pleading for their freedom. I was not!

My father signaled to me that it was time to go, and took a few steps to load the goods on my head. I felt as if I were drowning. If I went, I would be taking Jealousy's soul with me. If I didn't, I would be disobeying my father, and the consequences would be harsh.

"Fotso, didn't you hear me? It is time to go," he repeated.

"I am not going!" I surprised myself saying, with defiance.

My father looked at me as if he had misheard my answer or had not heard it at all; with a sarcastic smile on his face, he clearly and slowly stated, "I said, it's time to go." From his body language, I could tell he was eager to hear my response, to confirm what he thought he had heard.

"And *I* said I am not going."

This time, my words did not sound so foreign to me. The few seconds had provided me with enough time to think it through. I was not going.

My father pounded like a starving lion on a disabled antelope, and switched from the tire sliver to the electrical cord; but I was determined not to scream or cry. I agreed to bleed, but not to shed a tear. I did not hand him that victory. The swollen slits on my trembling body would reveal his victorious defeat. But as he did not stop, I finally yelled, "I will go now!"

He continued striking me for a little while and stopped. He then crushed my head with the heavy box and sent me off. I did not have enough courage to look at Jealousy. Between my sniffles, I could only listen to her exhausted and furious cries fade away with each of my steps. I wished she were able to hear my thoughts: "*I am sorry, Jealousy; I have to do it.*"

As I walked through the town, I contemplated going back home with all of them, claiming I had no customers. But in my heart, I knew that excuse would not suffice because a lot of people would easily offer the one thousand franc-asking price for each puppy. They were all adorable, descendants of a stray German shepherd and Jealousy, a golden retriever look-alike.

The best thing was to sell them and hope they would each fall into good hands. It crossed my mind that nobody would be more caring than Henry's mother. It had been a long time since I had last seen them, so I decided to head that way. Even if she did not buy a puppy, at least I would see them again, and maybe earn another hug.

Inside the box, the puppies whimpered and whined. I hurried across the city toward Henry's home. From the Central Post office, I decided to go uphill past the Presidential Palace, majestically located on the top of the hill. Each time I passed it, I shivered out of fear, knowing that the most powerful man of my country, President El Hadj Ahmadou Ahidjo, lived there, protected by scary-looking, heavily armed guards with scarred faces. But fear alone never dissuaded me from taking a closer peek at that mesmerizing white palace. As I passed by the steely main gate, I didn't dare look straight into the spacious courtyard. I knew hidden guards were scrutinizing me from all angles. I took a few sidelong glances and walked away.

About one hundred yards from the palace, an older man emerged from one of the administrative buildings, and called, "Hey, puppy seller! Here."

Excited, I hurried across the street.

"Let me see the puppies," he requested, taking the box down. "How many do you have?"

"Seven, sir... all very good ones," I pitched, struggling to catch my breath.

"Let me see." He opened the box, took the only all-black puppy out, and held it up right in front of his face, as if he were about to give it a kiss. After a moment, he declared, "You are right, I like them. How much again?"

"One thousand, sir."

He looked at me and started smiling. My heart was beating fast with excitement and hopes to make my first sale of the day; but at the same time, I was already being crushed by the grief from the anticipated loss of one of my little friends.

"Well... I am buying two" he said, reaching into the pocket of his suit.

After handing me two new one-thousand-franc bills sporting our president's face, he chose his other puppy and went back to the administrative block.

I was off to a very good start, at least for my father. As I continued my long walk through the city, people gave me the ostracizing looks I had expected. I managed to sell one more before heading to Henry's home.

As I approached the house, I was excited to show Henry the puppies. He would not have the chance to see the three I had already sold, but I thought he would love the four remaining. He would never expect me to arrive with merchandise other than bananas, as those were my specialty. But there I was, ringing the bell, with the unusual load of goods on my head.

Henry's mother had always been prompt about rushing to the gate at the first sound of the bell. This time, I was surprised by the silence from the other side of the fence. As I struggled to stand on my toes to peek through the keyhole, I heard footsteps behind me.

"Are you Joseph?" I heard.

I turned around. "Yes, sir," I hurried to answer.

"How are you doing?" the strange man asked. "Puppies for sale?"

"Yes, sir. Very good ones. Do you want to buy one?"

For a few seconds, my business instinct overcame my silent questions. My first instinct would have been to wonder how this European, whom I had never met, had come to know my name. But I hurried to do business with him, like a good Bamiléké.

"Don't go away... I will be right back," he said, turning into the gated residence next to Henry's.

I waited, but with no idea whatsoever of what I was waiting for. My hope was that he had gone to get some cash for a puppy or two. Or maybe Henry and his mom were in his house, and he had gone to get them for me. He returned and walked over to me. He picked the only black-and-white spotted puppy and handed me twelve hundred francs, two hundred more than the asking price, written in bold on all sides of the box.

"Sir, how much do you want him for?"

With my fingers crossed, I anxiously awaited his answer.

"It's okay, Joseph," he said, with his eyes on the puppy.

"Thank you very much, sir," I said, taking a look at Henry's gate, which still had not opened.

"Here, Joseph," the man said, handing me a small package neatly wrapped in a red plastic bag. "Mrs. Justine asked me to give you this when you came back."

I looked at him, puzzled, as I opened the little bag. I unfolded the newspapers it contained and discovered Henry's beautiful car and a little note:

> Hi, Joseph:
> We just wanted to let you know that we left Cameroon. We had hoped to see you before going away. You will forever be on our minds and in our hearts. Goodbye.
> Justine.

One of my shaky hands held the note, and the other gripped *my* car very tight. I didn't want to accept the fact that I would never see them again. I thought of all the lost hugs I had hoped for. In a fraction of a second, I relived all the good moments and desperately hoped that they could come back. All I could do now was say, "Thank you for everything," and put a smile on my teary face. I did not want to leave feeling sad. I wanted to leave as usual—grateful and smiling despite all. I would cherish all the wonderful memories and be forever thankful for my beautiful car, which I started driving away from my dreamland—for the last time.

It took very little time to sell the remaining three puppies, and I had a lot of money in my tiny dark brown wallet. My father would be ecstatic, but I did not want him to be. I did not want him to celebrate. I decided not to return just yet.

Many nomadic beef jerky sellers were bunched up in front of the *Les Portiques* movie theater. They sat behind their merchandise, chatting. The meat on their trays was visually juicy and spicy hot. The aroma waft into the atmosphere was mouth-watering. I thought about my mother selfishly chewing hers while I tracked down her lice and pulled her gray hair out.

As I stood in front of those vendors and salivated, the men looked at me with amusement. I wanted to devour the entire trays of meat and burp all the way home. I unzipped my little wallet and took out some coins. I then walked closer to the sellers, wondering if they would let a mere child buy some meat.

"How much are the skewers?" I bravely asked, though scared to death inside.

After a moment of hesitation, they each said, "Twenty-five francs" at the same time. I handed over fifty francs and chose the best two skewers of the entire bunch. The sensation of the meat in my mouth was thrilling. After each bite, the thrill felt evenly distributed to every single part of my starved body. Swallowing the first mouthful without chewing much, I silently screamed, *"Payback time!"*

The vendors realized I was serious and had money. They surrounded me, each promoting his jerky. I didn't care who I bought from, as the taste was the same to me. As my jaws started to hurt, I drenched in my own sweat but had no intention of stopping any time soon. This was my chance to catch up on years of no-meat. Even if my parents killed me afterward, at least I would die with the juicy jerky in my stomach and the wonderful aftertaste in my mouth. They would go crazy, and I would die happy. My stomach stretched out, inch by inch. Only a quick glance would tell everyone that something wonderful had happened to me.

Realizing I would never get full, my attention switched to a movie poster. A line had formed. They would be showing a Chinese movie next, all about fighting. A karate movie might teach me some new moves and tricks, which I could use to defend myself. They would come very handy against my father when he was drunk or on a rampage against me.

I got in line, extremely excited to purchase my very first movie ticket. I put my empty box at a corner of the theater, and it became the last thing on my mind. At school, I would have great stories to tell, just like the other kids.

As I set foot in the theater, I had sparkly eyes and a glowing forehead. I could not believe *I* was in there. Though it was dark, I managed to find a seat like everyone else, holding onto my car.

For many hours after, I got out of the theater and right back in, watching many more movies. With my freshly acquired fighting skills, I felt invincible.

As I walked toward the Central Market, I was drawn to stands with beautiful clothing, bright with stripes or some various other designs. What would my parents do if I spent all the money? Certainly nothing less than they would do if I went home at that point. No matter what I did from thereon, I would be roasted; so it might as well be for all the good reasons. I meticulously chose four shirts and three shorts that I thought would fit. Then, looking at the disinterested vendor, I asked, "How much are these all together?"

He reluctantly answered and I realized I could afford all the clothes I had chosen. I counted the money and handed it over. My new clothes smelled great, and they were just as I had always dreamed. I had waited my entire life to own them, and waiting longer—until I got home to peel off my old ones—would be foolish. So I walked onto the stinky public urinal behind the vendors, and soon emerged feeling like a totally different boy. The soft fabrics of my dark blue shorts and bright red shirt gently caressed my body. From that point on, my little skirt belonged in a dumpster. I knew I would face a horrendous punishment at home, but I didn't care. I would stand tall and proud of my renegade actions.

Sunset was approaching and I hurried home. I didn't want to arrive too late because almost no one would see the new *me*. First, I put my putrid shirt and skirt in the puppy box and threw it onto the mountain of trash pile on the street. Hours ago, that box contained things I wanted to keep—the puppies—but now, it contained everything I wished to discard and never see again.

I was nearing my neighborhood, and already receiving the attention I had long wished for. I made sure I walked slowly and stopped as often as possible to show off. It felt so good not to be the same filthy boy everyone knew.

I rounded the last corner. My home stood only minutes away. From afar, I saw my parents chatting in front of their shop. I was not afraid of arriving home. I was ready for anything.

My mother looked my way, but went right back to her conversation. She could never even guess that the decently dressed little boy she saw was her own son. Only when I crossed the wooden bridge next to our house did my parents realize the truth. Their discussion stopped and their jaws dropped. They looked at me as if I was an alien.

"Fotso?" my mother called, bewildered.

"Good afternoon," I bravely and politely said.

As I entered the house, I did not even acknowledge them more than I already had. I rushed into my room and threw my snack, the remaining money, and my precious car under my bed. I returned to the living room, put my other clothes on one of the chairs, and waited patiently. One thing was sure: they would storm in there any minute, for revenge.

"Fotso, did you sell all the dogs?" my mother asked.

My father, who appeared somewhat irritated and quite perplexed, followed her.

She was struggling not to let her emotions out, poorly crafting a smile on her furious and confused face. My father stood by our wooden armoire, ready to reach for one of the torture tools.

"Yes, I did."

Her follow-up question was obvious, but I ignored her dark snake-like eyes, and waited until she vocalized it. Sure enough, after a long and uncomfortable silence, she added, "So, where is the money?"

I handed her the wallet.

"There is nothing in here!" she spat. "Let me ask you again, *where is the money?*"

She was already incensed. A few weeks before, I would have urinated in my shorts from deep fear. That day, I was fearless.

"There is no money left."

"What?" She vehemently cut me off.

"Mother, I was very hungry and I bought something to eat… Also, I found these nice clothes and bought them."

In the middle of my answer, I saw my father reaching for the top of the armoire, and I slowly took a few steps back, knowing what was coming.

"Who gave you the permission?" he demanded as he came toward me. I ran around the chairs and tables as my father chased me. My mother spread out her arms, reducing my area of mobility with her large body. Knowing I could never get away, I gave myself up to their callous hands.

My father started to alternate between his belt in one hand and the electrical cord in the other. He also kicked me repeatedly with no concern for where his foot landed. I felt it punish my ribs and aching neck, and hoped he didn't thrash my face. I was once more determined not to let a sound out, and my stoicism, without a doubt, drove him crazy. As he showed no signs of giving up, I thought about using my new fighting skills against him. I already knew how to do back flips, just like in the Chinese movies. But was I tall enough to stand up to him?

"Don't beat me anymore!" I roared.

With one sudden push, I was up, standing in front of him, in pain and shaking. I looked straight into his eyes, and he looked back into mine. The belt was on the floor, and the cord in his right hand. "*If you lift it, I will defend myself!*" I thought. Couldn't that man see that I could not and would not take it anymore? Why couldn't he understand? What in the world could make them decent parents? Why couldn't my mother find in her dark heart a few crumbs of affection and compassion? She stood there, saying nothing. Her maternal instinct should have made her stop the beating that day and all the times before. She picked my clothes up and clutched them. Her eyes were still as sharp as ever but they no longer frightened me. Those days were over.

I decided to walk—not run—outside. I was going out there to do what all of my friends were doing—be a kid. On my way, I said to myself, "*If I sell, we share the money… That's how it's going to be from now on."*

After a very restful night, I woke up and washed the dishes. I was more than ready to go to school, with my money tucked into my little brown schoolbag. That day, I would not beg anyone for tiny pieces of doughnut and beans. I would buy my own. For once, I would fit in.

As I set foot outside, our main door opened and my father emerged, appearing very sleepy. With only partially opened and swollen eyes, he called me over.

"Give this to your teacher," he lazily said.

He handed me a large gray envelope, so light it seemed to contain nothing. I put it in my bag and took off.

Having joined a group of friends, I began to talk joyfully, exhibiting my new outfit. My confidence felt incredible. I had never felt so good about myself. As the distance to school shortened, I considered opening the envelope to see what was inside. My best guess was that my parents had written a note to my teacher, Mr. George—again—to tell him about everything that had happened the day before. He would be furious and would probably make me stand on one foot for hours. I did not want him to know. He was a wonderful teacher and I wanted him to continue being proud of me.

Though knowing it was wrong, I stuck my little finger through the unglued end of the envelope and carefully retrieved the paper inside. It was in handwriting I didn't recognize and had official stamps on both ends. As I skimmed it, I realized it was a birth certificate. Something immediately caught my attention: "Name of the Child—Fotso Joseph."

As I continued to read, my heart raced and I felt numb with confusion.

"Father's name: Todjou." *Not Fotso.*

"Mother's Name: Pauline." *Not Marie.*

"Residence: Bandjoun." *Not Yaoundé.*

"Profession: Farming." *Not Business.*

What did it mean? Did it mean *they* were not my parents, not my biological father and mother? I was a Fotso, just like him, and that would only make sense if he were my father. *"If they are not my parents, where are my real parents? Who am I? Why am I here?"*

A seed of joy started to grow from my cloud of confusion, and excitement spread through me. My gut feelings told me that *he* was not my father, and never had been; and that *she* was not my mother, and never had been. It made sense!

Looking back, they probably could not imagine that I would ever open it, much less be able to read the document. I had no idea what they knew about what I knew, as they never checked my schoolwork.

"Hey, guys! Wait for me!" I shouted.

My friends were far away and could not hear me. I started running to catch up. With every few steps, I whispered the same thing: "They are not my parents!" I finally caught my friends' attention and they slowed down, waiting for me.

My joy was uncontainable, and my confusion, almost unsolvable. I would have given my new outfit to know where my biological parents were. How could I get that priceless information? I always felt strange and incomplete. That was certainly the lost or missing piece from my life puzzle. I hoped to find it.

"What if my real parents are deceased? What if I never see them?" Those thoughts were scary. I already knew what my life was with a humongous hole in its center—a life in shambles. It would be even more disastrous if it continued. Despite my lingering questions and concerns, I could not conceal my happiness. Hope was mine, and I would hold on to it.

As soon as I entered the classroom, my classmates noticed the new me and started to applaud. They were celebrating my physical appearance, and I was celebrating with them; but celebrating more than my outer shell, I was celebrating my newfound hope. I was Joseph Fotso, proud son of Todjou and Pauline, whoever and wherever they were.

My life was never going to be the same. It was October 22, my birthday. I was nine! Finally, I knew my real age. It had been nine thorny years. Many times I had felt like giving up, but a few people had sustained me. Thinking of Mrs. Justine and Henry kept me going many times, lifting my body and my spirit. I had been rescued from desperation and despair by Sita Fidèle when I thought all was lost. She did more than secretly feed me through her window; she kept me alive. I had begged my way through school, almost always receiving crumbs from tiny giving hands. How could I ever forget the man who helped when I was tied up and humiliated? Just one day ago, I had discovered that Mrs. Justine and Henry were gone, probably forever, but now I had uncovered another hope to cling to.

When I got home from school, I was unable to look at my "mother" the way I used to. As I swept our little front yard and alley, I gave her some sideways glances. All that time, she pretended to be who she was not: my mother. She did not act or behave like a mother.

The local market had already closed, and my "father" would be home shortly. My eyes would certainly reveal my thoughts. Just by looking at me, he would more than likely be able to guess what I had done and what I knew. But I did not care. In just a day's time, I had lost all respect for them. For the time being, I had to play along.

As I stood up to dump the trash into the assigned receptacle, I saw my "father" standing not far from me, waiting for the thick cloud of dust to settle.

"Good afternoon," I robotically said.

"Did you give the envelope to the teacher?" he asked.

"Yes, I did."

"What did you say?" he asked again.

"*Yes*, I gave it to the teacher."

Obviously, something was bothering him, but I could not tell what. I had given the envelope to Mr. George.

"Come here," he ordered.

Without wasting a second, I stood only a step from him. He grabbed my left earlobe, which he pinched between his thumb and his second finger. I was perplexed, for I had given a true answer to his question.

"What did I do?" I defiantly questioned.

"Let me tell you what you did," he replied, squeezing a little harder. "How many times have I told you to say 'Papa' when I am talking to you?"

He then let go of my earlobe. Looking around, I realized that a little crowd had already built up. Sita, Nicholas, and Bébé were present. Evéline and Julie, the firefighter's daughters, were also there. A few bystanders had stopped, curious about what was happening. My "mother" was watching through the partially opened blinds of her window. All of my neighbors were listening, puzzled and worried. *I* was neither. After my declaration, the way they would look at my "father" would forever change. I turned my back to him and faced the wondering crowd. Gently rubbing my earlobe, heroically looking into the many supporting and encouraging eyes, and defiantly pointing at him, I shouted, "*He* is not my father!"

My voice was clear and sharp. The world stopped. Everybody was silent. Some stared at me, and over at him. Although I was not looking into his eyes, I felt his shock and embarrassment. He did not even attempt to speak. What could he have said? Keeping his mouth shut was dignifying for him. I was sure he had retracted into his shell, from which he would erupt and strike. But maybe I was wrong that time around. Maybe that was the switch that illuminated his consciousness and his humane side.

Head down, he started to shamble toward the main door, holding the brown one-strap bag containing the money from his daily sales. I sat on one of the steps leading to the house and in a very short time, everybody was gone. I decided to go in and face my "father." Why not?

With a few determined steps, I entered the house. He was seated at his usual place in the living room, with his wife on the couch across from him. The silence was awkward. I bravely walked to my room and did my homework. Then I got my toy car out of its hiding place. I wanted to go outside and play with it before total darkness set in. I heard my "parents" whispering to one another and did not want to waste time speculating what they were concocting.

Grasping my little car, I once again entered the living room. I was sending a strong message—my strongest yet. Normally, I would stay secluded in my dark room until the next day or until they called me for any reason. Walking through the room now, I didn't bother looking at them. My goal was to go outside and enjoy the last minutes of daylight like other kids my age were doing: chatting, laughing, running, playing soccer, singing, and shouting. As I got close to the door, I heard, "Fotso, where are you going?"

It was my "father's" cracking voice, sounding as if he had just woken from a very long and troubled night.

"I am going outside to play with my friends," I rebelliously said and kept walking.

I knew my words ripped them apart; but those words had to be stated, then or never. Outside, my friends gathered around me for a chance to touch my new toy. After standing at the doorstep for a few minutes, certainly wondering what was going on in our circle, my "mother" came over and stood by us, looking over our heads.

"Where did you get that?" she questioned, sounding vengeful.

"From my friend, Henry," I said, without sharing any additional information.

Without saying another word, she went inside. It would not be very long before I followed her, as it became increasingly dark. She was eagerly waiting for me, and I was anxiously waiting to see what would happen.

Having finished my fun, I proceeded to complete my chores. My "parents" watched me, without saying much. Questions were written all over their baffled faces. I transferred the first round of clean dishes to the house and then went back for the last. Jealousy faithfully accompanied me in and out. I was sure the vacuum around her was still unbearable. Until the day before, she was followed everywhere by her babies. This was definitely a different day for her, as it was for me. She had no one to care for, and I had a reason to hope.

After closing my door, I climbed into my bed and held onto my car as I dozed off. It provided me with a sense of comfort and reinforced my hope.

A distant voice awakened me. As I struggled to fall back asleep, the voice came to me, loud and clear, "Fotso, come here!" my *father* shouted.

I jumped up and out of my room. Both of them were in the living room, and they didn't look like they had slept at all.

"Who told you I am not your father?" he demanded.

"I read my birth certificate, and it was not your name."

"Who? You?" he asked, almost unbelieving.

"Yes, I saw it."

My bravery neared the borderline of disrespect, but I was speaking the truth. Though he tried not to be loud, avoiding waking our neighbors up at that time of night, his voice cracked with rage.

"Did I say that you could open it?" he angrily questioned, taking a few steps toward me.

I did not even try to back up, as I was completely ready to endure the pain.

"Now, let me tell you... It is the last time I hear you say I am not your father, or that she is not your mother; do you understand me?"

"Yes, I do."

"What did you say?"

"Yes, I do, *Papa*," I sarcastically answered.

"If you say that again, you will be in more trouble than you have ever been. Do you understand?"

"Yes, *Papa*, I do."

As he threatened, my "mother" stood up and went into my room. Each of her decisive steps resonated like a hateful fist into my stomach. After a few minutes, I started to wonder what she was up to. I hoped she was not going to come out with some fabricated story that I had robbed the shop, or stolen some food. Enough was enough!

She exited my room, holding my precious car and its control. She went into her room and came back without them. Looking at me triumphantly, as if she had just won a long-fought war. I was sure the two tears that instantly erupted from my sad eyes were victory trophies for her. I hoped they would be forever engraved in her memory as reminders of her cowardly, shameful actions against my powerlessness.

"Where is my car?"

Not expecting an answer, I lifted my shirt to dry my tears. I stopped crying, but my heart was bleeding. I would certainly never see or hold that magnificent toy again. As I trudged back to my room, I almost stumbled over a tray full of ripe bananas. The next day was Saturday, a big sale day. If all went well, I would make a lot of money for my "parents." But this time would feel different, without Henry and his mother to look forward to.

I found it strange that my "parents" weren't expressing their rage violently. How unusual was it that they had not reached for the tire sliver or the electrical cord? Those tools of torture were the only means of communication they knew. I felt they might be breaking down. As their bedroom door closed, I envisioned them whispering to one another, wanting to know what had happened to me. But that docile little boy, the one who would take *it* without challenging back, was gone. That obedient-at-all-costs part of me had died when I saw my "mother" return to the living room empty-handed, without my precious car. She should not have taken my car away! She had imprisoned my smiles, joy, and happiness throughout my life. Taking my toy away was her ultimate attempt to bury my dreams and hope. In the darkness of my room, a sense of revenge sprouted from my sadness.

I would never have thought that I could fall asleep without that car in my hands; but I finally did.

After a troubled and exhausting night, I headed to the bathroom. Once there, I could not turn my attention away from the storage room, adjacent to our tiny toilets. The room had tons of ripened bananas. If I could find a way to break in to steal some, I would not have to work with an empty stomach all day. My "parents" would never know.

From where I stood, the wonderful sweet smell of perfectly ripened bananas almost overpowered the nasty odors escaping the filthy hole in the floor. I was just a few inches away from the jackpot. As I daydreamed about what was inside, I discovered the door was not locked this time. With my heart pounding inside my chest, I eagerly but cautiously entered the storage room, shivering with excitement and fear.

I was welcomed by the unison of booing from an army of termites, so loud I was afraid my "mother" heard it. They could have been mistaken for a herd of little barking guards. The room was also a fertile ground for large rats. As my eyes adjusted to the semi-darkness, I spotted tails hanging limply from several burrows. The place was scary. Any child would have probably run away, but not me! I was there for a purpose, and I was not going to leave empty-handed.

Bananas were scattered all over the floor. I was completely astonished to discover an abundance of rotting ones. In my hunger, there had been days when I thought death was waving at me, as my belly ached with emptiness. There had been hours that I felt were my last. The now rotten bananas could have made those days and hours less painful. This thought enraged me and triggered an unspoken desire for immediate revenge.

I methodically selected the best bananas in the room. A pile of skins grew by the door. That was my Secretland. I would never be hungry again, unless that room was locked.

Upon exiting Secretland, I wiped my mouth with the back of my right hand and threw the skins in the toilet. The sun was bright, and life felt simply beautiful.

Chapter 7

Itchy Erodiis

Despite the crushing weight of bananas on my head, I kept my spirits up. I wanted to be pragmatic and go straight to where I was most likely to sale. With a stomach full of bananas and beads of sweat on my forehead, I climbed the hilly narrow street that led to the main road of my neighborhood. I didn't want to carry that heavy load for too long.

I passed by the Maison Blanche pub and approached the bridge to the train station. Amid the din of dilapidated vehicles struggling to go uphill, I heard screaming voices that seemed to be coming from excited children, interrupted by thunderous splashes. Curious, I made a left turn downhill to find the source of the excitement. It was coming from a lake-like branch of the Mfoundi River.

Several dozen kids, all boys, were having a great time. They were all naked and none of them seemed worried about their public nudity. Some were running as fast as they could, and then jumping very high before diving thunderously into the grubby stream. Others were skimming the surface of the water just by moving their hands and feet.

I struggled to resist the temptation, as swimming looked easy, only a matter of jumping in and beating my hands and feet—just like them. An older boy helped me get my load of bananas to the ground, and I took my clothes off. In just a few minutes, I would be one of those boys—splashing and swimming. I placed my clothes on my banana tray, and got ready to jump in. Adrenaline rushed through my body. I sprinted forward and within seconds, I was off the ground and in the water.

As the water engulfed my body, I started to pedal my feet and flail my arms frantically. The water was surprisingly heavy. I had the impression that I was not moving at all. The surrounding noise got dimmer, as if coming from a distant place. Breathing became impossible and I realized I was sinking. I opened my mouth to inhale and instead gulped down mouthfuls of mucky water. Panic set in and I knew I was about to die. Though kicking the bottom of the river hard propelled me upward, it allowed me to inhale only a breath of oxygen before I sank back down. Because I could not keep my head above water long enough, my numerous attempts to scream, "Help!" failed. Everything seemed to be in slow motion. Some mysterious force appeared to be dragging me downstream. I was losing consciousness.

Just as I gave up, I felt someone gripping my fatigued bicep. I felt an upward surge and suddenly found myself on solid ground, panting and catching my breath, shivering, coughing, and vomiting copious amounts of water.

"Never do that again!" a strong voice shouted.

At that point, I didn't care what they said and how they said it. I was just glad I did not die. My senses calmed down a bit and I started to breathe normally. Ashamed, I sat up. A few kids surrounded me. Just like them, I was not concerned about being nude.

Having recovered enough to stand on my shaky feet, I walked toward the spot where I had put my belongings, but found nothing.

"Where are my bananas… and my clothes?" I roared, in total panic.

For a split second, the crowd stared at me. A loud and brief laugh followed, and then they returned to business as usual. As for me, I turned each weed upside down. Unfortunately, my search remained fruitless.

As I started thinking about what to do, I heard, "They are over there."

"Where?" I anxiously asked.

All fingers pointed to an area with higher weeds. Rushing over, I knelt in front of my tray and buried my face in my palms. It was not loaded with bananas anymore, but a mountain of fresh banana skins. My clothes were nowhere to be seen. I had lost everything. Looking around, I noticed a group of kids staring at me discreetly. They became my prime suspects. Their unusually round stomachs were irrefutable evidence.

The boys left the swimming pool one after the other. I sat in the weeds for hours and couldn't even think about leaving. How could I? I was naked, with my home far away.

At the end of the day, people passed by only yards away from me, still stranded in the bushes. It quickly got very cold, dark, and scary. I was also extremely lonely. I would have given everything to get out of there. Frogs croaked endlessly around me. In the background of that scary amphibian melody, the place seemed to be invaded by ghosts, all approaching me. I had to get out of there!

With the empty tray hiding my private parts, I cautiously stepped out of the high weeds and tiptoed over to the road that ran parallel to the river. About twenty yards away, bright lights from an adjacent house broke through the darkness. Being that close to an illuminated area, I felt safe and petrified at the same time. I really could not afford to be seen. If I was sighted stark naked, I could be stoned to death; no one wanted an unclothed, psychotic stranger wandering around their home. I cautiously approached the house, planning to use my speed to flash through undetected. Three grown-ups came and sat under the invading lights. In desperation, I jumped behind a vehicle on the left side of the street. I hoped not to cough, sneeze, or even breathe. It could be disastrous. By intuition, I knew I was going to be there for much longer.

I sat, completely worn out. Bugs of all sizes invaded my space, some landing on my cold body, forcing me to chase them off very gently. I couldn't take any chances.

With my shaking hands on the handle of the car, I tried opening the rusty back door. It had been abandoned for many years, it seemed. Through a shattered window, I saw weeds, empty beer bottles, and garbage. I carefully cracked the window open, sneaked inside, and lied across the backseat. Despite the unbearable smell, it felt like a cocoon, a safe oasis in the middle of the Sahara desert. The bananas from that morning were long digested. The sensation of hunger had grown by the hour, and my grouchy stomach was angrily claiming its dues. Though discouraged, I knew I would find a way out of that swamp. I had to.

The men's passionate discussions bounced back and forth between politics and soccer. I hoped they would leave soon. I wanted to head home. While I waited, I resolutely damned all the boys responsible for my misery. I wished I could have revenge that would forever be engraved in their memories.

I started yawning almost every minute and hoped I did not fall asleep there, struggling to keep myself awake by thinking about all the thrills and turmoil of the past few days. As I struggled against closing my eyes, I heard the echo of a song that had sustained my spirit and hope many times, coming from a nearby pub. The song—*Motemo* by André Marie Tala—seemed, more than ever, written just for me. Tala was preaching love against hatred, and telling me *"a lonely child is God's child."* I listened closely. Tala's voice and lyrics felt just like the hug I needed that day.

The sharp crow of roosters awakened me. I had been sleeping for a while, but I was not sure for how long. I must have passed out. Looking through the feeble luminosity of a fading dawn, I was amazed by a magnificent facet of Mother Nature I had never seen before. It was a little foggy outside; and above and around the river, a distinct layer of white clouds lingered in the air, motionless. It almost seemed possible to grab one end of that mass of cotton and drag it away to clear the air and allow the eager sparrows to fly freely.

The sun was rising in the horizon. Before long, I would be warm again, but until then, I had to remain in that fetal position to pre-serve my body heat. Getting out was not an option yet.

As the morning warmed up, my goose bumps cleared and my muscles loosened. Not far away, a few boys were playing with marbles. But I was forced to remain hidden, captive in my nakedness.

The comfortable warmth gradually turned into horrendous heat. I had bravely tolerated the cold, but now the car had turned into a furnace that was slowly cooking my body. I needed to get out, unless I wanted to die in a horrible way—very slowly, one depleted cell at a time.

As I sat up and gazed through the dusty windshield, I heard splashing coming from the swimming pool. If I could join that crowd, I would feel safe and shameless. Being nude would only be normal.

I started to push the door open, less cautiously than in the night. In the middle of the day, a squeaking sound would not surprise anyone. It was vital that no one saw me getting out of that vehicle. Once on the road, I would appear to be a regular little boy on the way for a swim.

Looking around, I cleared the possibility of anybody being nearby. Like a frightened rabbit, I jumped out of my fortress and on the road. The pool was only about fifty yards away, and I would be there in no time. With each step, I sensed my excitement and relief grow.

At the pool, one of the boys gave me a vicious look. I remembered him being the guardian angel who had pulled me out of danger the day before. As he started coming toward me, I declared, "I am not going to swim today, big brother."

"Very good! Don't!" he replied, before turning away.

Intimidated, I didn't dare go any closer to the pool. I could not imagine being elsewhere right then; so I wisely agreed to anything they said. They all were my heroes now, despite being my villains only one day before. I sat near the same spot where I had lost everything. The sun rose higher in the blue sky, and I came to appreciate being refreshed by the water drops often landing on my sizzling body.

As I gazed around me, my eyes stopped on the various amazing outfits and shoes on the grass just steps away. Then I felt the same adrenaline rush I had felt when I was reaching for my father's bank. The internal voice prodding me to help myself became irresistible. No one was paying any attention to me anymore, and so my interest shifted from my desire to feel safe to my unstoppable quest for normalcy.

Having stood up, I walked to the improvised locker room. When I reached the matching striped shirt and shorts I targeted, I was unsure about how to get the job done. If I were caught, I would likely be beaten until I died. They would never realize that I was just a child digging deep for survival. All that would matter was that I was a thief. Overwhelmed by my emotions, I almost blacked out. I bent as if reaching for my feet and instead, I discretely grabbed the outfit, and slid my muddy feet into the shoes. No one said anything. I started to move deeper into the bushes with my prize, which I folded into a small bundle. I disappeared behind the high vegetation and put my clothes on.

Out of the bushes and satisfied by how well my new outfit fit, I reached the busy adjacent street. I hurried to get away from that neighborhood, where someone could recognize my clothes. I was not out of danger yet, but I started to breathe easily for the first time in twenty-four hours.

At the top of the Montée Caveau hill, I recognized someone I looked up to, Erodiis. He was a teenager, and sold bananas too. His load of the day was fresh and seemed heavy.

"Hey, Erodiis!" I called.

"Fotso, is that you?" he questioned, obviously surprised by my clothes.

"Yes, it is."

He had no idea about what had happened; but I knew it would not be long before I told him. He liked talking with me and was always very concerned about me. Our encounter was fortuitous and I wasn't going to let it slip away. I decided to ask him for some bananas to eat.

"What's going on?" he asked.

"First, I am very hungry. Can you please lend me some bananas?

I will pay you back."

His insistence to hear everything first forced me to tell him all of my misfortunes very fast. After intently listening, he said, "Listen: you can get all these bananas."

"What?" I asked.

"Yes, you can... They are my pay for the month."

Life looked brighter. If I were to get the bananas, I would certainly be out of trouble. With this possibility, my "parents" would not suffer any loss of cash.

"Thank you very much, Erodiis."

"But I am not going to hand them over to you here; it has to be where no one will see."

"Really? Where do you think I can get them?"

"Let's just walk together until we get to a good spot, okay?"

"Let's go!" I said, very excited.

As we walked, I was very eager to own his merchandise. In my naïve opinion, I was sure we had passed a multitude of *good spots* where the bananas could have been handed over to me. I had already suggested five of them, all turned down. On my last suggestion, Erodiis furiously attacked my lack of good judgment.

"Do not bother anymore," he said. "Let's just walk. Do you want the bananas or not?"

"Yes, I do." I replied, almost begging him not to change his mind.

The all-boy Nkol-Ewé school was not far away, majestically occupying a considerable flank of the Nkol-Ewé Mountain. The school playground was completely deserted. I believed it would be the perfect transfer site and had the feeling that was where we were heading.

But the sharp right turn he made took us through an insane sinuosity of rundown houses in a flood-prone neighborhood. I hoped he had not just been teasing me. I would never forgive him.

A few weeks before, I had spent a whole day in those same bushes with a giant cobra. I had promised myself never to go through that same place again. But there I was—hopefully for the last time. As we passed near that area, I was argus-eyed, trembling and not saying a word. But I quickly regained my determination to get the bananas and lessen the trouble I was already in. In a way, I felt ready to go head-to-head with that giant snake again to reach my goal.

We finally passed the dangerous area and started uphill toward the Mefou Private Middle School, not far from the *Mvog-Ada* local market. The bargaining voices made one loud and continuous rumble. One of those voices was certainly my "father's," trying to attract more customers to his charcoal stand, with his face and hands blackened by his merchandise.

Erodiis and I emerged on an uninviting little trail, covered with high weeds and shrubs, and not visible from the main road. The bush was thick and still. The sun was at its highest point in the sky, and the day was dry and dusty. He was sweating profusely, crushed by the heavy load that was about to become mine. As my dizziness worsened, I thought it would not be long before I succumbed from exhaustion.

Right below the fence of the Mefou Private Middle School—where the bush was the thickest—Erodiis stopped and stared at me. He then looked around, certainly to make sure we were alone. The banana transfer had to be absolutely secret.

"Follow me," he said, forcing his way through the thick bushes.

"Okay," I replied, in a very low tone, as I didn't want my voice to betray us.

We disappeared behind the surrounding vegetation. My excitement became overwhelming. I would first eat some, and then take possession of the whole batch. What could be more thrilling at that moment?

With the tray on the ground, Erodiis lied on the grass, out of breath. I knelt to lessen the chance of being seen from the footpath. Crickets and grasshoppers flew noisily above us, crisscrossing one another. A merciless current traveling back and forth in my stomach continued to torture me. *"Why should I wait any longer?"* I questioned inwardly. *"We are secluded, and it's now safe to proceed."*

"I am going to have this one first," I said, reaching for one of the biggest bananas of the bunch.

"No, wait!" Erodiis erupted, jerking the fruit back.

"Why? There is nobody around."

"Exactly! *Nobody*. Scratch me first," he said, without pointing to any spot. His voice was trembling, and I didn't know why. He should not be breathing that hard anymore.

"Where are you itchy?" I asked, eager to eat some bananas before leaving with the rest.

"Here," he replied.

It was hideous to even think of putting my hand where he wanted—inside his shorts!

"Why can't you do it yourself?" I questioned. "You can reach in there."

"You don't understand yet. Just do it, please. Don't be afraid."

I knew I should not have been reaching in there, but yet I took a step to do just that. Erodiis stretched the elastic waist of his shorts, making enough room for my hand. As I hesitantly approached the itchy spot, he was trembling. He was not the same anymore. He had become a soft giant that appeared to be voiceless. He peeked at me through his half-closed eyelids. As I brushed his private part, he made a hissing sound. I pulled my hand right back out. I did not know what was going on, but I didn't want to touch *that* again. I had never touched anybody's private part and had never imagined I would.

"No!" I said, stepping away from him.

"If you don't want to scratch me, it is not a big deal. You can still get all my bananas."

"When? Now?" I hurried to ask.

"Yes, now. You just have to lie down on your tummy, and nothing else. Even if you are not itchy, I will scratch you. It will feel good; you will see," he reassured.

Without thinking about it, I lied on my belly, waiting for him to scratch me. I knew I had to play along to get what I wanted. Soon,

I would be out of there with my tray of bananas. The sound of his footsteps on the dry grass indicated that he was moving toward me.

"You better hurry up because I am getting sick of being in here," I worriedly declared.

He stood above me, with his feet on both sides of my body. He then knelt down, with me between his legs. I didn't dare say anything. I was more confused than ever. "Scratch me and let me get out of here!" I said. His trembling hands slid my shorts down, without any resistance. I didn't see a single reason why I should have stopped him from scratching me. After all, scratching never hurt.

As my shorts reached my knees, he proceeded to lie on my back, almost crushing my tiny body with his heavy weight.

"Don't worry," he whispered in my ear. "It will not hurt."

One of his hands in between my shoulder blades held me down. Even if I wanted to, I would not have been able to move at that moment. At the same time, he diligently spread my legs apart. His breathing became irregular and scary. As I wiggled under his body mass and whimpered to express my discomfort, he pulled his shorts down in one sharp movement.

"Remember, it is not going to hurt. You will like it. Believe me, it's good," he reassured again.

In my frail mind, I wondered what it was that was not going to hurt. I knew Erodiis cared about me and if he was so reassuring, I just had to believe him and let him scratch me. His lower body got more in contact with mine, and I felt him shake. I thought that was definitely not how one scratched. Something was most probably going on, something I could not comprehend yet.

As he let all of his body weight rest on me, he continued to hold me down very tight. I felt something strange touching me, moving on and in between my thighs. His movements became ferocious. With my back wet with his sweat, I felt him sliding on me.

"It might hurt a little now, but don't worry; it won't be for long," he said, with his cheek on mine.

A loud voice inside of me started screaming, "*This is not right!*" As his hard private part forced its way into my anus, I almost blacked out. I felt as if I was not going to survive the excruciating pain. With his hands on my neck tightly pinning me to the ground, I could barely breathe through the everlasting minutes that followed. My face was slammed on the ground where I was forced to inhale—when I got a chance—the obnoxious smell from the mixture of dead grass and tortured weeds. Powerless and with no chance to scream, I agonized as his hardened private part continued to slide violently in and out of my anal sphincter for even longer. I foresaw death. I knew I had to wake up then, or I probably never would. If I didn't act right away, I didn't think I would be alive much longer.

"No, Erodiis. I don't want this!" I yelled, gasping for breath. "I want to go now."

He fought fiercely to continue his act, but I was not going to let him. He could kill me if he wanted. I was small, but not weak. I became enraged and tried to flip myself over. The grip was tight and he had no intention of letting go. In his struggle and battle, he put his hand on my face to hold my head down, creating a golden opportunity for me. With some of his callous fingers on my lips, I managed to slide two of them in my mouth, between my incisors. Then I bit very hard, without worrying about tasting or swallowing his blood. If I let go without securing my safety, only God knew what would happen. As he slightly slid off of me, I elbowed him hard in the ribs. He screamed loud enough to alert people on the main road. Unfortunately, I didn't think anyone was close by. I then got out from under him, despite him trying furiously to hold me down. Having freed myself, I pulled my shorts back up as I bolted away.

"Please, wait!" he loudly pleaded.

I stopped and looked back, ready to take off again if he came any closer. He was not the powerful Erodiis anymore, the one who tricked me with bananas. He appeared weak, submissive, and vulnerable.

"Don't go away, please."

"No, I am out of here. I don't want your bananas anymore! Just leave me alone!"

I didn't think he realized that his shorts were still down. He didn't seem to care anyway. His facial grimaces expressed intense pain and fear.

"Please, don't tell anybody," he begged.

"I will!" I roared.

"Here, get some bananas," he bargained.

At that point, I had nothing to lose. I thought about making the most out of that gruesome situation, and instantly decided to make him a puppet.

"Stand where you are, and throw me some, one by one. If not, I will tell your parents," I ordered.

He obeyed and threw me the first fruit, which I devoured without taking my eyes off him. I then skillfully caught and ate the next ones, one after the other. While I ate, I regained more of my senses and felt an increasing pain from my anus.

With a full stomach, I started limping away, desperately trying to conceal the throbbing from my behind. Still in shock, I was very confused by what had just happened to me. I wondered if that was what men did out there, if it was normal. Deep inside, I knew it was not. My shorts became wet on the backside and, after passing my fingers over the spot, I realized I was bleeding. Seeing blood instantly magnified my pain, and shame unexplainably set in me. Telling could be terribly humiliating and, though proud for having stopped Erodiis from killing me, I made his secret mine also.

On the long walk back home as I continued to bleed and leak a horrid fluid from my anus, the same questions surfaced with each sigh, "*Why me? Why at all?* When I finally arrived home, my "mother" stood with both her hands on her hips. I could not tell if she was expressing her anger or her relief, after my unexplained absence. I was not sure whether or not *they* were worried and had turned the world upside down to find me. I did not believe anything could be worse than what I had just lived through. So I was very calm. Being home felt terrific—strangely.

"Where have you been?" she finally broke her silence. "What happened to the bananas?"

"They were stolen, and I couldn't come home."

"How were they stolen?"

"I was in the Mfoundi and by the time I got out, they were all gone."

I guessed she had not *turned the world upside down* for me. I could tell from the grave look on her face and the fury in her misaligned eyes, that she was about to turn my world upside down for her bananas and her money. With her hands squeezing the back of my neck, she pushed me forward, into the house. In spite of how I entered, it felt wonderful to be home.

"Now, tell me where everything is; and don't even try to lie to me," she threatened.

"I already told you. That's what happened," I courageously said.

"Did you eat my money again?" she asked, breathing hard.

"No, I did not. What I told you is true," I resolutely replied.

She reached up for one of the tools. I was ready for the cruel strokes. This time also, my voice was not heard. I did not let her have that pleasure.

After the tough days I had just had, my "parents" still had not woken up, and I wondered if they ever would. I believed they would forever remain in that dormant state. To *them*, I was just a thief and a liar. To me, I was not. Taking without asking had always been imperative to my survival. I gave up on them. If I didn't get out soon, I was certain that the following weeks, months, and years would be the same for me. With no voice, no power, and no consideration, I asked myself, "*Should I escape from this jail, or stay in?*" Staying was absolutely worthless. Yet escaping seemed dangerous. Monstrous predators like Erodiis were probably out there, walking up and down the streets, ready to prey on vulnerable children like me. And opportunists like the ones at the swimming pool were ubiquitous, waiting for perfect occasions. Even though corporal punishment would cease if I escaped, the future would still be very uncertain, and possibly perilous.

Staying made a lot of sense.

Chapter 8

Creatures of Death

(1977)

Years went by, and my life remained on standby. I was now thirteen years old.

Through this time, I survived by searching through dumpsters and mountains of trash to collect discarded plastic and glass bottles, meticulously washing them and secretly selling them to palm oil retailers in local markets.

The banana business flourished. But with Secretland off limits to me, I had to take without asking. Even though it technically made me a thief, deep down in my heart, I knew I was not. I had to survive. I needed to see the next day arrive. I was too hungry and in too much pain not to fight for my survival by *stealing*.

Through those years, I repeatedly raced against our dog for leftover bones, which I would suck shamefully, but relentlessly. I disliked it, but could never resist the opportunity to have a taste of bones and tiny fibers of meat when I was lucky. Tired of sitting and wishing for leftovers, I often stole meat from my "father's" dinner in boiling pots, each time engulfing it very fast to avoid blistering my mouth, and almost passing out from my constant fear of being caught and the excruciating burning sensation trickling down my esophagus.

I still had no idea who my real parents were. Finding them became taunting and obsessive over the years. Ultimately, I was compelled to only daydream about them, asking myself many questions that always went unanswered: *"Where are they? Do they know I am here?*

Do they think about me? What are they like? Why am I not with them? Will I ever meet them?"

One day, I sat on a bamboo chair on the veranda of our house, unable to move. My left knee was extremely swollen and unbearably painful. It felt as if there were little creatures wiggling inside with needles and pins. That had been going on for about three weeks, getting worse by the day. Unlike everyone else, Sita slowed down as she approached me, worried.

"What happened to your knee?" she asked, without making any eye contact.

"I fell during a soccer game."

As I finished my sentence, my "father" appeared from around the corner. The timing could not have been any better. She lashed out, "Have you seen your son's leg?"

"Yes; what about it?"

"It's really bad… he could lose it."

"He will be fine, trust me."

"No, he will not! You must take him to the hospital."

Sita's rage was visible. As they talked, I inspected my knee, terrified by what I had just heard. Physically and emotionally paralyzed by the excruciating pain, I silently asked, "*Why? Why me?*" In case he didn't want to take me to the Healthcare Center, nothing would stop me from limping the two kilometers to get there. I couldn't afford losing my limb.

"Go wash your legs, Fotso," my "father" ordered.

Having struggled to stand up, I headed into the house. My feelings were mixed. I was afraid that my voice would be one of those I often heard, desperately screaming from the Nkol-Ndongo Medical Center. Nonetheless, I just had to go and take it like a man. So I left with my "father", hoping everybody saw us—*us*—walking together. At that one moment, I strangely felt loved.

As we approached the medical center on the Nkol-Ndongo hill, my heart began to race. The screams inside were loud, and I could not help but tear up. As slow as I was already walking, I began to walk even slower. I knew what was waiting for me in there.

After filling out the paperwork, a nurse gently took me away from my "father." I was sniffling and shaking like a leaf in high winds. I had heard horrible stories about hospitals, some of which led straight to death, which I feared.

She cleaned my knee with a white cloth soaked in alcohol. The smell reminded me of the care Mrs. Justine had provided for my injured toe the last time I had seen her and Henry. Remembering their love and compassion momentarily cheered me up, and I believed I could survive anything.

Sitting in front of me, the nurse held my leg between hers. Then she reached over, grabbed a scalpel, and burned its tip in a tiny flame powered by kerosene from a small bottle. I screamed as the tool struck my kneecap.

"Do not move," I heard her say. "You will be fine."

She then opened the door and called for one of her colleagues, who was big and seemed very strong. I had no chance at all.

"Now, this will hurt, but it has got to be done. Please hold still, okay?"

"Okay, madam," I answered, in tears.

The man's powerful arms held me down as she aimed the tip of the scalpel at the crusty area of my knee. As she pushed it in, her face depicted disgust. She suddenly jumped away as a dark brown fluid erupted from my wound, and immediately covered her nose with her palms. I pretended not to mind the stinky odor. It was my leg after all.

She used a white cloth to wipe the filth running down my leg. As soon as she started applying some pressure to purge my joint, she yelled, "This is too much!"

I looked at her, unsure of what had suddenly become too much.

"Let me get your father in here. He must see this. This is absolutely unbelievable," she said, storming out.

She returned alone after a short while and, despite the disgust she was still expressing with every part of her body, she continued to apply pressure to my knee. The smell was still very strong, as if coming from a putrefied piece of meat. Looking closer at the cloth she used to hold the thick pus, I was sickened. I saw small maggots swimming in the grubby cesspool. Even *I* started gagging at that point.

How in the world had I hosted live maggots—creatures of death—in my living body? I thought they only infested dead and decaying organisms, but I was wrong, because I was definitely alive.

After purging the horrid fluid, the nurse sprayed the larvae with alcohol. She poured the same liquid into the hole in my knee and wiped the wound with big cotton sticks until it was clean. As she gently wrapped my knee, I felt relieved and grateful.

"You are ready to go home now," she declared, helping me up.

"Thank you so much, madam, I said, as I learned to use my new leg.

"I could not find your father... Don't forget to come back in three days, okay?"

"I will come back, madam. Thank you."

At that moment, the world seemed brighter than usual. I went out to look for my "father" through the crowd of patients and caregivers. After circling the waiting area a few times and not finding him, I decided to walk back alone, imagining him in a pub, drinking his beers. But I was not mad. He had done what he could, and I was fine.

Chapter 9

The Stranger

My knee healed quite well and I started moving around normally. It was a Saturday, about noon. Most of the residual noise came from various kitchens and dining tables. It was lunchtime.

I sat in the side yard washing the dishes dolefully. I had been there for a while, and the end didn't seem to be near. The pile was still very high, and my water reserve depleted and grimy. But I was too tired and hungry, too lazy and unmotivated to go to the public fountain for additional water. My supply had to be enough.

My "mother" exited the kitchen. Though I didn't know what she was cooking, the aroma suggested she was making one of my favorite meals. I couldn't help but salivate profusely. She locked the kitchen before heading to the living room with my "father's" lunch. She knew well by then that had she not locked that door, the next thing she would see would be me burping very loud after eating everything. I had pledged not to miss such chances anymore.

As I resentfully resumed my chore, an older woman rounded the corner and advanced toward me. Almost at the same time, my "mother" shouted from the living room.

"Fotso, hurry up!"

At the sound of my "mother's" voice, the woman froze, as if she did not want to be noticed. I ignored her and focused on obeying my "mother." The stranger stared at me, and the pile of dirty pans, pots, bowls, and plates in front of me.

"How are you?" she asked.

"I am doing well," I replied, looking straight at her, with a little more interest than a few minutes earlier.

The Stranger

My "mother" heard us. "Who is it?" she questioned, up from the couch again.

"I don't know," I answered, after checking the woman out one more time.

My "mother" crossed the doorstep and *exploded* as they saw each other.

"Oh, Mama, it's you?"

"Yes, it is me," the woman replied.

"Be very welcome. How was the trip?"

"As you know, very tiring," the intriguing visitor said.

"Of course, Mama. Let me take your bag. Please, come in."

My "mother" opened the kitchen door and invited the woman she called "Mama" in. Her demeanor had changed. She was very talkative, smiling, and not intimidating at all. She was the kind of woman I wanted as a mother, certainly not the one raising me. With her hands behind her back, the visitor followed her into the kitchen, and I became unable to hear much of their conversation.

"Joseph... Joe?" I heard after a few minutes.

It was my "mother's" voice. For the very first time, she had called me by my first name, Joseph, and my nickname, Joe. I was astonished and quite confused. What did it mean?

"Did you call me?" I inquired.

"Yes, I did. Like I already told you, it's time to eat. Stop what you are doing and come have your lunch while it's still warm."

In a fraction of a second, I stood at the doorstep as my "mother" continued her charade.

"Since I finished cooking, I've asked him countless times to come and eat, but he did not want to. That's how he is, Mama."

As she talked, the woman's eyes inconspicuously explored me from head to toe. In my mind, I was screaming, "*Liar, Liar, Liar!*" How could she be so cold in her lies with me standing only a few feet from her? I had spent many weeks, months and years waiting to be invited to eat, but the invite seldom came.

Anyway, she had said it was time to eat. No one ever begged me when it came to that. I entered our tiny kitchen and my "mother" pointed to one of the corners. "Joe, there is some couscous in that white bowl, and the okra soup is in the pot here."

"Okay," I said, resolved to obey.

"If you do not feel full, feel free to eat more, as usual."

Wow! I hurried outside to get a bigger bowl than what she already had for me. I acted fast, before she changed her mind. I had no idea about the kind of game she was playing, but I certainly wanted to be the perfect teammate. She continued to talk animatedly with our visitor, without ever taking her eyes off me.

I chose the largest ball of couscous and put it in my bowl. Then I turned around and faced my "mother," as the pot with the soup was right in front of her. Prior to taking the few steps that put me at hands reach from her, I defiantly looked at her. She wanted to intimidate me, but her steely eyes really did not affect me at all. I had grown past that. I made sure I picked the biggest piece of boneless meat in the pot and as much soup as my bowl could hold. I was so close to her that I heard her breathe. She exhaled anger and rage.

I devoured my first round of couscous. As I ate, the visitor observed me, as if she were recording how much I was enjoying my lunch. She was probably very appreciative of all the care and love my "mother" was providing me. How ironic! But I didn't care.

I was already in trouble and could not get much deeper, so nothing could stop me from enjoying that moment. Surprising my "mother" and the stranger, I proceeded to fill my bowl a second time, choosing another big ball of couscous and showering it with some okra soup and more meat. I was planning to store enough food in my belly for at least the next two days. My "mother's" look became grave.

As I continued to devour my lunch, my "mother" could no longer take it. She exited the kitchen with some lame excuse. I continued eating without even lifting my head. I knew that at any time she could burst in and take it all away. After completing the second helping, I started to prepare for my third, intermittently burping, as the visitor finally broke her silence.

"Do you know me?" she whispered.

"No." I answered without taking my eyes off my juicy pieces of meat.

"Really? You don't know who I am?" she insisted.

"No, I don't," I replied after glancing at her.

"…I am your mother," she added in a low voice.

I looked at her once more, incredulous and overwhelmed by a sudden rise in my emotions. She had caught me off guard and I didn't know how to behave. Speechless, I hesitated to reach for the rest of my meal. I was probably supposed to jump up and down and hug her. But my immediate desire and determination was to clean out the soup pot. I knew I had to hurry.

My "mother" returned and continued piercing me with her eyes. As I licked the bowl with my fingers, proudly burping, her eyes ordered me to get out; but I was not finished yet.

"I have to tell you something, Mama," she said, visibly annoyed.

"Go ahead, Marie; I am listening."

"Fotso steals a lot, everything he sees; he is a renegade."

For a short while, it seemed as if she was talking about someone else. I knew I didn't steal a lot, and certainly not "everything" I saw. I stole food when I was starved and maybe some money when there was no food around. To me, it was survival, not theft. She had never imagined how ashamed I felt each time I was forced to take without asking.

"I know," The stranger—my mother—said. "Just by looking at him, I can tell he is a renegade thief. He looks nothing like any other child out there," she added and I detected sarcasm in her tone.

The silence that followed her answer was uncomfortably heavy. The two women could probably hear me swallow the last bony particles I had been swirling and crushing in my mouth. Though they faced one another, they seemed to be avoiding eye contact. For a few very long minutes, my "mother" spoke not a single word. Instead, she rearranged the overly stuffed kitchen shelves, and appeared to be very dedicated to it. My *real* mother—if it was true—stared at me, and I furtively glanced over at her. It was not easy to start talking with her. I was confused about what exactly to say or ask.

My "mother" finally broke out of her mutism to ask, "Joe... are you full?"

"Yes," I replied.

My inner voice shouted, "*You've got to be kidding me!*" Having accomplished my mission, I headed outside, and not back to the dishes. Instead, I invited four friends to play marbles. I was certainly too full and too heavy to even think about a soccer. My food had to settle first.

Being outside with a big smile on my face, my energy level

increased. I played marbles with enthusiasm. I enjoyed every second of the game, while constantly thinking about the woman in our kitchen.

It was still very hot, and we were all sweating. In the horizon, I heard the rumbling of powerful thunder and saw raging lightning blaze the darkening sky. It got windier by the minute and the clouds started moving faster, shadowing our neighborhood. People rushed by, trying to beat the big storm.

Just as I got ready to aim and strike, the stranger emerged from the house. She waved at me and I rushed over to her, excited.

"Did you understand what I told you?" she asked.

"Yes, I did: you are my mother." I replied.

"Do you want to go home with me?"

I instantly answered, "Yes!" without thinking about it. It did not even cross my mind that I had no clue as to where I agreed to go. Knowing where I would be heading was not as important as leaving where I was. I hoped to finally see the end of my nightmare.

My mother appeared worried. Although I had just met her, I sensed it. She was staring at me and I knew it was a look of concern. It was very similar to Sita's look when she saw me tearing up after a relentless punishment or to Mrs. Justine's on each of my visits. My mother slightly folded her lower lip inward and looked over at my friends, probably comparing their physical appearance to mine. If only she could imagine how delighted I really was, she would have understood that she had nothing to worry about. I was not the thief I had been labeled. I was Joseph Fotso. I was born again. Deep inside, I knew this was the very first day of my new life.

"Go back where?" I finally asked, emerging from my daydream.

As I waited for an answer, she looked at me, seemingly surprised by my question. She probably did not understand that I had lost my identity over the years. She did not know that my "parents" had systematically stripped my identity from me with each merciless beating.

"To the village, Bandjoun," she replied. "You can at least come and spend your summer break with us."

"Yes, I want to go!" I begged, almost cutting her off in mid-sentence.

My dream was to leave my house—that horrible house—go as far away as possible, and never come back. Without knowing anything about her village, I already thought of it as my Promised Land, a place where I could simply be a child, where I could smile and bloom.

She confided to me that we would be leaving in about two-and-a-half weeks, after I finished up my school year. Those would be the longest weeks of my life, and I doubted I could wait that long without breaking down. My heart also sank when I realized I would be leaving all of my friends. It meant I would not see Sita anymore. I was not sure how to handle that imminent separation. It was going to be one of the hardest things to endure, but ultimately it was the only option for me. I would just have to carry all of them in my heart.

As she said goodbye and started to leave, an instant radiance illuminated my horizon with hope that I would be given new outfits for my trip. I had to be recognized in the village as "the kid from the city." I had to be different from any other kid: up-to-date in fashion, and clean! I wanted to arrive as the new me. All kinds of clothing styles paraded through my mind. I became excited, vividly picturing myself in things that had never entered my wildest imagination before.

The crystal curtain of fast-moving rain furiously coming down on us from the Nkol-Ndongo hills forced me to run for cover. I wondered if my "mother" would let me in. I would not blame her that day. I had eaten almost all the couscous and meat despite her silent warning. I knew she would be livid.

I entered the house and saw her on her favorite chair. As I prepared to pass by her on the way to my room, she abruptly stood up to block my way. I knew she was expecting me to escape from her, but I did not. She could just get me. It would be easier for me and for her.

"Did I ask you to eat all that food?" she asked in a raging voice that was shadowed by a thunderous sound from the storm.

I knew what she meant but I didn't even attempt to answer. As expected, she grabbed my arm and started using the tire sliver on my body. She was vengeful. I knew it. She was enraged. I felt it. She was hateful. I saw it. But I did not scream. Not that day. Never again!

One week had gone by since I met my mother, and absolutely nothing had changed. I became anxious and worried. My "parents" were behaving as if I would not be going away in just another week. I did not want to go anywhere in my old clothes.

Being on a soccer field usually took my mind off everything and made me feel like the happiest boy in the world. Not on this day. Only my unconditional love for the game kept me on that stony field. Because my teammates played fearlessly, as they all had shoes on, an idea crossed my mind:

"Hey, guys, stop!" I shouted.

"What is it?" a teammate asked.

"I don't think this is fair. All of you have shoes on, and I don't. Do you think it is fair?"

"Not really… but you, *Bami*, cannot even buy some shoes?"

Feeling crushed and rejected, I lashed out. "Don't you ever say that again! I am a Bami, and nothing can ever change that."

Realizing they were listening to me, I decided to go for the jugular. "To make the game fair, why don't you all take your shoes off?" I asked.

To my amazement, they all reached down and complied.

"All shoes over here, guys!" I joyfully said, pointing an area adjacent to the bushes.

The game resumed and went well for a while. I had to act very quickly because almost everyone was limping and complaining about the sharp little stones. Before long, they would certainly give up and put their shoes back on.

I kicked the ball far into the bushes, and everyone rushed in to retrieve it, with me last. On my way in, I discreetly dragged a pair of shoes I had targeted, which I quickly secured under the weeds before returning to the game.

The fun came to an end. One after the other, the players put their shoes back on and left the dusty field. I decided to keep a close eye on the owner of *my* shoes by pretending to be looking for something in my book bag. He was looking around, extremely worried. I could tell he was not so sure anymore about where he had placed them.

"Where are my shoes?" he questioned, as loud as he could, with a trembling voice.

Though I felt bad for him, I just could not let such an excellent opportunity slip by. My journey was only a week away, and I desperately needed shoes to avoid going to the village barefooted.

"Fotso, have you seen my shoes?" he asked, already in tears. "My parents will kill me," he added.

"Please, don't ask me. Look at me; do I look like someone who wears shoes?"

The answer to my question was obvious—with my exposed, ugly toe nails—and he did not feel the need to address it.

"Please, help me look around... please."

"Okay, let's look... you over there and me over here."

I headed around the hiding place to cover up, making sure I appeared genuine. Knowing I should not be doing this, my heart was beating very fast as I stood on the shoes. In the darkness, it became harder to see anything through the weeds, let alone a pair of small brown shoes. It was time to give up.

"I am going home," I declared.

As I left the field, he followed me, barefooted and limping. My conscience slapped me, but I had no choice but to follow through.

About three hundred meters away, we had to go in different directions. He was almost home, and I still had a significantly long road ahead of me.

"Goodbye, Fotso. Hopefully I retrieve my shoes tomorrow."

"I will see you tomorrow," I said, feeling very ashamed of myself.

He disappeared, and I ran back to the field. With him out of my sight, I felt much better. It was a relief not to see his teary eyes or hear his crying voice. I went straight to the spot, retrieved *my* shoes, and jogged back home. I did not feel comfortable with anyone looking at me. It seemed like they all knew about what I was holding in my bag so tightly.

Stepping into our house had a taste of victory. They could never imagine what I had just achieved. From the dining table, my "parents" silently watched me as I cautiously shut the door, sweating and gasping for breath.

In my room, my shame dissipated, replaced by excitement. While I contemplated my shoes, my mind was drifted to solving my next problem. I was a big boy, and it was time to obtain my first pair of underwear. I decided to use my savings from bottle sales to buy some. At that thought, I reached deep into the messy corner of my room and grabbed my wooden piggy bank. As I stumbled on the mess, my father heard a sound he knew all too well and didn't waste any time to investigate it, "Fotso, what's that?" he asked.

"It's my money," I answered, confident that it was not going to be an issue.

I heard his footsteps coming toward my room. Soon enough, he stood at my doorstep.

"Your money!" he said sarcastically. "Since when do you work? That's my money; give it here!"

For a moment, the idea of fighting him crossed my mind, but I knew I would never win such a battle. All I could do then was plead my case.

"I swear it's mine. I sold bottles at the market. Please, ask around."

"I don't want to hear it! You got it from the shop. Give it here!"

He grabbed the piggy bank without looking at my begging eyes, which would have proven my veracity. So I lost my hard-earned savings, four hundred and twenty francs. He stepped out, jiggling the bank. The sound of clanking coins pierced my heart and I instantly burst into tears. I heard him crush my little wooden bank, and that sound fed me with a burning desire for revenge. I took a brief peek at him counting my earnings. As I stepped back in my room, I heard a knock on the main door.

"Who is it?" my "mother" asked.

"It's me, Sita Fidèle... I have this for Fotso," she said. "Where is he?"

"Here I am, Sita!" I yelled, bouncing into the living room.

She handed me a pair of light brown pants, which I grabbed from her instantly. My hands were trembling. I could not believe that I, *Skirty Fotso,* would be wearing pants. Picturing myself with two hands in *my* pockets, I sensed my confidence shoot up. So I started dancing around, unable to muzzle my emotions.

"Thank you so much, Sita." I said, drying my tears with my hands.

"It's important that you have them," she said.

As she proceeded to leave the house, my "parents" followed her. They got outside, and I heard them walking further and further from our home, providing me with an opportunity.

Without wasting any time, I rushed into the shop. Knowing exactly what I wanted and where it was, I reached for the cash register and opened it. My trembling hands grabbed a few bills and coins with one swift movement. Back in the living room, my entire body was shaking. My heart was pounding so loudly that I thought it could be heard yards away. I inwardly reminded my guilty conscience of my innocence. I had not stolen from anyone; I had just taken back what belonged to me. I had dug in stinky and filthy dumpsters with my bare hands, washed out the bottles, and sold them for almost no money. Saving four hundred and twenty francs (about $0.85 US) was hard labor, and I deserved to get my earnings back.

In my room, I hid the money in a hole in my dry mud wall. I shifted my focus back to the pants, which I held up in front of my unbelieving eyes. Just then, my "parents" entered the house. As excited as I was about leaving, my feelings were mixed. In just a few days, I would go away and probably never see my friends again. After losing Mrs. Justine and Henry, I knew how harsh such a separation could be. Nicholas, Jean Emile, Sita, and several others would enter my history book. It would be a living history, as I would carry them in my heart forever, especially Sita. I was the product of caring strangers, and that would never be forgotten. I would always let my best memories soothe me and guide me through the bumpy journey of life.

After school the following day, I headed to the local market. Standing in front of an underwear vendor, I got confused by the many types, styles, and colors to choose from. My first instinct drove me to a white pair, which I bargained for, bought, and squeezed into my book bag. On the way home, I looked at people with a different mindset, almost feeling like telling every one of them, "*I will soon be wearing what you are wearing!*"

Upon arriving home, I heard my real mother's voice. I had not seen her since our first meeting. As I stepped in, I inwardly wondered whether or not to call her, "*Mom*" or "*Mama.*" Something heavy seemed to be crushing those words in my heart, and I knew it would take a lot of lifting for me to use them. I just hoped she understood.

"Good afternoon," I said.

"You are back? How was school?" my mother asked.

I could not remember the last time—if ever—someone had asked me that question. There was no doubt in my mind that I would be safe. I saw it in her concerned eyes, and heard it in her attentive voice. I would leave that torture house and never come back again. With my latest acquisition, I felt complete and ready to go. My pants, shoes, and underwear symbolized the beginning of my new life.

Chapter 10

I Was Him, Proudly.

As we left Yaoundé early that morning, embarking on a two-hundred-mile, forty-eight-hour journey to Bandjoun, I abandoned everything and everyone I had ever known, leaving them behind to head into what was still a mystery to me.

The trip was hectic. I could not count the number of times our yellow Renault bus got stuck in deep mud in the middle of nowhere, often in the middle of the night. Despite all, I was very excited about my first car ride. It felt wonderful to be seated in that van—next to *my* mom—watching the trees move backward while we sped forward. I almost wished the ride would never end, but at the same time I was eager to get to my village and begin my new life.

Being with my mother, I already felt safe and cared for. Mama Marie's steely eyes, the electrical cord, the tire sliver, my vain pleas echoing off of deaf walls, my "father's" mercilessness and carelessness, all seemed to be things of the past. *I*, as I had known myself for thirteen years, was no more, for I was just a boy in a car with his loving mother.

Bandjoun was nothing like what I had imagined in my daydreams. The kids running around looked like they had not taken a bath in months. The layers of dust on their bodies made me an oddity. Though they looked at me with envy and admiration, I wanted to rip off all of my nice clothes to fit in. Happiness was apparent. Most importantly, it seemed contagious. I felt like I belonged.

Walking up the hilly road, I worried about when we would arrive at my new home. I was so eager that I almost turned into the front yard of every single hut on the way. Every man we met looked like he could be my father, but none of them had been so far. I could not wait to see him and to be his boy.

After rounding a few corners off the straight road and going down a winding hill, we arrived at a compound with several mud huts. I heard my inner voice yelling, "*This is it.*"

"This is home," my mother said, closely monitoring my reaction.

"Really?" I asked.

"Yes, this is your home."

So that was it. Finally! Overwhelmed by my emotions, I remained speechless for a while. I was disappointed because I had hoped and prayed for a nicer house, but ours was not different from those I had seen along our way.

As I acclimated to my new environment, I spotted a swarm of kids running toward me from a heavily vegetated area downhill, repeatedly yelling, "*He is here.*" After getting to me, they began competing to shake my hand. They were simply happy; as normal as that seemed for them, it just did not make sense to me at all. They all seemed to be holding on dearly to the first piece of clothing ever made by man, since the darkness of time. It crossed my mind that this was what I must have looked like not long before; but unlike them, I had been the unhappiest kid on earth. I had always known what I did not have, and I guessed they didn't. I felt they were well-cared-for minds and souls in needy bodies. They all seemed to have what I had missed all of my life. I would have traded everything I had for a little piece of that carefree joy and happiness.

Across the front yard and above the vegetation surrounding the central hut, a thick white smoke was dissipating in the air. A strong smell of tobacco wafted over to me. As the oldest kid held my hand and pulled me toward that hut, the smoke momentarily stopped rising above the plants. A sudden loud cough resonated.

"It's Papa," one of the younger kids declared.

"Yes, it is our father," another ascertained.

I Was Him, Proudly.

My heartbeat accelerated and my eyes opened wide. I advanced to meet my father, my real father... Even without knowing it, I had been waiting for that moment all of my life.

Since I had come to know that he was alive, I had envisioned many images of him. I wondered which image would resemble him. Was he going to be old and frail, like some of the village men I had seen so far? Or was he young, athletic, and perhaps able to kick a soccer ball with me sometimes? Was he going to be poor or was he rich despite my negative first impression of his home? Was he a loving person? My mind raced with possibilities, as I shook with high emotions.

He finally emerged from the greenery, and some of my questions were answered instantly. That was my father—finally, toddling barefooted toward me, without speaking a word. He had stopped smoking and was holding his pipe loosely. He seemed to be trying to run, but could not. He was almost completely naked from the waist down. He was also wearing what looked like the very first piece of clothing ever made, ripped, and barely clinging to his frail

My Father

body. In place of shorts or pants, he just had a piece of fabric clumsily wrapped around his waist, which failed to protect his private parts. He was almost as naked as I had been in Yaoundé just a few months before.

I realized that all that time I had been the miniaturized image of my father. I was him, unknowingly; I was him, proudly. He was not rich and not young. I had thought I would be profoundly disappointed if my father happened to be all that he turned out to be, and all that I had never wanted him to be. But instead, I felt instant pride at being his son.

He managed to climb the little slippery slope between us, and approached me, with his small eyes locked onto me. Just like with my mother, I asked myself whether or not I should jump all over him and hold him tight. He simply held me on the shoulder, and said in our native language, "Welcome home, son."

His voice was soft and a little shaky. Overpowered by emotions, I was unable to say anything. He proceeded to shake and then held my trembling hand. He gave me a dim smile, which revealed his dark brown teeth. That happy facial expression instantly spread, and everybody started to smile and laugh. My smile was a sign of relief or liberation, and theirs was certainly a smile as usual. I had retrieved my long lost roots. I had a father.

I dropped the little bag I was carrying in the tiny veranda of the house and started trying to fit in. I knew I would not have to try very hard because I saw myself in all those kids. Even though I looked a little different, I was one of them deep inside. With those sincere smiles, they were what I was aspiring to be.

Two women came out of the other two huts and converged in the area where we stood. One of them was holding a cane with one hand, and her back with the other, grimacing with each step. The other was singing a traditional welcome song for me. A lot of words were mumbled, due to the lack of her front teeth. In a move that defied all of my wildest imagination, she spit onto my palms, hissing in a fine mist, and rubbed them against one another until her saliva dried off, as she repeatedly said, "May God be with you! Welcome, son."

The other woman came closer and said, "Welcome. We are very glad to have you here."

Although it was flattering to be the center of—positive—attention, I became totally confused, asking myself who all those people were. After ordering the other kids to take a few steps back, the woman engaged in a conversation, which made me wonder if she had read my mind.

"Do you know who we are?" she asked me, after pointing the other woman and then herself.

"No," I replied, with no attempt to guess.

"We are your father's wives," she said, in a tone of pride.

My father's fortress (top right) surrounded by his wives' huts: first (bottom right), second (top left), and third (my mom's)

"I am the first, and she is the second," she added, pointing to the other woman.

Astonished, I started wondering how many siblings I had. Maybe all those children surrounding me were my brothers and sisters.

My father emerged from my mother's house holding a bread-and-sardine sandwich, something everybody adored. It was *the* proof that someone had just come from *the city*, the expected thing everyone waited for without voicing it. It magnetized all the kids who instantly surrounded him. I behaved as if I didn't care at all. But I was dying to get a bite, just like everyone else.

Using his long nails as a sharp knife, he cut the bread into tiny pieces. In a voice just above a whisper, he reassured that every one of us would have some, visibly excited about what he was doing.

He finished passing on the pieces of sandwich, and each of us held onto them dearly, making sure no crumbs escaped. After worshipping my share for some time, I finally decided to take the prized food into my mouth. As I joyfully bit a tiny piece, I noticed my father licking his fingers. He had not eaten a piece of *his* sandwich at all. How in the world was he not thinking about himself? A new day had certainly come for me, filled with the reality of selflessness and a true sense of caring.

The night was approaching fast, and the darkness began to envelop everything. It was dark outside, but very bright inside me. No one there could see the beam of light effusing from every fiber of my being. Its rays would illuminate my *way*. I sensed it.

The next few weeks, I was flooded with new friends, among which Philippe Tala and Joseph Toche, with whom I bonded.

After a long day, Philippe suggested we take a bath. I wanted to refuse, but how could I? I was the cleanest guy around, straight from the city, admired by all, and I had to live up to that standard.

"Okay, let's go," I reluctantly said.

We arrived at the bank of a small stream flowing through a forest of bamboo trees, and I took my clothes off, just like him. Having realized that I was by his side, he looked at me and inexplicably burst into a hysterical laugh, holding his belly, intermittently stopping and laughing each time louder and longer than before.

"What's so funny?" I asked, perplexed.

He looked at me wiping his watery eyes and said, "My friend, you have women's underwear on."

I looked down, thinking, "*What is he talking about?*" He was obviously hallucinating.

"That's not true," I objected.

"Yes... It is a lace panty, brother. Men do not wear those."

I realized the mistake I had made, not knowing any better. I tried to play it down to conceal my humiliation. The first underwear I had ever worn were women's.

"I will throw it away as soon as I get home," I promised.

"My dear friend, are you kidding me?" he asked, having stopped laughing for a second. "You should get rid of it right here, right now. I don't want to think about what you are wearing each time I look at you."

I wanted to beg him not to spread the news but thought that doing so would bite a big chunk out of my pride.

Chapter 11

Never Again!

One late afternoon, a few months after my arrival, my father came up from his hut, carrying a medium-sized, long-necked calabash and a twisted cup made out of a goat's horn. Because of his well-known desire to feel warm at all times, he chose to sit on a spot where the sun was the brightest in my mom's dusty front yard.

From my mom's little veranda, I silently observed him. I loved him, but had not expressed it, as I had no idea how to. Though I was never taught how to express love verbally, I had learned how to recognize it, feel it, and cherish it. As he sat down, unwillingly exposing his private parts, he looked at me and said,

"Come here, son."

I stood up and walked to him, thinking he wanted me to pour him his drink.

"Hold this," he said, handing me his exclusive cup.

For the first time I held his century-old goblet. He asked that I came lower, so I kneeled in front of him.

"Hold it tight, okay?"

"Okay, father," I answered in a voice almost as soft as his.

He then proceeded to pour some kind of white drink from the calabash into the cup. The wonderful smell of the liquid was one I had never experienced before, and I wondered what it was.

"Drink it; it's palm wine. It's sweet," he said, carefully putting the dark brown container back on the ground.

Intrigued but excited, I took a sip of the milky drink. I instantly fell in love with the sweet taste and emptied the whole cup in just a matter of seconds. Being served by my father seemed to have made it even sweeter than it already was. Not long prior, I could barely dream of a drink, or of my *father* pouring it to *me*. That moment reinforced my sense of security and prodded me to let go of my past.

The following day, I discreetly trailed my father and discovered where he harvested the wonderful drink. Then I took matters into my own hands. Each day, I made sure I got there before him and selfishly emptied the receptacle into my stomach. My father complained about someone or a wild animal stealing his wine. I never dared say anything.

After about two weeks, I arrived at the palm trees that produced the wine. As I eagerly lifted the white, dirty receptacle to my thirsty mouth, the smell of tobacco forced me to turn around and look back. My father stood about ten yards away, looking at me. I felt awful, caught red-handed. It felt as if I had reached for my *father's* bank again, and unbearable images of my *crucifixion* flashed before my eyes. I was definitely ready for whatever forms my punishment would take. I deserved it.

"How are you?" he surprisingly asked, walking toward me.

"I am good, Dad," I replied, my heart pounding and my eyes wide open with fear.

"Come here."

For about fifteen minutes, he meticulously taught me the art of harvesting palm wine. Then to my surprise, he declared, "From now on, this belongs to you. Take good care of it, okay?"

"Okay, Dad. I will. Thank you!"

We then poured the drink into his calabash and started walking back, with him holding my hand all the way home. I couldn't comprehend why my father was not mad at me but instead, expressed attention and love. Deep inside, I slapped myself with no mercy at each step we took.

"Son, your name is Fotso," he continued, "and I named you

after the King of Bandjoun. He was a man of honor and dignity, and I want you to be one too, just like him, okay?

"Okay, Father. I will be."

The incident was my wake-up call. My miserable life in Yaoundé had changed who I was born to be. I was not in need anymore, but I stole. Whether I liked it or not, it really was stealing this time. I was not born to be a thief. I knew it. That white drink helped me retrieve my true self. I vowed never to steal again in my life. Never again!

Chapter 12

Why Not Us?!

July 1978, one year after I arrived in the village, my father organized a family reunion to bring all of his children under one roof for a day or two. It was scheduled for the last Saturday of that month and would be held each year on the same day. That occasion was the perfect one for me to find out if any of my siblings had made it big in life. I had always wished to have a very successful, rich brother or sister. I prayed that some of them would come to the reunion driving beautiful cars. One after the other, every single one of my father's kids arrived, many of whom I had never met. One after the other, they came on foot. No rumbling engine in our front yard! No smell of smoke from an exhaust pipe! It sank in that all of my father's children were poor.

I was, however, extremely satisfied to finally get to know all of my siblings. Having grown up feeling lonely, isolated, and unloved, it was surreal to be surrounded by so many caring people paying so much attention to *me*, the latest addition to the family.

Throughout the meeting, we prayed, talked, joked, and danced to the melodious sounds of drums. I dreamt eating rare foods that we did not ordinarily eat: rice and tomato soup with fish, fried chicken, spicy plantains and pork, and grenadine soda. But none of that was served.

Around 3 a.m., I went to my room. As I lied in my bamboo bed under my cotton covers, a sudden cloud of sadness shadowed me. I was not sad because the reunion had ended. I was not sad because there had not been exquisite food, and not because I was temporarily separated from my brothers and sisters. My sadness had a lingering taste of fury. I was deeply troubled, for I had discovered misery profoundly embedded within my family.

I was forced to realize that hope had bypassed my family. Out of more than a dozen children, only Irene, one of my elder sisters, had a seventh-grade education. All of the others had dropped out before ever reaching the fifth grade. I asked, "Why *us?*" and the only answer I could ever find was, "*Maybe it was meant to be.*" But that was absolutely unacceptable. Furious, confused, but determined, I vowed to work relentlessly to revive hope and to be its face in my family. One day, wonderful sounds of a rumbling engine would be heard in our front yard! That day, my family would smell the fantastic smoke from the exhaust pipe of *my* car! We would devour the rare dishes I expected in vain.

At the break of dawn, I rose up from my bed with a burning desire to challenge my destiny. As I opened my tiny wooden window, I realized its panel offered a great surface for writing. With the dim luminosity from outside, I managed to retrieve my only black marker and transcribed my determination:

LES AUTRES, POURQUOI PAS NOUS?!
(Others, Why Not Us?!)

With all odds against me and no real role model to follow, that line on my window fueled each day of my life.

Throughout the six years that followed, I grew closer to my father and all of my other siblings. The eight miles between my home and my middle school was certainly an obstacle, which I successfully conquered. My days started at 5 a.m. with a long walk, and ended around 10 p.m. when I arrived home from school through rain, dust, and the darkness of night. That distance made me want *it* even more. Very early on, I had understood the undeniable value of education. I understood it was my only door to daylight, my only key to greatness. Education was the way I relentlessly searched for during all the years I spent in Yaoundé. It was my way. Only education would lift the heavy weight holding me down, and break through the many social barriers and castes that existed around me and around the world.

Challenging my destiny

In 1980, prior to my last year of middle school, I devoted my three-month summer break to hard labor and earned about 18,000 francs (about $36 US), 13,500 of which I used to purchase a rusty women's bicycle. I knew that money could buy a lot of lunches and snacks. I knew it could definitely attract a lot of pretty girls. But I considered my bike one of the most important investments I would ever make in my life. It helped me cruise through distances and grades. To me, it represented the hammer that would crack the poverty walls surrounding me, the hatchet that would cut off the long legs of the social ladder.

It was 1983. I had just graduated from high school with honors and was praying for a government scholarship to be able to continue my education. If I were a recipient of the scholarship, I would go back to Yaoundé where the only university in Cameroon was located. I would return to the place and people that had seen my fears and tears reunite with my friends. However, I would leave my family behind. There was no doubt in my mind that it was what they all wanted me to do. I was the torch carrier of my family. All hopes were on me.

Before I could possibly head back to Yaoundé, I decided to seek answers to questions that had burned inside of me all of my life.

As I entered my mom's hut, I found her seated by the fire. Her feet still had a layer of fresh mud, so I knew she had just come back from a hard day of harvesting corn and peanuts. She was definitely exhausted and certainly hungry.

"Welcome, son," she said.

"Thank you, Mama. How are you?"

"I am just tired from all the work... I was wondering when you were going to come."

"The school year just finished, Mama."

"Really? How did it go?"

"I passed. Maybe I will be going to college in Yaoundé."

Before I even completed my sentence, my mom started to praise and thank God. At that moment, I understood the true magnitude of my achievement. I had done what no one else in my family had ever accomplished.

My father heard my mom's prayers, which spiked his curiosity. As he approached, I also heard my sisters' voices coming. It was a full house that night, and I hoped they would provide me with the answers I needed.

In the midst of the celebration, I was burning inside and could not wait any longer.

"Can I please ask you all a question?" I firmly demanded.

"Of course, go ahead," my mother replied. "I know your brain is always wandering. What is it this time?"

"Well, you know I was given away... I just want to know why."

I had the impression that everyone seemed to be very

uncomfortable and distant, displaying a smile to hide their discomfort. Apparently feeling cornered, they just looked at each other, none of them wanting to speak. I patiently waited. Finally, my mother broke the silence.

"Son, I have always told you that you are unique. You were born with a unique gift."

"What do you mean?"

"Son, you were born with a bracelet on your left wrist."

My sisters watched my reaction. They stared at me and I sensed their eyes even though I was not looking at them. My mother continued, "No child is born with a bracelet. Absolutely none! That is why you were special. Had I kept you, some jealous person would likely have killed you. I had to protect you, and so I did so the best way I could."

I was immobile, listening to my mother. She agitated some wood in the evening fire. As my father came and sat beside me, my mother added, "Do you understand?"

"Yes, Mama, I do," I replied.

I knew that even though I had been hurt in my childhood, she had kept me alive.

"Being born with that bracelet meant that you were a prodigy, that you were one of a kind. It meant that you shall accomplish great things on earth."

Hearing this forced me to take a deep breath.

"Son, you are our moon and our sun," my father added. "Without you, we would live in the dark with no hope for light... You shall see things that we can't."

"So that is why we had to give you away to my little brother in Yaoundé where no one knew the truth. But had I known how much you suffered in my brother's hands, I would never have hesitated to come and get you. Never!" my mother continued. "We hope you understand, son."

"I do now," I affirmed.

As they spoke, I knew I still had the birthmark on my wrist. It was about a quarter of an inch wide, slightly protruded, in the shape of a true bracelet. Everything suddenly made more sense. I understood and forgave my parents. Surely I would have made the same decision if I were in their shoes and believed what they believed. They had just wanted to save my life. It was likely that I would have been killed because of the shiny dark brown birthmark that encircled my left wrist. That revelation allowed me to find myself and put all the pieces of my being together. Having that answer allowed me to hold my head up high and accept my "gift," as it was a vital part of what had made me who I was.

Chapter 13

The Worst

(1985)

Being my family's first and only high school graduate, I never intended to stop there. About four months after my graduation, I was thrilled to be one of the recipients of merit scholarship awarded by the government. My dream of pursuing a college education was about to become reality. Without any financial aid, I would never have been able to afford my room and board.

Coming back to Yaoundé was a homecoming filled with glory and triumph. I was heading to college to pursue my crusade against destiny, feeling very proud of my achievement. I was not *Skirty* anymore, and no one would dare tease me, laugh at me, or reject me. I held my head up, not down, as I walked through the same bumpy, dusty path I used to take each time I carried a load of bananas often much heavier than I. But I knew I would never lug such a crushing load again. I was gradually smiling at life, enjoying every second of it.

For the first time since I had left Yaoundé about eight years earlier, I was returning to what used to be my home to see the people who for thirteen years I thought were my parents; the people who had tortured me. As I crossed the last wooden bridge that led to the front yard where I used to play soccer and marbles, I laid my eyes on the column where I had been tied for a whole day and felt that same pain all over again. I saw the entrance to the shop where several times I'd had to take money and food without asking, in my quest for survival. I remembered being caught with coins in my mouth. I would have done the same thing again if I had to. I had no choice then and no regrets now.

After walking up the stairsteps to the door between the kitchen and the main house, turning my back to Secretland, I knocked several times. As no one seemed to be home, I decided to venture inside. With each cautious step, I remembered every tear I had shed in that living room. The wooden armoire had not been moved. The tools of abuse—the electrical cords and the tire sliver—were not on top of it anymore, but I still seemed to hear my cries and pleas, and to feel the burning pain from each merciless strike. I looked at the spot where I had been forced to mop my excrement off the floor with my bare hands. Anger and fury tamed my confidence and pride, and became overwhelming, punctuated by the same questions, *"Why? Why me? Why at all?"* But my silent questions seemed to echo against the same old deaf walls.

As I sat on one of the brown couches, the squeaking sound from an adjacent door—my "father's"—surprised me. It was Tino—my "father"—coming out of his room. For the first time in eight years, I stood in front of the man I used to think of not only as my father but also as my executioner. With a split-second glance, I took in his physical appearance. He had lost some weight, judging by his protruding cheekbones. His creased brown shirt fit flimsily and his hair had a lot more gray than what I remembered. He appeared to have shrunk, as I was now almost as tall as he was. But in fact, I knew that *I*, the used-to-be little boy, had grown from less than four feet to approximately five feet nine inches.

He walked toward me, surprise in his red and tired eyes.

"Hello... is that you?" he hesitantly asked.

"Yes, it's me. How are you?" I replied, looking him straight in the eye and extending my right hand to shake his, but unsure what his reaction would be.

After an awkward handshake, he invited me to have a seat on the loveseat that used to be my "mother" Marie's. He sat at his usual place, right in front of me, with the brown wooden coffee table separating us. I made every effort for us to look into one another's eyes, but he did everything he could to avoid eye contact. He no longer was the same terrorizing man I had known. He seemed to be as powerless in my harmless eyes as I used to be in the tight grip of his fury and hatred.

"When did you arrive and what are you here for?" he finally asked after a long silence.

"I got here a few days ago. I will be attending the University."

Another long period of silence followed. He definitely had nothing to say, and there was nothing for us to talk about. My sudden presence was not the recipe to spark a relationship; and only God knew if I wanted one with him at all. His body language screamed his growing discomfort, and I wondered what was going through his mind. Was he afraid I was going to prosecute him? No! I was not there for that. That—if it had to be—had to wait for another time. Just sitting in that house without fear empowered me. The paradigm had shifted.

"Where is Mama Marie?" I asked, raising my voice for her to hear in case she was in another room.

"She is not here anymore... We separated and she went back to Baleng, her village, near Bafoussam... I have a new wife now, but she is not back from the market yet."

I had expected to meet Mama Marie again and look in her steely eyes that day. But I couldn't; and I was not sure if or when I would again.

After about fifteen minutes, it was time for me to leave. As I said goodbye and stepped outside, feeling taller and stronger, I saw my friend, Nicholas, just arriving home. Though we had not seen each other in years, we instantly recognized one another. Being together again felt wonderful. We sat in his veranda and spent hours remembering our past, sharing our present, and dreaming about our future.

Then I heard Sita coming home through her backyard. My heart instantly began to beat fast with excitement and I ran in the house.

"My son!" she cried, "Is it really you?"

"Yes, Sita."

Then, to my surprise, she screamed even louder, "My son is back! *Á Sanghó Lobà, Ná Sôm wã jïtà!* (Dear God, thank you very much!)"

She hugged me, and I felt as if I had my mom in my arms. Frankly, to me she was just that in so many ways.

"How are you? You grew a lot... I am the happiest mom now... my son is back! *Á Sanghó Lobà, Ná Sôm wã jïtà!*"

During the hour I spent with her, she did not take her eyes off me. She clapped her hands regularly to show her amazement. She was genuinely as excited and thankful as I was. That day was the very first of many to come, and I was more than ready to embrace them all.

On my way back to Ngoa-Ekélé, the university quarter, I couldn't help but think about Mrs. Justine and my friend Henry. The sadness of never seeing them again shadowed the joy I had just experienced. What would Mrs. Justine have thought if she could see me now? How was Henry? I had to contain my frustration and keep going.

I enrolled as a freshman in the Faculty of Sciences and rented a tiny room in *Bulawayo*, a privately owned dorm in one of the many valleys of Ngoa-Ekélé—La Colline du Savoir (Knowledge's Hill). My scholarship was 30,000 CFA francs (about $60) per month, half of which went to my rent. For the first time in my life, I had an income; I felt as if I was already cracking the surrounding poverty walls. After receiving my first pay, I went straight to a local market, bought a whole chicken, and ate it all in one sitting. It was my way of celebrating my new life and marking my adulthood. I had found a long-sought sense of normalcy.

After spending my adolescence with an imaginary girlfriend I conveniently named Justine, I found myself increasingly gripped by the power of my first crush. Since my senior year in high school, my attraction for a girl I had met during my summer break in a different city, Douala, grew bigger. Her name was Stella and everything about her was beautiful: her smile, her voice, the elegant way she

Joe, the freshman, at the University of Yaoundé in 1985

walked, and her overall aura. Just seeing her filled me with inde-scribable joy. I was in love for the first time in my life, and I did not wait to tell her in my way, writing her letters and poems. She lived in Yaoundé and attended the Leclerc High School; so another reason for my excitement over coming back to Yaoundé was that I would be close to her.

Reuniting with Stella brightened my love life. Even though I was almost certain that she did not love me, at least not as much as I loved her, to me she was my girlfriend.

Though Stella and I met often during my freshman year, all of my attempts to see her suddenly failed the year after. I became frus-trated and confused, as I had no idea why she had vanished. Many times I came close to abandoning my search. I had reached my peak of perseverance. But before I gave up, I decided to allow myself one last chance. That day, as I walked up the hill by the Inter-Army Military School—EMIA—I prayed to be fortunate enough to spot her in the crowded street. It was about 3:45 p.m., right after school dismissal.

Passing by a parked yellow Toyota KE-70 taxi, I furtively looked inside just in case she happened to be the passenger. To my surprise, she was. Stella was sitting on the far right side of the back seat. She behaved as if she did not want any eye contact with me, as she steadily kept her head down, and I understood why: she was pregnant. I could not miss her round, protruding belly, not well hidden by her tight uniform. My heart sank.

Silently standing only about three yards from her, I instantly grasped that I had lost her. After a very long minute, the taxi drove away. Resuming my lonely walk uphill, I realized that she was forever gone. In a split second, I experienced how much love could hurt when it went south. But I had to *swallow* my tears, keep my head up, try to forget her as quickly as possible, and continue my way.

As great as my life on campus seemed to be, the atmosphere within Cameroon had started to change. Upon the forced resignation of President Ahidjo on November 4, 1982, Paul Biya had taken power. Since then, an economic crisis had slowly and steadily ravaged the country. We—the vast majority of the Cameroonians—believed that the new President and his corrupt government were filling their personal pockets with revenues from *our* country's assets, including natural oil and gas, gold, bauxite, the Douala seaport, agriculture, and telecommunications. It became increasingly difficult for me to behave as if everything was alright in the face of my nation's lingering unhappiness.

The next election, on April 24, 1988, was the first in which I would vote. The only candidate—yet again—was President Biya, the incumbent. Other potential candidates were either too scared to stand up to him or too busy stealing from the country. We could only vote for Biya whether we liked it or not.

As I arrived at the polling station located next to the Ngoa-Ekélé post office, the large number of armed soldiers guarding the premises and parading the street surprised me. I took a deep breath and stepped inside the little concrete building where absolute silence reigned. The quiet signified fear. No one dared speak his or her mind loud; freedom was still a faraway dream.

I walked to a small desk where two election officials sat. At each corner of the room a soldier stood, straight and frighteningly still, with a grip on his heavy gun. I had never been so close to machine guns, and my heart began to pound fast and hard. A fine mist of sweat layered my forehead. I was scared to death.

"What's your name?" I heard, from one of the officials.

"Joseph Fotso," I answered, trembling.

Hearing my name, he looked up and I knew what he was thinking—without a doubt: "*Bamiléké!*" As with almost every other Cameroonian, my last name revealed my ethnic origin. Fotso was a name a lot of people disliked. It was a name I grew up hating myself, desperately trying to dissociate myself from, but now one I had learned to respect, appreciate, and praise. As a child, I had felt ashamed for being a Bamiléké. Now I felt extremely proud to be one, as I knew—from my own experiences—that the Bamiléké people were relentless survivors and business-driven men and women.

So there I was, a Bamiléké, standing tall in the little room, looking straight into the eyes of officials from the president's tribe—*Béti*—and about to cast my vote for a candidate I resented. As one of the officials skimmed down the voter list in the big registry book, I asked myself what to do.

"There you are," he said, pointing my name in the book. "Sign here."

I held the blue pen tight to prevent my slippery fingers from sliding down as I scribbled my signature. I asked myself if I was really going to vote for President Paul Biya. And again, a loud voice inside me yelled, "*No way... never!*"

"Insert this ballot in this envelope and put it in the box here," the other official said, handing me the items.

At the same time, as one of the intimidating soldiers moved a little closer to me, I thought I would collapse from fear. But as soon as I received the ballot bearing Biya's picture and the envelope, I made the risky decision to enter the voting booth that was placed in the middle of the room, and which offered very little privacy. As I set foot inside, I thought I was doing the right thing, standing up for my beliefs. I had decided not to vote for Biya. So as discreetly as possible, I crumpled the ballot and put it in my pants' front pocket in one swift movement. Then after acting as if I had inserted the paper into the white envelope, I turned around and walked straight to the large wooden ballot box on the table, with all eyes on me. As I was about to cast my vote, I realized just how transparent the envelope was. Everyone saw that it did not contain President Paul Biya's ballot. I was betrayed and vulnerable. That meant that I was an enemy. Silence reigned. I had to hurry and get out of there.

After inking my thumb, I rushed outside, hiding my discomfort and fear, and praying not to be followed by one of the many informants on our campus.

Despite my withheld vote and certainly that of many millions of others, President Paul Biya won the election by an overwhelming majority (99.9%) and continued to strengthen his grip on power, systematically appointing people from his tribe to key government positions. One had to be a loyal member of the President's political party, the Cameroon People's Democratic Movement (CPDM), to succeed, for the most part. For the majority of Cameroonians, it became extremely difficult to make ends meet. Even the 435 million dollars (over 215 billion CFA francs) borrowed from the International Monetary Fund in 1989, with the promise of putting the country back on its feet, did not serve its purpose. We rolled our sleeves up to work harder and harder as the President and his government mismanaged the country and got richer and richer. But there was absolutely nothing we could do. We just had to endure in silence.

As Cameroon continued to slide into darkness, students' transportation and food privileges were suspended by our unconcerned government. Those of us living off campus found it almost impossible to afford to get to our classes. Additionally, eating became a lot more expensive—almost unaffordable. Thus, students became very unhappy and a lot more vocal than the almighty government would have liked. Through it all, I managed to obtain my bachelor's degree *summa cum laude* in Zoology and then my master's degree in Biochemistry in 1989. I enrolled as a doctoral student in the Biochemistry Department of the University of Yaoundé.

Over those years, the government continued to be indifferent to university students. Our anxiety grew into a tension, sustained by the arrogance, carelessness, and selfishness of government officials. Professors' salaries were slashed by as much as fifty percent, and student scholarships were suppressed. Left with no income, my dreams and aspirations of making it became just that, dreams! And I was only one of the tens of thousands of young men and women sharing the same loss of hope. There was no motivation to teach and absolutely no drive to learn. Life became unbearable. No one knew what the next day had in store.

With the growing uneasiness and rumors of an imminent students' strike, the President and his lackeys ordered hundreds of armed soldiers, undercover agents, and tanks onto the campus, in an attempt to frighten us. They did not want the world to hear from us but to continue having the illusion of a peaceful country, on its way to prosperity, unity, and equality. They had to muzzle us. They turned the campus into a military fortress, as there seemed to be one soldier for every few dozen students. Horrifying sounds of gunfire were sporadically heard at nights. Our government was at war against its own people—the powerless students and teachers it was supposed to protect and serve. AK-47s and tanks were met by our silence and scorn. Even though we were unarmed, we knew we would never be disarmed.

One afternoon, a few days after the beginning of the occupation, I powerlessly lied on my bed, desperately hoping to catch a nap. Though my eyes were closed, I couldn't sleep. I kept thinking, meditating, and brainstorming—instead. I had the impression of having entire films of untold horrific images of our lives parading in my brain. The loneliness of my semi-dark little room became a silent partner who listened to my voiceless thoughts without challenging them or judging me. I wished I could go out and express myself through a bullhorn, but I couldn't. One never knew who was listening. The government's ears seemed to be always tuned in, and its reach was very long. They had already attempted to muzzle some of the more outspoken including Senfo Tonkam, who had escaped captivity and was in hiding.

We, students, were more than just our families' hope; we were our nation's future, and what was happening was beyond even the most ruthless of imaginations. Hope from education was the cane that helped us stand. It was what sustained us when there was nothing to eat. It was what kept us going. And they were taking it away, torturing our dreams, and murdering our future.

I broke into a sweat and decided to open my windows. I was tired of being a prisoner in my own room, my own *home*. Increasingly, something inside me pressed me to step outside. So I stood up and went to the door. I heard a few of my friends, including Pierre Néabo—or Piné as we called him—whispering outside. Like me, Piné was a doctoral student in Biochemistry, and we both lived in different buildings of the *Cité du Savoir* dorm, where I had moved.

Despite having a pleasant taste of freedom from being outside, I was exhausted and starving, with no will or power to resist the urge of finding food. As I headed up the deserted stony hills from our dorm complex to local shops, I caught a sight of a helicopter crisscrossing the blue sky.

When passing a few other students on the narrow pathway, we exchanged quick glances, and the voices out of our frustrated eyes were very loud and audible miles away, up to the deaf ears of the Unity Palace, the presidential residence. The need to voice our oppressed thoughts was huge. But how could we? The government was merciless and we all feared being arrested at best, and gunned down at worst.

About one hundred yards away from the *Orly* gathering point, the major crossroad in the university quarter, I came across Rogers, one of my neighbors.

"Let me show you something, Joe."

He pulled me close and took a creased piece of paper out of his pocket. He seemed very nervous and was shuddering. He looked up and down the street, and even in the surrounding bushy areas, as if he wanted to make sure no informant was hiding there. What was it? I could only tell by his unusual body language depicting fear, it was something very serious.

The helicopter flying by forced Rogers to delay showing me the paper. It was so close to us that we could see the hatred in the eyes of the two soldiers sitting on its edge. That demonstration of might was unnecessary; we only held pens and papers, not machine guns. We could shoot words, not bullets. But there was no doubt that they were just puppets, and the strings were being pulled from far away, in the luminescent Etoudi Palace. We wished they remembered that we were their brothers and sisters, and that while they fought us, the masters were busy selfishly looting our nation and stealing what belonged to all of us—our heritage. We started to walk back to our dorm.

The piece of paper was still in Rogers' right hand and I was dying to know what it said. Without consulting one another, we walked just fast enough not to give any impression of running away.

"Take a look, Docta," he said, finally opening the folded paper. "This is dangerous!"

Skimming through the black-on-white text, I was flabbergasted by the first few words. Rogers had every reason to be as nervous as he was.

DIRECT ACTION FOR LIBERATION

Enough is enough! Before independence, the Bamiléké represented misery; today, they represent wealth. They have bought our lands and women with beer.

They belong to the Western mountains where they came from! Our tribe is sacred. Danger to anyone who accepts these illiterate and money-loving bastards.

Together, we must stop them. Our tribe first, our tribe only!

Signed, National Front

I came from the mountains of the West—Bandjoun, and the shocking words I read seemed to be a massive gun pointed mercilessly at my temple. Their authors were cutting our national unity with tribal knives, destroying the multifaceted roots of our society.

"Where did you get this?" I asked, in a state of shock.

"It's everywhere on the street up there."

We stopped talking, as we both understood that it was time to get out of there. The clock was ticking. Wishing one another good luck, we separated and headed back to our rooms. I felt the heat in all senses of the word and was sweating profusely. Getting back into my little room was reassuring. I sat on my squeaky bed, with both of my palms on my chin supporting my head. Thinking of those I had always had around me, I did not see tribes but diverse people. After digging deep inside and hesitating between different ways to vent, I chose to express my feelings on a piece of paper:

> *Steps from light,*
> *You fight.*
> *Steps from felicity*
> *You inspire pity.*

The Worst

On pedestals of love
You scare off doves.
In the darkness of your skin lay love,
And you nurture hatred and not love
In the abyss of your pain.

Of all screaming voices
Without choices
Of the agonizing humanity,
I hear some yelling
Others praying
On the shore of the bloody sea.

This world of blood and tears
These words of wars and fears
Are not the ones I conceived
So many years ago
In the dawn of my days,
With little on our trays.
With a ways to go,
They ought not to be the ones I perceive.

If to my crushed pen is given the order
To restore some order
In the vast necro-toll
Rising in all poles,
From its bleeding tip and ink
In a blink,
These words will flow
Without any flaws:
Bami or Béti
Hutu or Tutsi
Peuhls or Touareg
Black or White...
Had any chosen?

Our difference
Should be a reference.
I would be me, never you;
And you, always you;
Always and forever.
I would rush to your weaknesses
Prey the weaknesses of my strengths.
The world, a better place,
Will grow smiles on your face,
With ashes from tears and blood.

I could have gone on and on, but I stopped there. I wished my words could eradicate the message of hatred and war. Unfortunately, I was the only one with access to those thoughts; but I hoped and prayed to be only one out of many millions who would repudiate those incendiary documents.

As I lied back down in my bed, loud noises began from far away, certainly from the campus. Our frustrations had built up to a point where they could not be held in anymore. We had started to let it all out at our own risk. It had just been a matter of time for our frustrated voices to be heard.

The helicopter picked up speed and began to maneuver as if in a war zone. My heartbeat became uncontrollable. That sea of shouting voices made my decision very easy. I had to get out of there that same night. But I was not capitulating. I was just not ready to die, and I wanted to keep my family's hopes and dreams alive.

After that aggression, things became a bit calm. But danger waited just around the corner—the danger of being trapped with nowhere to go; the danger of being arrested for fighting for our right to fairness; the danger of being killed for standing up to the President and his government. One could almost sniff it and smell it. As the moonlight dimmed, the time to escape arrived. After locking my door, I ventured outside. It was about one o'clock in the morning, and dangerously quiet, so quiet one could hear the soft breeze blowing by. Under my feet, the ground became spongier as I approached the river of our neighborhood. The increasingly high vegetation helped my discretion. I was shivering from the cold of that hour and the consuming fear growing inside me. A sudden noise drew my attention and I instantly stopped to listen, ready to take off. After a few everlasting minutes, with my heart pounding and my feet barely touching the ground, I advanced, almost counting my hesitating steps. My imagination could not help but picture an AK-47 on the side of my head, with an angry finger on the trigger.

It wasn't very long before I heard sounds again. I noticed a slightly open dorm door on the other side of the river. My curiosity grew from passive to obsessive and devouring. Cautiously advancing, with my eyes wide open and my senses heightened, I was extremely scared. Any minute could be the last one of my life, but I still wanted to see. I wanted to know!

The voice became clearer as I got closer. Its imploring tone was like a sword in my heart. In an attempt to increase the acuity of my hearing, I stopped breathing.

"Please! Stop! For God's sake," I heard.

"Quiet!" a deep and angry voice ordered.

I riskily approached the room, step by step. I thought of a robbery in progress. No other explanation could really hold. I got to the point where I could finally sneak a clear peek through the tiny opening of the door. A sudden spasm shook my body and cold sweat dripped down my forehead. It was not a robbery, but I truly wished it were.

Two soldiers in uniform were holding a fellow student at gunpoint in one corner of the small room. The student was crying silently, and tears were flowing profusely out of his exhausted eyes. Every now and then, he glanced at the opposite corner. I cautiously stepped sideways to see what he was looking at, and time froze: another soldier was fulfilling his bloody and diabolic desire by raping a woman. She no longer showed any sign of life other than sporadic neck contractions. At that moment, I wanted to burst in there and turn one of those firearms on those wretched men. But how could I?

After the weary and sweaty soldier triumphantly lifted his body off the woman, I realized she was pregnant. My heart dropped. As one of the other two started unzipping his pants, I turned around and began to tiptoe away. If those soldiers knew I had witnessed their crime, they would have turned the world upside down to find me.

Turning around and walking away filled me with a crushing sense of uselessness. But what could I have done? I was sure I would ask myself that question for the rest of my life, and would probably never find an answer. I was deeply disturbed, hurt, and doubted I would ever heal.

Numb, I walked back to my dorm room. Those heartless puppets, those ruthless soldiers were more than welcome to come and get me. As I persisted on finding one single reason that would halt my consuming guilty feelings over abandoning that woman, I fell on my bed and slid under my covers. The rest of the night would be long.

The next day, the sun was shining, and more students emerged from their hideouts. My head ached. I couldn't sleep through the few hours that separated me from dawn. I decided to walk back to that place to uncover the outcome of the horrendous scene I had witnessed.

From a distance, the shadow of a woman under a mango tree in the front yard of the dorm drew my attention. I was torn between wishing that person be the woman I'd seen the night before and wanting her not to be her. If it was her, I would be glad she was still alive; but how sorry would I be for not lending a hand when she desperately needed it?

The woman was resting on a little wooden bench, vaguely and steadily looking straight at her door. As close as I came to her, and as noisy as my footsteps purposely became, she remained unmoving. She seemed completely unaware of her surroundings. She gently rubbed her round belly with her right hand as if it hurt. Realizing she was the one, I assembled all of my courage and approached her.

"Hi, cousin," I politely said, calling her by an endearment shared by all, and struggling to conceal my shaky voice.

She looked at me, and said "Good morning, cousin," unexpectedly sharing a smile, which came as a beam of light in my obscure view of the world.

Her face appeared very familiar. I remembered thinking how beautiful she was each time I ran into her on campus. She still looked very pretty, but I couldn't get past what she had just suffered. Asking her how she was doing would be cruel, and I didn't dare attempt to. I had already gotten an answer through that priceless healing smile. Without saying more, I continued my route to nowhere.

Chapter 14

The Jewel

(1990)

W e—Cameroonians—aspired to democracy, tired of witnessing our great nation kidnapped by self-centered politicians and their families. Weary of going to bed with no hope! Despite our pleas to restore fairness across the country, assistance to college students and hope for younger generations, Paul Biya, our "deaf and blind" President, pushed on, building and securing his way to everlasting power. It became certain that he was determined to ever lose an election only to almighty death. Our society became like a dormant volcano, boiling and rumbling from deep within, only awaiting a spark in its cracked crust to explode and unleash its hot and uncontrollable magma.

Looking the nation in its exhausted and bleeding eye, Augustin Kontchou Kouomegni, the Minister of Information, shamelessly claimed *zero death* through the only TV channel—the government-owned Cameroon Radio Television (CRTV)—and the many loyal radio stations. I personally did not know whether or not any of us had been killed, but nothing would have surprised me. Anyway, did it really matter? We had all been killed in so many shocking ways. They had drowned our motivation, hopes, and dreams.

Lectures slowly resumed, taught by unmotivated professors. In fact, we all individually fought hard to regain our lost determination to hatch from our poverty shell. Each day was a day to wrestle with, as any of us could crack under the unthinkable emotional weight of uncertainty we each dragged around. Nonetheless, we kept hoping that the incendiary battle from the past weeks would illuminate our ways to success. We did not have the right to hit rock bottom.

As the sun set on June 09, 1990, I sat at my tiny little study table, struggling to read a few biochemistry lecture notes. My mind was set on the Soccer World Cup, which had started the day before. I couldn't wait until the rerun of the opening game of the competition between Cameroon and Argentina. In the meantime, as I wandered between laziness and lack of motivation, some distinctive footsteps caught my attention. It was my friend Piné, who came over and invited me to his cousin's wedding celebration.

Piné and I braved the dust of the dry season and soon arrived to the party house. As we entered the tiny rectangular living room, we greeted a few of the guests. While Piné wandered around for a sweet spot, I managed to squeeze myself into a tiny space between an armoire and the loveseat that was reserved for the bride and groom. Covered with a pure white cloth and ornamented with a few rose petals, that seat was sacred and no one dared even come as close as I was.

I sat in the corner, silently scrutinizing the other guests and secretly sniffing the exquisite aromas from all the foods I couldn't even see.

The happy couple finally made a grand entrance and the crowd became euphoric. As pleased as I was for them, I was starving and wanted things to speed up. So I was relieved to see all the food arrive shortly after.

Right after we ate, many people got up and began dancing to local rhythms and melodies. Not I. Every now and then, I lifted my head to admire the bride and groom just inches away. The room was noisy and very annoying, as almost everybody danced and sang at the same time.

Out of nowhere, a silhouette appeared on the dance floor, disrupting all of my asocial feelings. It was a girl, slowly making her way through the cheery crowd. My heart stopped, along with time and everything else around me. She was amazingly beautiful and I did not need all the time in the world to see it. So I instantly engraved that unique and precious sight in my memory and started to cherish it.

Just a few minutes prior, I clearly wanted out; suddenly, leaving became the very last thing on my mind. I had not had a chance to say a word to that girl, but my heart already whispered and sang to her at each sighting.

She approached the newlyweds and came so close to me that I could hear her captivating voice. I watched her, with my thoughts navigating between how well she wore her light-blue-and-white pants and shirt, and how smooth her skin appeared. In that room, I no longer was aware of anything or anybody other than that enigmatic, intriguing creature.

Wonderful sensations traveled my body. For a long minute, I stared at her. She glanced at me and I found myself looking straight into her gorgeous eyes. Focusing on her with all the confidence I could muster, I became captive of her sudden smile. It was *the* smile I spent my teenage years only dreaming about. I managed to smile back, though not certain this fairy beauty had smiled at *me*. I was *nobody*, and a lot of people in that room were probably far more deserving of that gift.

She ended her conversation with the groom and walked toward the back door. As she disappeared, I felt as if submerged in a thick cloud of darkness. I looked at the spot where she had stood and willed her reappearance. No magic happened and I returned to reality, hearing some of the lousiest voices ever, sensing the floor shake from dance steps, and smelling the rising dust.

Then I started blaming myself for not having gone to her, even just to say, "Hello." As I tried to understand and justify my lack of action, she came back on the dance floor and stood in one corner, amused by all the fun of the moment. My heartbeat sped up again, but this time, despite my insecurity, I kept my composure and approached her.

"Hi," I said, looking her in the eye.

"Hi," she replied.

"Would you please dance with me?"

For long seconds, I agonized to hear a "Yes" or see a nod.

"Not now… What about the next dance?" she said.

"Sure…"

As I began to digest her unexpected answer to *me*, she entered a small bedroom right across the dining room. Every single cell of my trembling body was triumphant, for I had just talked to that mesmerizing girl and gotten a promise of a dance. It was surreal.

Another song began. My time had come. I stood on the dance floor, not sure if I should start dancing and hope she joined me, or return to my seat and hope she came and got me. Time stretched on, as seconds seemed to last forever. As I took a few steps toward the middle of the room, I heard her voice behind me. Turning back, I saw her looking at me. I started dancing, putting on the moves of my life, and easing toward her. She stood still, staring at me. I felt awkward but didn't have a choice. About three feet from her, I considered giving up. At that moment, she started dancing too, slowly, and smoothly. We met face to face and our bodies seemed to melt and fuse into one, as the *Zouk* dance required me to hold her by the waist.

I wanted to tell her how beautiful she was and how gracious and healing her smile was. I wanted her to know how soothing her voice was and how refreshing her perfume smelled. But I did not. I let my genuine silence speak loud for me and say all the unspoken words of my exuberant senses, the words I was not able to say.

The music ended but we remained glued to one another. I was still not aware of anyone or anything around us, and it seemed like she wasn't, either. As the guests got invited to have a seat to share some ceremonial roasted peanuts, I wished I could be somewhere else, alone with the girl. I would gladly give up all the peanuts in the world for her.

"Can we talk?" I asked, with confidence this time.

"Sure," she replied. "Let's go behind the house."

Without wasting any time, we sequestered ourselves in the backyard as she suggested. As we sat on the wooden bench by the wall, it seemed as if we were the only two beings left on earth. The half moon illuminated the yard. Even though I didn't want God's eyes right on us, I had the pleasant feeling that He would not disapprove of us being there—together.

"My name is Joseph. What's yours?"

"Chantal," she replied, almost whispering.

"That's a beautiful name. Where are you from?"

"Bandjoun," she said.

As we conversed, an undefined force drew us toward one another until, shoulder to shoulder, we could not move anymore. In a bold move, I took her right hand and, without saying anything, she started squeezing mine, just hard enough for the message from her soft fingers to be clear.

I knew I was in love. Chantal was the girl of my dreams, my soul mate. There was no doubt in my mind.

The door opened and an elderly woman stood at the doorstep, staring at us. We untangled—out of respect for her—and increased the distance between us. I did not know who she was, but she had given us a silent warning. We had to get out of there.

"Can I see you tomorrow?" I asked.

"Yes. I will tell you later where; for now I have something I want to say now before we leave: I was dying to dance with you, but I just had to tease you first."

"Really? Very funny…"

I followed her back into the noisy room, my eyes sparkling. I was a new man with a priceless jewel deep in my heart. As the rest of the evening went by, we evaded all distractions, exchanged glances, and spoke to each other with our eyes. I was saddened when the party came to an end, because I would no longer be able to look at her.

I arrived home around 3 a.m., went straight to bed, and was unable to sleep for the rest of the night. Each hour seemed like an eternity. Time teased and tortured me.

Tired of waiting around doing nothing but praying for time to speed up a little, I rushed across town to the cross-section where I would be meeting Chantal. It was 10:15 a.m. on Sunday, June 10, 1990, and I was forty-five minutes early to my rendezvous. I tried to guess what corner she would appear from as I walked down one of the dusty and crowded streets. About 150 yards down, she popped up thirty minutes early. Only then did I really realize she was not the product of my fertile imagination. She was real!

"Hey, Chantal, how are you?"

"I am okay. You are already here?"

"I just couldn't wait anymore."

I wanted to jump up and down and sing to the world how much I loved her, but I decided not to proclaim it just yet. We then talked about everything like identical twins separated at birth and finally reunited, which revealed how much we had in common.

During the one month that passed, I met her older sister, Anne, who seemed to like me. Over that month, Chantal told me about a number of men, some very wealthy, who were willing and able to put up a considerable chunk of their fortune to marry her. On more than one occasion, she went so far as to ask me to help her choose the lucky man. I was, of course, crushed and very scared, scared of losing the girl of my dreams to one of those deep pockets. Those rich people always got any girl they wanted and as many as they desired. I had nothing but my heart to offer her.

We then traveled to Bandjoun, our birthplace, to spend the rest of our summer break. As we walked through some woods one afternoon, I felt ready to help her choose the right man, a man who would live for her, who would not hesitate to stand between a hot bullet and her.

"I have someone for you, Chantal," I said

"Really?"

"Yes… I know who will make you the happiest woman on earth."

Judging by the look on her pale face, she was eager for me to reveal my choice. I reached into my pocket and pulled out an envelope.

"In here is *the* guy. Remember: if you don't like my choice, feel free to reject it. But I know him very well, and no one will ever love you like he does. He has been waiting to marry you."

As I finished my sentence, she ripped the envelope open and pulled out a picture. I could hear my heart pounding. I stared at her to see her reaction. She sighed and moved closer to me.

"Joe, you made me very nervous. Why didn't you tell me it was *you*?"

"I couldn't do it in any other way."

"Thank you, Joe. I want to marry you, too."

Hearing these words from her seemed surreal to me. We fell into one another's arms and I wished that moment would never end.

"I love you and will never stop loving you," I whispered in her ear.

"I have never had feelings for any of those men... From the first time I set my eyes on you, all I wanted was you, and no one else. I love you too, Joe."

Not long after, I was introduced to most of Chantal's family, especially her mother, Mama Therese, who gave us her blessing. A few members of her family including her cousin, Nestor, and her brother, Jean Rockefeller, voiced opposition to our union, because they would only get "respect, and nothing else" from me. They would have preferred a heartless but wealthy brother in-law to a loving but broke one. Always standing by me was Chantal and her unwavering support, materialized by her rejection of the richest man in Cameroon, who happened to have the same last name as me—Fotso. She had a unique opportunity to own the *world*; instead, she chose me, the penniless student. I felt loved, knew I was loved, and could say it with confidence then.

The day finally came to take my fiancée home to my parents. If they didn't like her, I could lose my love. This debilitating thought made me extremely nervous as we started the descent to my mother's house. Crossing the doorstep was nerve-racking. My mother was seated in front of the red-hot fire, using a bamboo pestle to swirl the steamy contents of a big aluminum pot. She lifted her head and said, "Welcome, princess."

"Thank you, Mama," Chantal replied, with a bright smile on her face.

"I had been waiting for this day to come..."

At that point, I was certain that my mother would not stand between my sweetheart and me. She stood up and started a long massage session, identical to the one I had received the first time I set foot in Bandjoun, the day I met my father. In my culture, massages from grandmas were synonymous with blessings. My mom was blessing Chantal.

As we got closer to my father's hut, we saw him sitting and sunbathing on his dusty front yard, and feeding the visiting chickens some corn. He turned as he heard us coming, and unsuccessfully attempted to stand up.

"Welcome," he said, in a very inviting tone.

"Thank you, Papa," I replied, helping him up.

He took a look at the both of us, and threw the last handful of corn he was holding on the ground. As the domestic birds noisily rushed to the grains, he continued,

"So, this is she?"

"Yes, Papa," I hurried to answer.

After a long pause, during which he visually scrutinized Chantal through his tiny eyes, he said, "Welcome, my queen. Always be welcome here; do you understand?"

"Yes, Papa. Thank you very much," Chantal said, gently squeezing my hand.

"May God bless you. May Bandjoun's God always protect you from all harm. May my ancestors always sweep your paths and clear them from any pines."

"Thank you, Papa," we both replied.

At that moment, I heard my mother calling me. I released Chantal's hand and rushed back to her hut. As I sat down, she started enumerating all of Chantal's qualities. "She is a great girl; we are truly blessed." She went on and on, delighted. After about an hour, wondering what was taking my fiancée so long to join me, I went back to my father's.

As I approached the hut, I heard the sound of splashing water. They were no longer in the front yard. I rounded the corner and realized that Chantal had stripped my father of his clothes and was giving him a shower. My father was over a century old and had not bathed in over a decade. His now-cleaned clothes had not been washed for years. He had always vigorously rejected all attempts, stating that showers would get rid of the protective outer crust that had built up on his skin over the years. What was even more mind-boggling was that Chantal's beauty was striking and no one would have thought she would readily dirty her well-manicured hands. But she did just that. She would be my wife, the woman who would share my joys and sorrows. There had never been a doubt in my mind, and that day reinforced it.

My father had pushed his dignity aside and allowed Chantal to bathe him. That meant Chantal was now a part of my family. They had mutually accepted one another.

She finished her chore and emerged, sweaty, wet, and dirty. I was speechless. How could I have said, "Thank you"? Only my love could show her how grateful I was and would forever be.

Chapter 15

Living on Love and Fresh Water

S till under tremendous pressure from the endless social turmoil, President Paul Biya instituted a multi-party democracy against his beliefs, with promises of freedom of speech and assembly. He, however, continued to have a very heavy hand through the National Security forces, local police, and secrets agents, acting in the dark of nights or in plain view to arrest numerous opposition leaders. Thus the democracy so loudly offered was a false one, and one not to be accepted.

The dormant social volcano erupted in the form of *Villes Mortes* (Dead Cities) in April 1991, a social disobedience movement that crippled major economic activities, including public transportation within and between cities, seaport, airports, local markets, etc. The country became paralyzed, forcing the president to declare a state of emergency, establishing himself as a smooth ethno-fascist dictator, protected by his well-paid iron-fist army, flying under the radar of the international community, with his dishonorable tracks well-covered by France. Biya himself, president of a free and sovereign nation—supposedly—boasted about being "France's best student."

Two years crawled by, two years during which my love and commitment to Chantal was challenged constantly by my precarious financial situation. I was now a Research and Teaching Assistant, and would normally be earning some money. However, despite our pleas, the government had suspended all allowances to the university's teaching assistants. Thus, I was not able to buy my beautiful fiancée a single tube of lipstick or nail polish, let alone to fulfill her recurrent, monthly feminine needs. Therefore, we were supposed to have broken up because we were poor and could barely make ends meet, pressured by wealthy men still fighting to win her. But we stuck together. Our love for each other withstood all attacks.

Although Chantal had found amazing ways to cope in every situation and adversity, looking at her always brought tears to my eyes. Agonizing over the possibility of losing the love of my life, I went to bed every night ashamed in the pure secrecy of my mind and soul. But she stood firm by my side in the name of love. Her beauty kept me fighting and hoping; her support and tender words of kindness kept me strong; and her splendid smile and constant display of love, which never faltered, kept me going.

Having postponed our wedding several times for financial reasons, we finally decided to get it over with. August 19, 1993, was the day I would say, "I do" to the woman of my life. We chose to hold our wedding in the village to keep the cost down. As we got closer to the scheduled time, I felt butterflies in my belly.

Now standing across the table from the civil servant who would unite us in front of God and men, Chantal was extremely beautiful, wearing a white gown cut to her knees. After some routine ceremonials, the civil servant finally asked the questions I had waited so long to hear.

"Mr. Fotso, do you take Chantal as wife for the rest of your life, for better or for worse, in sickness and in health?"

"Yes, I do," I said, excited but still extremely nervous and shivering.

"Ms. Chantal, do you take Joseph as husband for the rest of your life, for better or for worse, in sickness and in health?"

"Yes, I do," Chantal said, sharing a look that said, "*We made it!*"

"Chantal and Joseph, you are now husband and wife... you may kiss," the civil servant declared, after having us sign the marriage certificates.

Mr. and Mrs. Fotso, happily receiving their marriage certificates from the hand of a Civil Servant on August 19, 1993

Holding my copy of the certificate reinforced my new mission in life, which was to make that woman—now my wife—the happiest woman on earth. It was my pledge and I would make sure it never faltered. Failure was not an option. I would fight relentlessly the rest of my life and give until I had nothing left to give, to keep my wife smiling.

After living on so much love and fresh water, and almost only on love and fresh water, the horizon suddenly looked brighter. On April 26, 1994, less than a year after our wedding, I defended my doctoral thesis and passed with honors, earning the right to be called "Doctor Fotso." It certainly was a new day for us. I would soon be able to afford to feed my wife and the little one growing in her.

We had waited three years to get married, and we refused to wait any longer to enlarge our family. Encouraged by my vain hope for recovering my unpaid salary at the university, we got pregnant and expected our first child in May. It became as exciting as it was scary. How would we welcome a child in the world? It was more than just being able to feed our baby. What if he or she had some major health issues? As grown-ups, we could go to bed hungry, cuddle and hold on to each other all night until dawn liberated us with the hope of a better day ahead. But babies wanted it "right here and right now!" As scary as it was, we knew we would starve ourselves to death, if necessary, to feed our baby.

I applied for an Assistant Professor position in the Biochemistry Department at the university and was very hopeful. I had excelled in school and had always thought education would bring me security. But despite all of my efforts, I gradually lost any hope of being hired. The university was for the most part a government affair, and I had the wrong name—Fotso—for that or any other position. I was a Bamiléké vying for a prestigious job in an institution governed from a distance by the president's inner circle. I was fairly sure that if my name were Biya, Atangana, Onguéné, Essono, or Mballa—thus from the President's tribe (Béti)—I would have been hired in a heartbeat. Tribal origin, not merit, was the criteria. I was sequestrated by bad luck and my name, powerlessly surrounded by the unfair grips of tribalism. I knew I deserved a position at that university, and more so than some of those with names that rhymed with alignment to President Paul Biya, his government, his opulent Party, his tribe, and other non-Bami loyalists.

It was a Sunday afternoon and for about three hours, Chantal had been enduring an incisive pain. Ever since I knew her, it was the first time I saw her in tears. Lying on our bed, she was often unable to cry out loud, as the pain had kidnapped her distressed voice. I felt powerless. Not being able to alleviate her suffering tore me apart. I wanted to help the woman I loved, but couldn't.

Some bloody fluid started to seep out of her; and so I decided to take her to the hospital. She barely stood as we walked through the bumpy path to the main road. In the back of my mind, I started brainstorming about ways to get some money. Without any, I didn't know how I would get care for my wife and our newborn.

We arrived at the hospital, the *Maternité Centrale*, and Chantal was admitted. Hearing women screaming inside the huge concrete brick building got me worried. So I instantly gave my wife the only thing I could at that moment, my supporting words: "Be strong, sweetheart; I love you."

Her answer was a soothing glance and the beginning of a smile, which was cut short by a sharp pain in her belly.

Without any information, my imagination rolled. My wife could die. The thought that I saw her smile for the last time the previous day set in, and I ferociously fought it. My wife had been in labor for about forty-eight hours. If I could at least see her, I would hold her hand and comfort her. I would whisper in her ears words that had held us up in times of adversity. But I couldn't; I was forced to wait and hope for a nurse to emerge with some good news. I was floating in a confusing world of fear, prayers, hope, and reality from which I could not escape.

A little after 5 p.m. on May 17, the heavy double door finally opened. I wanted to hide from the bad news just steps away from me; yet at the same time, I wanted to jump toward the nurse to hear the marvelous news that my wife's life was out of danger after all, and that our baby—my son or my daughter—was well.

"Mr. Fotso?" she called.

"Yes, madam," I hurried to reply, shaking and almost ready to release my bladder's pressure.

The nurse smiled. "She gave birth to a girl at 5:17. Your wife is very weak, but will recover."

Obviously, she did not need her to say more, as she had just said what I was yearning to hear. Though I was dying to storm in that room and hug my wife and my daughter, I could not. I was forced to wait!

"What name are you giving your daughter?" I heard her echo, as if she was hundreds of yards away.

"Mylène Fotso." I replied.

"Congratulations, Mr. Fotso; your daughter is very beautiful."

"Thank you, Madam."

The nurse waited, and we both knew she was waiting for a tip.

She knew I was a doctor, but certainly did not understand that though I had been teaching at the university since my graduation, I had not received a single franc. She did not understand that I had to walk about five miles every morning, and five miles back, to fulfill my teaching responsibilities. She did not understand that we had walked miles to make it to the hospital. She couldn't imagine how broke I really was. Despite the chunk of keys I had collected over the years and held as if I owned houses and cars, I was probably the most broke of all doctors. I only survived by borrowing money from everyone I knew—until I ran out of lenders—my only collateral being my faded hope of being formerly hired one day at the university.

"They will be out soon, and will spend the night here," the nurse continued after the awkward moment. "Here is the list of what you need to buy for her and the baby. You will also have to pay the hospital fees to be allowed to take them home."

"How much are the fees?" I asked, torn between my excitement and my worries.

"6,000 francs."

"I got it. Thanks a lot, Madam."

She turned back and vanished behind the doors once more. After about ninety minutes of torment and agitation, I saw them coming out of the delivery room. Chantal was being pushed on a wheelchair, tenderly holding our baby. She looked extremely pale, but I read joy and relief in her wearied eyes.

"Hi, Chan. How are you?"

"I am okay."

"She is very beautiful… Thank you, sweetheart, for being so strong; I love you," I said, taking our daughter.

As my wife climbed on her bed, I held our baby with an overpowering impression of holding an angel. She was sleeping, and it seemed like she would never open her little eyes. I knew I was holding a precious flower that had sprouted and blossomed out of a love tree, fertilized by the endurance and determination of two people. As I looked at her, I secretly pledged always to protect her, take care of her, and never to let her go to bed hungry. I vowed to give her everything I had lacked, starting with the unconditional love from a father. I vowed to help her be the best girl and woman she could be. But I knew that at that instant, if she asked for anything other than her mom's breast milk, I would not be able to provide. I was still very far from turning my words into concrete actions.

A night went by, and the time to go home arrived. The Maternity Center handed me an invoice, which I was supposed to take to the cashier with my payment. Because I was broke, I thought about flushing my honesty down the toilets, and sneaking out with my wife and my daughter. After running away, they could use a portion of my unpaid wages from teaching at the university to cover those fees.

I decided to give it one more shot before giving up. I thought of a good friend of mine, Louis Wafeu, who had dropped out of college for business, pressured by his heavy family responsibilities. He had always had a big heart, and could probably help.

As I stepped out of the crowded room, I was overwhelmed with a sense of being a total loser, not being able to provide for my daughter on the very first days of her life. However, my sense of a true fighter quickly overpowered that negative thought of *me*. I would fight for my daughter and my wife, until I was exhausted to death.

I arrived at Louis' office at the Nziko retail center, where he was busy as usual.

"Hey, Fots! How are you?" he asked, keeping an eye on his calculator.

"Things are not going well, Louis," I hurried to say. "Chantal is at the hospital, and we need some help to get out."

"How is she, and what do you need?" he asked, pushing aside all the paperwork and the calculator.

"She is doing well; we have a girl... Here is the list, in addition to 6,000 francs."

After about forty-five minutes, I gratefully exited the store with everything I needed: a blue portable bathtub, a blue blanket, some first-aid medicines, diapers, baby soap, lotion, some baby clothes, a towel, and some money.

Back at the Maternity Center, My sister in-law had arrived. She informed me that she had already paid the fees and that we were free to leave. All of a sudden, I had some extra money in my pocket. I couldn't remember the last time I had 10,000 francs (about $20) to spend, and it came in very handy.

Chapter 16

Fireworks of the Dark Abyss
(1990)

Time passed and little Mylène was soon walking and speaking fluently, armed with an impressive vocabulary built from the age of nine months, when she started talking. I continued to teach without pay at the university, borrowing money to make ends meet. I was in so much debt that I became annoying to almost everybody. I had the impression that a lot of people, including some of my own siblings, whispered, "Here he comes again" each time they saw me. For years, I had not kept my promise of paying off what I owed. So I had no credibility whatsoever. I was considered a crook, and my shame forced me to distance myself from all of my creditors.

After failing to make it in my own country, I turned my focus to finding a way out, a way to go anywhere else in the world. I could not continue to live like a starved rat fed with only hopes and dreams that would never come true. It was time to escape from that burrow.

Luck smiled at me when my mentor, Dr. Esaïe D. Tamboue, left Cameroon to the United States, where he had obtained his degrees several years earlier. His trip opened the door to new hopes, as he recommended and facilitated my admission to Kansas State University, Department of Animal Science and Industry in 1995. With this admission on hand, I applied for a US non-immigrant visa and obtained a devastating refusal, followed by many other attempts, all to no avail. Over time, I had been at the US Embassy so many times they probably recognized me each time I tried. After more than a year of trying, I came to understand that it was a lost battle. My destiny had a tight grip on me, relentlessly holding me down in the perpetuating poverty abyss.

As I went to bed one hot night of March 1996, I was about to make a decision that would impact our lives. After sorting through the very few options I had left, I had to choose between opening a car wash business on the Mfoundi River, by the Caisse Hospital, and immigrating to a neighboring African country, as I had no means of traveling to a Western nation. The car wash would certainly allow me to afford a yogurt for my daughter every now and then, and would simply be a short-term fix to a very long-term problem. Emigrating, on the other hand, would open new doors. In another country, I would be more than just a Bamiléké. I would be a qualified and motivated young man eager and ready to contribute to the prosperity of the country, and fighting for his survival and that of his family. Emigrating would allow me to untie the rope—my tribal origin—unfairly used to shackle me down.

I needed to break away, free myself from prejudice and injustice, and start my life on a leveled field. After hesitating between several French-speaking nations, including Gabon, Chad, and Central African Republic, I settled for the latter. I just had to take the train from Yaoundé to Ngaoundéré in the North, and shuttles from Ngaoundéré to Bangui, the capital. But how could I leave my beautiful wife and my little daughter, without knowing whether or not I would make it or when I would be back? Each time I thought about this move, my reason advised me that it was the right thing to do, but my heart begged me not to abandon my family, the two people I loved most in the world. I was cornered and had my back against the thick wall of poverty. I was sick and tired of feeding my family with roasted corn. My wife and my daughter deserved a lot more than that, and I was ready to offer them what they truly deserved—normalcy at the very least.

After many thoughts, I refused to be the first doctor washing cars for a living in my own country. I opted to emigrate and hit the road. Traveling in one of the characteristically noisy train wagons, I held my small luggage very tightly. It contained everything I had for the trip: my birth certificate, my passport, my diplomas, some food items, and some money. It was obvious to me that I would have to be killed or incapacitated before losing possession of that precious little bag.

As we entered Bangui, I realized I was not home anymore. I began to feel scared, for I didn't know where to start. In my tiny notebook, I had one name, given to me back in Cameroon by an acquaintance with diplomatic connections. He assured me that this person would help any stranger, because he was Christian. However, it was Sunday, and the Cameroonian Embassy, where he worked, was closed. How would I find this needle in that haystack? He could be walking right past me and I would never know it. All I had was a name.

Invigorated by my hope of getting some assistance from security guards possibly, I headed to the embassy where I found no sign of life. The last piece of my crumbling world seemed shattered. How could I just start walking through that million-person city and ask everyone a name? Returning home crossed my mind, but just for a fraction of a second. I was there, and I had to make it work for me. Hope was the last thing for me to give up.

As I continued to motivate myself, I heard footsteps. A man in a hurry was approaching. The closer he got to me the closer I got to crossing the street to distance myself from him, from potential harm. I was in unknown territory, far from everything I had known all of my life. Having caught up to me, the man started talking, to my relief.

"Hi, how are you?" he asked.

"I am doing just fine," I answered.

On the one hand, I tried very hard not to give him any clues that I had just arrived and was scared to death. But on the other hand, being overly cautious could deny me the help I needed. So I made the decision to open up and ask for the residential address of my recommended helper.

"Don't worry; I know where he lives... I will get a *mototaxi* for you," he told me.

The man went away and came right back on a noisy motorcycle that was trailing a long and thick line of black smoke in the hot air, almost giving the impression of never to dissipate. We sped on the bumpy, dusty, and narrow streets of Bangui, and I felt as if I was riding to safety. Before long, my mototaxi stopped.

"That is the house," he said, securing his 1,000 CFA franc (about $2) pay.

As I knocked at the door, my heart was beating hard. I was very excited, having the feeling of a long overdue family reunion. A young girl, about fifteen years old, opened the door.

"Good afternoon; is your father home?" I asked.

"No, only my mother is."

"Hi, madam," I politely greeted the girl's mother as she entered the living room.

"Hello," she replied, intrigued.

After I introduced myself, she continued, "My husband will be back shortly; come on in and have a seat."

I was extremely hungry and the exquisite aromas escaping from the kitchen sent hunger pangs barking in my grouchy stomach. I distracted myself by looking at the many pictures hanging on all walls, among which Jesus Christ and His mother, Mary. Those reassured my sense of being at the right place, my sense of belonging.

It did not take long before the girl's father came back. As he entered the house, I stood up to greet him. Then I proceeded to tell him why I was sitting in his living room.

"Sir, I need some help... for just enough time to get on my feet, and I will be out, on my own."

The way he looked at me—as if I was kidding—frightened me, and I intuitively sensed that I needed to be more convincing.

"Sir, you are the only person I know here. There is nowhere else I can go..."

"I would really like to help you, but we do not have any spare room in the house," he finally said, ripping my heart open.

"It is not a problem; I am ready to sleep on the floor, sir." I pleaded.

"I am sorry; we cannot help you."

At that moment, all of my thoughts focused on my daughter and my wife. They were the shoulder I needed to lean on, the ones who would help me carry all the weight of unfairness and injustice. I had silently promised them a much better horizon, but I was still standing at the doorstep of failure.

"I will get a taxi that will take you to the Ambassador's residence. I am sure he will be able to help. God has a way for you," he said, inviting me to the front door.

"Thank you, sir," I replied, with a crisp smile on my face.

My smile was just a way of hiding my inability to comprehend what had just happened. The minute I sat down in that living room, I would never have guessed that only an hour later, I would be kicked out like a scabby stray dog.

The majestic front gate of the Ambassador's home instantly gave me not only the expected sense of opulence, but more importantly, a rock-solid sense of hope, born from the ashes of the hopes that were crumbled in the house I had just left.

The Ambassador, Mr. Christopher Nsahlai, was unexpectedly welcoming. From the beginning, he gave me the impression of being a wonderful father, as he joked with the kids I assumed were his.

"How was your trip?" he asked.

"Very tiring, Excellency," I courteously answered.

"I know; you don't have to explain. It is a very long trip," he added.

"But when you know why you are enduring it, you don't feel the pain at all." I said, in an attempt to direct the conversation toward my goal of finding refuge.

"Where are you staying here in Bangui?"

"His Excellency, I've come to ask for your hospitality. I need a temporary place to stay."

"What are your goals, and how long would you stay?"

"His Excellency, after my graduate degrees, my fruitless job search, and my unsuccessful visa applications at the US Embassy back home, I have not been able to make it. Being here is a new opportunity for me, and I intend to find a job as soon as possible."

"It is not easy here either—the economic situation is at best the same," he said.

"Here I am not just a Bamiléké, His Excellency... and you understand what I mean. Also, I know I have tried everything in Cameroon, and I have yet to try anything here." I argued. "Sir, I would greatly appreciate it if you could let me stay here while I get settled."

"What about hotels? Some are very affordable."

"I do not have enough money for that, Excellency. A single night at any hotel will certainly empty my pockets. That is how much money I have, sir."

"I am very sorry, Mr. Fotso. I wish I could help, but I can't. The house is full of people. There is honestly no room left, not even for one more," Mr. Nsahlai said, reeling me back to my starting point.

"I understand, sir. Thanks a lot for receiving me."

Of course that was a big fat lie. Each corner of that residence and the adjacent guesthouse could be a mansion to me. I would not have minded sleeping on the couch, the floor, in the kitchen, or even on the porch. There was definitely room for one more person, but I had to head out in the true unknown.

"Good luck, Doctor," he said, shaking my hand.

Once on the other side of the fence, a quick thought urged me to go back to the Embassy of Cameroon, where I had started earlier. After all, I was Cameroonian and it was my undeniable right to be on Cameroonian territory. They would have to use bulldozers to move me from there, if they so wished.

With no cars or pedestrians passing by the Embassy, I put my hand through a hole on the gate panel, and pushed down the L-shaped knob on the inside. As it opened, I stepped in, hoping to have left all of my bad luck behind. A quick inspection revealed that all doors of the main building and the attached little one were locked. But at least I would not be sleeping out in the open, at the mercy of anything and everything. No matter how I spent my night, I was already lucky enough to be within fences.

After checking and double-checking all nooks to make sure there were no places that could accommodate me better, a parked vehicle in the backyard, a Peugeot 305, became my only hope for a shelter. A thick layer of dust and mildew covered its windshield, and its windows were shattered and halfway down. Its tires were all flat, and the door handles were missing. That car had probably been there for many years after suffering fatal damages. I forced the back door open and, as I bent a little closer, I noticed a nasty smell emanating from inside. In spite of the stench, I was ready to make that car my new home, my safe haven. I slid my luggage through the cracked door and sat on the edge of the adjacent veranda.

Total darkness set in, and it got a little chilly. It was time to enter what would be my fortress for the unforeseeable future. The more comfortable driver's seat became my bed, and I started my count-down to sleep, using one of my shirts as a blanket. As I closed my eyes, I realized how quiet and peaceful I was deep inside. After the rocky two days I had just endured, I found an internal oasis, an unexpected equanimity. This peace was very short-lived. Being in that filthy vehicle battling ferocious mosquitoes reminded me of the night I had spent in the abandoned car as a child, when my clothes were stolen at the *swimming pool*. At that time, I thought those moments were the darkest of my life. But there I was again. My nights would be long, and I had no way of escaping.

After a few days, I acclimated to my new life and established a routine. Around six o'clock every morning, before the workers arrived, I took my shower using the carwash hose, right in the middle of the yard.

As I left the embassy that mid-morning, I noticed army cars, armored vehicles, and soldiers crisscrossing Bangui's streets. They all looked very tense, almost on the brink of pulling the trigger. Bangui suddenly seemed to be under siege. Just like in Cameroon, the President of Central African Republic, Ange Felix Patassé, was said to have brought his country to its knees, and to be holding onto power at all costs. The vast majority of the population was tired of living in total misery while the president and his protégés unfairly lived a life of opulence. In addition to the widespread unhappiness, some high-ranking soldiers were power-hungry and ready to over-throw the sitting president—*on behalf of the people*. So the president had to protect his power.

Being in that country suddenly became frightening. After a few hours outside, I chickened out and returned to the embassy where everyone already knew me. Though they all downplayed what was happening, I was scared to death.

It was May 5, 1996, just about a week after my arrival. The night was dark as usual. I was in the car, struggling to get some sleep. I wished to just black out and wake up the next day. But that didn't happen. I also wished to have my daughter and my wife right there with me so I could hug them all night long. That didn't happen either. I realized it was not healthy to wish for such things. Reality was there with me and I had to face it.

A sudden crackling sound split the night open, crushing my fragile heart with each pop. The rattling sound was from gunfire. *It* had started. I was extremely vulnerable, trapped in a hole, with no safe way out. Just a little time had elapsed since the beginning of the shooting and it felt like it had been hours already. I stepped out of the car and stood in the yard, ready to duck back in. The dark sky seemed to be an endless screen for the display of red-hot bullets, crisscrossing one another from all points. The accompanying noise got louder and closer by the minute.

As the intensity of the fight heightened, I tiptoed to the gate and stood on a stack of concrete blocks, where I was startled by a sudden loud noise. I found myself lying on the ground, without any idea of how I got there. Only then did I realize that a second before—or perhaps a tenth of a second before—a whistling sound had preceded the noise. I had been shot. The bullet had certainly shaved my hair or pierced through my skull.

I rubbed my head with both of my hands to divert the warm fluid flowing down my neck from my scalp. As I did, I left my last thoughts to Mylène and Chantal, and to everyone else that had displayed a genuine love for me. I wanted to close my eyes with them in my mind and heart. I imagined them—no one else—taking my hand to the doorstep of Paradise.

As minutes passed by, still being alive surprised me. Back up on my feet, I realized that a sudden burst of sweat had wetted my scalp and upper body. Hurrying back to my fortress, the Peugeot 305, I scanned the ground to locate the bullet that had missed taking my life by just a few millimeters, and spotted it right away. It was shiny and metallic, clearly standing out on the unfinished pavement, a little distorted from the impact and still very hot. I squeezed it in my hand, thinking of it as my lucky charm. I had just dodged that bullet and escaped my death. I also knew it could just be a matter of minutes, hours, or days before I ran out of survival options. But at least for that instant, I felt safe in my car.

Sunrise uncovered a lawless town. Sporadic gunfire was still heard, but a few embassy workers reported for duty. The first one was the Ambassador's administrative assistant, who had arrived early and caught me naked in the backyard. The homeless secret of the *"Doctor"* was out and I was sure all respect for me would vanish.

The many following nights, red-hot bullets in the dark sky gave the impression of some kind of fireworks celebration. It sadly was not a celebration, but a true display of the uphill and rocky path of democracy in Africa. Democracy was a word a lot of African presidents, including Paul Biya and Ange F. Patassé, were—unfortunately—still unable to *spell*, let alone implement. Power was what they lived for, and they were willing to do anything to keep it. I asked myself whether or not they ever thought about us, the people, atop their golden pulpit. My answer was, *"No,"* with the exception of one selfless son of Africa, Nelson Mandela. To him, I scrawled a few words—a wish and a prayer for Africa, that *Promised Land* of our ancestors:

To Nelson Mandela

May your raised fist
Pedestal of freedom, justice and peace
Power-lifts all hurdles
And diffuse this raised light
On the darkened summits of Africa,
And the dark abysses of this Africa.

Despite all the blood and fire, I refused to give up hope on Africa. I knew the light might not reach me in time, but would certainly reach Africa's sprouts one day. My brittle bones would then rise and stand up from six feet under, join our ancestors' souls on the dance floor of Africa's birth, and move to the sounds of liberty, equality, and harmony.

In the midst of this intensifying war, I decided to find a way to get back home to my wife and daughter. It had been almost a month since I left Cameroon, and I had no news of them. I had tried hard, and it had not worked for me. But I had not failed. It was just time to get back to my family, and I would rather die trying. I was officially a war refugee. But I refused to sit there and wait to be slaughtered. I was resolved to return home, to my ancestors' land.

As frightening as it was outside, two Central African acquaintances offered to escort me through the nearly twelve miles that would lead to safer ground. No one was supposed to be out and if one chose to be, it was at his or her own risk. The further we went from the city the larger the crowds, as it got safer and safer. But I sensed undeniable hostility in the eyes of some men. If I were not accompanied by my two guardian angels, I would have become another war casualty.

As I stepped into the dusty car that would take me back to northern Cameroon, we secretly exchanged addresses and phone numbers, promising one another to meet again in life.

I headed back home, back to uncertainty within my country, in the tight grip of destiny, but to the priceless warmth of my wonderful wife and my lovely daughter for whom I had to keep my head up.

Chapter 17

Light in the Dark and Darkening Tunnels

For forty-eight hours after leaving Bangui, I endured an excruciating hunger, heat, and extreme fatigue. I survived this exhausting odyssey and entered Yaoundé again. I was about to finally see and hug my wife and my daughter. My fate had forced me to be away from them for a month, but I was back to them, where I truly belonged. They needed me, and I needed them. We would continue living on love and fresh water. It didn't matter anymore.

Approaching our rental apartment—which we had not paid for in about a year and a half—I was so excited that I became unable to hear the usual brouhaha of our neighborhood. Covered with dust from head to toe, I looked like I had been six feet under and back. But who cared?

Seated on the edge our tiny veranda and looking at the flank of the adjacent hill, my daughter and her mom had not noticed my arrival. I decided not to make it more of a surprise than it already was.

"There you are!" I screamed.

"Papa Joe! Papa Joe!" Mylène started singing, running to me while flapping her hands.

As I squeezed my two girls simultaneously, I felt a wonderful sense of relief. Chantal looked even more beautiful than ever, and Mylène had enriched her vocabulary.

"Papa Joe, where were you?" my daughter asked, struggling to squeeze her little hand in my luggage.

"I am here now, okay?" I replied.

"Are you going to leave us again?"

"I don't think so. I will make sure I don't."

I knew I was lying, because I didn't want her to be upset. She was two years old, with only two teeth in her mouth. She would never have understood why I had left and would certainly be trying again. I was determined to beat the weeds to follow my way. For the moment, I enjoyed hugging my wife and playing with my daughter again. They were my safe harbor. They were what I had been fighting for all those years. They were what I would keep fighting for.

Upon my return, I neared depression. We still had some family and friends who truly cared, but others took great pleasure in making fun of us. They repeatedly gossiped that I was a doctor, but a miserable one who couldn't make ends meet. They bashed my education and the efforts I had made to provide for my family. To them, I was just doomed to fail. True, I was an educated man with no money; we were poor and lived a miserable life. But I was strong.

For more than three months after Bangui, our lives remained stagnant. However, Dr. Tamboue relentlessly worked with my potential advisor at Kansas State University, Dr. J. Scott Smith, to renew my admission papers. Coincidentally, I heard about a new consul being appointed at the visa section of the US Embassy. I got ready to apply for a visa again. I knew this was the last chance for me, for us, and it had to work. It just had to.

On September 5, 1996, after reassembling all of my paperwork, I was—once more—ready to approach the US Embassy. A few days prior, I had taken a trip to Bandjoun to receive my father's blessing. Despite his age, he still remembered that out of more than a dozen children he had fathered and all of his grandchildren, I was the only one to graduate from high school. He told me that I should never stop moving forward, because Bandjoun's God had great plans for me. He reaffirmed that His hands would always be shielding me.

"Go get it," he said, "My ancestors will be sweeping your way. Tell them (at the Embassy) that you are my son, a Todjom (a native of Bandjoun)! They must not steal what's yours. Go get it!"

This time, I decided to bring Mylène and Chantal to the interview. I needed their support. We would instantly celebrate if a visa was granted, or lean on each other's shoulders if my destiny happened to take the same course.

As we passed by the Central Market, I ignored my daughter's plea for doughnuts. It was only about 6:30 a.m. for a 9:00 a.m. appointment. I chose to be one of the first, rather than to get there later and wait in line for hours. Almost everyone wanted to immigrate to the United States, and I didn't want to put off my window of opportunity. At the corner of the Abbia movie theater, my heartbeat skyrocketed at the sight of the American flag topping the ominous white building. I was walking to my destiny, which was in the hand of someone in there. I hoped *they* listened to my father. I hoped they rewarded my struggle and my determination that day. I hoped Mylène and Chantal left there with radiant smiles on their face.

My turn got closer. After the lady sitting beside us, I would be next. I was prepared for a war on the battlefield of my life. The first battle was definitely about keeping my nervousness to a minimum.

"Mr. Joseph Fotso," I finally heard.

"Yes, sir," I said, jumping off my seat.

After just a few short steps, I stood in front of the glass interview booth, politely staring at the officer who was holding my fate into his hands. I had learned a few English words, which I believed were munitions to the guns I brought on that battlefield. However, the consul's body language urged me not to pull the trigger just yet. Flipping through the multiple pages of my application, he was very calm. Almost too calm!

"What's your name, sir?" he asked, finally looking at me.

"Joseph Fotso, sir."

"Where do you work?"

"I teach biochemistry at the University of Yaoundé, sir."

"Since when do you teach?"

"Since May 1994, after I got my doctorate, sir"

"What's your salary?"

"Sir, I don't have any. I have never been paid."

"So, you work and you are not compensated for your work?"

"That's right, sir."

"Do you know why?"

"No, sir."

Things were going very well. So far, he had not asked any questions that I had trouble answering. But tricky questions could still be on the way.

"I have a history of your prior visa applications... Am I right?" he continued.

"Yes, sir. I have been here many times and my visa was denied."

"I see... Were you told the reasons for the refusal?"

"No, sir."

"Were your applications identical to this one?"

"Yes, sir. I had the same application each time."

After pausing, he wrote some notes on my application. I attempted to see what he was writing, but couldn't. My heart was pounding. I had been there before, too many times. I had seen them do exactly that before delivering the bad news. From experience, I knew he would slam a red-ink stamp in my passport to prevent me from applying again for a long time. He would then tell me that my visa was denied, without any explanation. In fact, we had heard those devastating refusal words numerous times already that day.

"Are you married, sir?" he surprisingly continued.

"Yes, sir. My wife and my daughter are here." I said, waving my family over.

"You have a cute daughter... If you were to go to the United States, would you leave them behind?"

"Yes, sir. I wouldn't have any choice in that case."

He asked Chantal and Mylène to return to their seats, and continued to take more notes on my application. In my mind, I thought, "*This is it!*" I knew it wouldn't be long before he handed my passport back. I inwardly screamed, *"I am my father's son, a Todjom, led here by his ancestors. So please, do not take away what's mine. I am here to get it."* As expected, he closed the file folder with my application, opened my passport again, and looked through. Time completely stopped and nothing seemed to be moving around me. The room became very silent. As everyone prepared to hear the feared decision, something inside me wanted it to be delayed a little bit more.

"Mr. Fotso, your visa application is approved. Come back in the afternoon with 175,000 CFA francs to pick it up."

"Thank you, sir... Thank you."

I turned back, showered by everyone's envy and admiration, and Chantal's relieved smile. We did not want to hug right there; but we squeezed each other's hands so hard we could hear the bones crack. Looking at my "cute" daughter—even though I had no idea whatsoever what "cute" meant—I knew that new doors had just opened for us.

The new battle became about how to afford the $350 visa fee. I did not know how in the world I could put together that fortune in such short notice. I asked my family to return home without me. I had three hours to find the money, so I had no time to waste. I knew I could go to my friend Louis for help again. A little part of me, where my pride resided, was reluctant. But every other fiber of my body screamed at me, *"Just go!"*

I listened and hit the road. As I jogged through the crowd in the women's section of the Central Market, I was very anxious and sweating profusely. The Nziko store where Louis worked was not too far; I was eager to get there.

As usual, Louis was drowning in paperwork. This time, he stopped just as I stepped in.

"Did you get it?" he asked.

"Yes, I did!" I answered, as excited as I could be, with my mind obscured by my insurmountable problem.

"Wonderful!" he said, applauding.

"But I need 175,000 francs by 2:00 p.m. for the visa..."

"Joe, that's a lot of money, but not a problem." Reaching into one of his pockets, he continued, "This is all of my savings. Take this and go get that visa."

How could I say, "thank you" for a fortune, for that selfless act from my friend? I just let every single cell of my grateful body express it.

After a few weeks, I finally came to realize I was not dreaming. I often woke up several times a night, just to hold my passport and feel the visa. I secretly kissed the Swiss Air plane ticket that my mentor, Dr. Esaïe Tamboue, had graciously bought for me. I would be leaving Cameroon on the evening of September 29, 1996, around 11 p.m. In the meantime, I stopped running away from my lenders. I had hope and assurance that I would pay all of them off. I was not a crook anymore. I looked any of them straight in the eye and felt no shame. My dignity was restored.

I was astonished by the newfound respect for me after my visa. All of a sudden, I was *somebody*. My presence was noticed wherever I went. Some that had been laughing at me had a sudden change of heart. There were exquisite foods everywhere I visited, made especially for *me*, as if it were the very first visit of an honorable guest. But *I* was the same, not more *honorable* than *I* had always been.

The time to depart came. We decided to gather at my sister-in-law's home for a farewell party. I tried to use my photographic memory to immortalize everything around me because I didn't know the next time I would see that again. My father could not make the trip to Yaoundé, but we had had some unforgettable moments when I went back to the village to say goodbye.

"I know God will always be with you," he told me. "He will hold your hand and walk you through every door, until you find *it*. My wish for you is hearing that you caught a *panther* or a *lion*; and you will."

He was articulating his words, often pausing to exhale the thick smoke from his pipe. In his eyes, I could read the words that his mouth had yet to let out, as they seemed caught up in a slow transition from his brain to his tongue. Pride was written all over his wrinkled forehead, and joy all over his frail, century-old body. For him, as for my whole family, it was surreal that I was traveling abroad, so far away, to a "white men country," as we called it. It was something they thought was meant for others, not for us, not for me. But why not us? Why not me? I wrestled with destiny to make it happen. I was opening a door that had been locked for too long, a door to freedom, hope, and prosperity. Being the very first to ever cross that doorstep, I was my family's pride.

As my father talked, one question repeatedly popped into my mind: "*Will I see him again?*" Who knew? He had made it that far, and he could always go further than his 119 years. I hoped and prayed he lived longer, so I could bring him a panther or a lion's skin, when I got *it*.

"I know I will never see you again, and you will never see me again. But don't worry; you have all of my blessings, and they will always be with you. Do you understand?"

"Yes, Father, I do."

"Come here, give me your hands, and let me touch you again," he said, bringing me near tears.

He placed my palms together, and started rubbing them gently against one another, sporadically spitting in between. After several rounds of that treatment, he reached over to his mud hut and forced a dry piece of the building block out.

"Here, son. This is all I can give you. Take it with you. My hands built this house a very long time ago. This will be your source of strength."

"Thank you, Father... Thank you very much."

The time to depart came, and we both knew it. I was afraid of turning away, but I had no choice. It was time to go hunt panthers and lions.

"Father, I must go now, it's getting late. May you remain as healthy as a rock. Thank you for everything."

"Before you go, son, remember this: one day you will hear that I am no longer around. I don't want you to cry when it happens.

Don't cry! May God be with you."

"Thank you, Father... Thanks again."

We shook hands, and briefly hugged, before letting go of one another. Holding my little block of dry mud, I stepped out of the bamboo fence surrounding the hut. As I rounded the corner to my mother's house, I looked back. My father had not moved. He was standing exactly where I left him, steadily beaming at me with the tiny orifices between his eyelids. Hurt, I ambled away, engraving that tear-jerking image of him in my memory.

Upon leaving Bandjoun for Yaoundé, reality set in. I grasped that those glances at my father were my last. As difficult as it was to accept, I knew it was true. Fortunately, my daughter's presence helped me tremendously. I enjoyed her as much as I could. She got more beautiful and more interesting by the minute. How would I survive without her? Most importantly, how would she survive without me? I had already experienced that once before, and I knew it was not easy. And yet, the time to part was nearing again. I was not sure she understood this, but I had to go. She would be very far from me, but always in my heart and mind.

Exhausted by the party, I retreated to the room that was reserved for my wife and my daughter, to alleviate my lingering headache. I lied down on the bed and my eyes landed on an English dictionary. Hoping to improve my vocabulary, I picked it up. My rest time would certainly serve a bigger purpose.

After flipping a few pages, I came across a folded piece of paper in the middle of the dictionary. I opened it, already amused. I thought it was one of my wife's graded English tests, which would reveal her weaknesses. As I unfolded the paper, I realized it was not at all what I thought. It was a letter, in my wife's handwriting. My heart sank at the first words:

> *Dear Father Ernest,*
> *I just want to tell you how much I enjoy and cherish our relationship. My dream is to see you and*

*hear your voice every day God has created. I enjoy the
pleasure you have been giving me, and I pray it never
ends. I will soon let you know when I will come over
(…).*

All yours,
Chantal

I fell back on the bed—holding the same piece of paper that was
so anodyne and harmless just a minute before—with those words
of betrayal still resonating in my brain. My heart felt ripped open.
How was it possible? Father Ernest was a priest officiating at the
Christ Roi parish in Bandjoun. While I was out struggling to make
ends meet, my wife had met him on several occasions—to pray, I
had thought. I knew now that this man of God broke God's will
and ridiculed His trust. He covered his white gown with everlasting
shame. A multitude of questions flooded my mind: *"How did God
let this happen? Why me?" How and why did the woman I loved more
than anyone in the world do this to me—the man she had vowed to love
and cherish in sickness and in health?"*

Deep inside me, there was a seed of doubt. Despite the piece of
paper I was holding, everything was only speculation. Only Chantal
could tell me the truth.

"Chantal?" I called, loud enough for her to hear amidst the
noisy crowd.

"Yes, Joe? I will be there in a moment," she replied.

"No, I need you here right now!"

I heard her footsteps rushing in my direction. I was burning
inside, but I knew I had to keep my composure. The door opened,
and she stood just a few steps from me.

"What's going on, sweetheart?" she asked, with her trademark
smile.

I knew I had to avoid letting her beauty divert me.

"What's this?" I inquired, fighting hard to hide the trembling
of my voice.

"What?" she asked, zooming in on what I held.

"Listen to what you wrote: *Dear Father Ernest, I just want to tell you how much I enjoy and cherish our relationship (…)."*

I lacked the strength to continue and stopped. Chantal's smile vanished, and she silently stood in front of me. I believed she was probably trying to find some explanation. Just a few words from her could have meant a world of difference at that moment; but she kept me waiting. Eager to hear anything, I continued, "Can you tell me what this is, Chantal?"

She opened her mouth, but not a word came out. I couldn't tell what she was feeling. As she remained silent, I decided to bring in her sister, Anne, in an attempt to force a few words out of her.

Anne stormed to us in a fraction of a second, sensing my unusual tone of voice.

"Yes, Joe, I am here; what's going on?"

"Anne, listen to what my wife, your sister, wrote to the priest: *Dear Father Ernest, (…)"*

All of a sudden, Chantal grabbed the letter out of my hands and tore it to pieces—shamelessly, looking at me straight in the eye without blinking. As I stood up in indignation, she stepped back, stuffed the little pieces of paper in her mouth, and started chewing. At that moment, looking at her, I was not sure anymore who she really was. I thought all those years that I knew her. Not anymore! All I seemed to know then was her name. She definitely was not the woman I almost died for, not the woman my heart had hosted since June 09, 1990. She was not the woman who induced goose pumps all over my body each time she touched me, even after six years together. She was not the person I shared my bed with every night.

"Chantal, what are you doing?" Anne asked, as indignant and shocked as I was.

We still had not heard a word from her. As she swallowed her mouthful of mashed, inked paper, a tear flowed down her left cheek, reflecting the dim light from the tiny window. That tear seemed to be a mixture of so many things, of which I could only guess a few— shame and guilt, perhaps a silent plea for forgiveness. But how could I forgive? Trust was crushed and love, just there a moment before, already seemed so far away. It would almost take the impossible to reach it again.

"Why?" I finally asked, still in my state of confusion and shock.

"I don't know. But it is not what you think, Joe. Nothing happened between the priest and me. Please, let's not talk about it now. I want you to have a good trip."

"Are you kidding me? How can I?"

"Please try! I just don't know what to tell you. Rest for now, and come out for the final farewell. Remember that I love you, Joe."

"Please, do not go there... Please."

She stepped out as I finished my sentence, and closed the door behind her. Nothing around me mattered anymore. If I were told that my trip to the US was cancelled, it wouldn't have mattered to me. Half of me had just left my heart, my body, and my soul, never to come back again.

I decided to join the crowd in the living room. I had stopped being the same, but I had to pretend being just that. My daughter was certainly asking herself why I had started squeezing her so hard for so long. I was not ready to let go of her innocent little body. As for her mother, the process of letting go had already started, although she smiled, laughed out loud, and occasionally leaned on me as if nothing had ever happened. I was disgusted, and claimed to be too tired and excited to eat.

We arrived at the airport, where I took care of all pre-boarding procedures. Only time stood between me and the panthers and lions. It was time for me to go and get what was mine. But as close as it was, it still seemed not to matter much anymore. My drive was gone. I was only an empty shell of who I used to be. But I knew I had to stay strong and focused. I was fortified by the resonance of my father's words, still fresh in my mind. I knew God would hold my hand and walk me through every door, until I found *it*. I knew my father's ancestors would be sweeping my way.

Everyone understood that I needed a private moment with my wife and my daughter; so they stepped away from us. I struggled hard to keep up the smile. I was never a hypocrite, and did not like smiling when I didn't mean it. But it seemed like one of those times when I had to be one.

"Joe, try to forget everything, please," Chantal said.

"I don't understand, and I am not sure I ever will, Chantal. I don't understand why you did that to me. I have to get going... They are calling."

"Goodbye, sweetheart," she said, hugging me very hard.

"Goodbye," I replied, forcing a smile.

I held onto my daughter, as if I would squeeze her into my carry-on luggage and take her with me. Against my heart's will, I handed her back to her mother, and she instantly burst into tears. She finally understood I was leaving them—*again*. I emptied my pockets of the last CFA coins I had left, putting them in the little pocket of her pink dress.

I turned away and walked straight ahead. Looking back would be too painful, and I made sure I didn't. That was it. I had struck light in the dark tunnel of my existence, and the darkening tunnel of my future was in search of the distant beam.

Chapter 18

My Daughter's Prayer

I arrived in the United States of America, country of panthers and lions, on the evening of September 30, 1996. After landing at O'Hare International Airport in Chicago, I was picked up by an acquaintance, André, who happened to be a *Todjom*—a son of Bandjoun—just like me, and who had been living in the US for a while. I would stay at his apartment before my trip to Manhattan, Kansas.

I was in America, the land I had dreamed of. As I exited the terminal dragging my three-piece luggage, I felt fireworks inside me, immediately countered by the incisive and penetrating shock of the ambient cold. In central Cameroon, I had never experienced temperatures below approximately 60 degrees Fahrenheit, which was considered almost freezing.

Although paralyzed by this cold—with only my suit to protect me—I remained lucid enough to admire the major differences between the now primitive world I had left behind only twenty-four hours earlier and the bright one I just entered. The lights from street posts and buildings were blinding. The streets were tarred and clean, with no mountains of trash obstructing them. No cars emitted trails of thick smoke, or seemed to be held together by their last screw. From a distance, the crystal-like skyline against the clear twilight sky was amazingly beautiful. I instantly fell in love with Chicago and imagined the first wonderful pictures of me that I would send to my parents, which would make them even prouder.

We arrived at André's apartment and, after chatting for about three hours, he and his wife Solange went to bed, leaving me alone in the living room. I sat on the couch where I would be spending my nights, relieved and thrilled to have finally made it. I was also still extremely tormented, although I believed I had done a good job concealing my hurt and bleeding heart, keeping all personal turbulences below my flabbergasted skin.

Alone, time seemed slow and endless. Even having a surprising choice of more than one TV channel—hundreds of them!—did not keep out troubling memories of my last hours in Africa. I wished I had had a nightmare right before leaving my wife and my daughter. I wished an alarm clock went off, or someone tapped me on the shoulder and told me, *"Hey, wake up! You have been sleeping for more than twenty-four hours now."* But no such thing was likely to happen. To shorten the night, I started to look through my carry-on, hoping to redirect my capsizing thoughts. Among other things, I came across a birthday present I had given my wife earlier that year, on February 14. It was a small $0.20 post card, on which I had laid down my feelings and my commitment.

02/14/96

"My sweetheart,

On this day,
Valentine's Day
You came to life
In the middle of the night.
Thus, Love is you.
Of all vultures around you,
I am the one without a roof
Over my genuine roots
Who always will shelter you,
Who always will stand by you.

The one whose love for you
Matches the faith in you,
Always more today
Than yesterday.

Original present (in French) to my wife

    Holding the card in my hands, I was conflicted. In front of God, Bandjoun's God, and men, I had vowed to love that woman for better or for worse. Should I look away and let her down at the first drizzles of a storm? Drizzles? Actually Not! What happened was a hurricane, powerful and destructive enough to erase a history of blue skies. Remembering all the misery we had endured together, all the hurdles we had crossed, all the love we had professed for each other, I became enraged. All that for nothing! But I was still very confused, torn between six years of wonderful memories and the few hours that had shattered the pedestal on which my wife stood.

Our future together was uncertain, but I had a daughter left to fight for, and it was my duty not to waiver. This was the Land of the Free and the Home of the Brave; I had no choice but to be brave. I was ready to hunt panthers and lions wherever they were. I was ready to follow the path swept by my father's ancestors and hold the door opened by the hand of God. I was ready to chase and catch my destiny, or to continue fighting it if need be. I was not going to sit and wait; I was determined to go straight up to it and get what was mine.

After spending about a week in Chicago acclimating to my new life, I traveled to Manhattan, Kansas, where I lived with Dr. Esaïe Tamboue and his children for a few months. I struggled with English and the American accent; it was a battle I had to win in just three months, before the beginning of the semester in January 1997. I had to stop being scared of what people would think of my linguistic abilities, or being ashamed of my strong and maybe funny accent. So I was determined to use that time wisely. In addition to reading and socializing, I learned English, one spoken word at a time, by watching Oprah, Maury, Ricky Lake, various movies, and news programs every day. By the end of December, my accent still seemed to be glued to my tongue, but I was able to understand and entertain conversations.

Around 8 a.m. on January 6, 1997, I officially set foot on campus for the first time. I wore the same suit I had worn on my trip, because it was my best outfit. As Dr. Tamboue drove me to Call Hall to meet my advisor, Dr. Scott Smith, I noticed how awkward I looked. Almost all the other students rushing from all directions wore *only* blue jeans, sneakers and various styles and colors of jackets. I wasn't sure then if something was wrong with me or with all of them. It had to be all of them, not me.

As I stepped out of my mentor's vehicle, I was nervous, thinking, "This is it!" That was where success—not failure—awaited *me*. I remembered the words still written on the window of my childhood bedroom in my village: *"Les autres, pourquoi pas nous?"* Now, *I* too was there, in the land of opportunity.

We opened the door to Call Hall and I took a deep breath. Dr. Smith's office was on the second floor. I silently wondered what type of person he was, what type of boss he would be. We knocked and his door—my door or trail to lions and panthers—opened to a tall, bald, very inviting man.

"Come on in, guys," he said.

"Thank you, sir," I replied as we stepped inside his library-like office.

"Welcome to America… you finally made it, hein?" he continued with a smile. "So what do you think?"

I giggled a little before adding, "Sir, I don't know where to start… but thank you so much for the opportunity. Thanks for waiting through the whole process, too."

That was one of my first conversations in the real world, and I was proud of myself for not fumbling.

"You are very welcome… I am glad to have you. I think I understand the situation you were in, in your country, as many are in other countries in Africa and other parts of the world. I have had many international students in my group, and I get it… So, are you ready?"

"Yes, sir… I have been ready for a very, very long time."

"Great! Well, I am going to take you around and introduce you to the other members of my group and to the other faculty members in the building."

My mentor left, and I was abruptly left to be on my own in the jungle of my new world of certainty.

Kansas State University was very welcoming, just the right place for me to be. I enrolled in an inter-departmental Ph.D. program, with a focus on chemical analysis and toxicology. Despite the high intensity of my classes, I took advantage of every opportunity that came my way. For instance, I volunteered as a DJ at the Kansas State University radio station, KS DB92, where I co-hosted two musical shows, *Reggae Extravaganza* and *Into Africa,* with my friend Siendou Ouattara every Sunday. I also made the Kansas State University soccer team. But after learning that what I called football was known as soccer in the United States, my dream of playing in the gigantic Kansas State University football stadium vanished. Nevertheless, I was a Wildcat!

To keep my word to all of my creditors back home in Cameroon, I used most of my student wages to pay them off, starting with my year-and-a-half unpaid rent. In only a few months, I was debt-free in Cameroon, and almost wished I could return just to experience great feelings from walking in public proudly, head up, without any fear of being sequestrated by one of my numerous lenders.

My daughter, my rock

I seldom spent more than about three days without talking to my family. While it was not the same with Chantal and probably never would be, hearing my daughter's voice was always very energizing. What would I have done without her? As tiny as she still was, she became my rock. Imagining how she was filled a lot of voids around me.

My father passed away almost a year after I last saw him. Though his passing was expected, I was distraught. But I did not cry. I had to respect his will. I used those moments to reflect back, and revisit everything I had learned from that great man who had let me go on a hunt for lions and panthers in a faraway world. I had not had a chance to catch any yet, and when I did, I would no longer be able to take any panther or lion's skin to him. He would have deserved it.

My father's funeral

I would only go to his grave and shower him with palm oil and present him branches of peace tree, like my family did for our ancestors. I would do so to celebrate him.

The distant presence of my daughter opened the door to my heart, and her mother tiptoed back in. Over the next two years, though my wife worked hard to mend fences, I was not very sure how successful she had been. I thought about divorcing her, as it was impossible for me to accept her relationship with Father Ernest, the Catholic priest. But then I envisioned my daughter growing up without her mother. Chantal was a wonderful mother. We had always been a happy, inseparable trio, and that was all Mylène knew. She could never guess how close we were to never reuniting again under the same roof. She would be devastated, and I wanted to keep her stable and happy at all costs. It was a paralyzing dilemma.

After much thinking, after listening to my wounded heart, I found myself on the verge of a major decision. My daughter needed her mother, and I was going to make sure she had her around all of her life. Moreover, time seemed to have a healing effect, as Chantal was slowly moving back into my heart. My loneliness, my compassionate nature, the power of forgiveness, and my need to love and be loved all acted to force me into reconsidering the decisions I had made—at least subconsciously. I decided to get my family to the United States with me. I was dying to see my daughter, and I wanted to give my wife and me a second chance. Who knew? Things could work out. Things could come back to where they were before the unforgettable night I discovered crushing words on an anodyne piece of paper. I would take that chance, at the very least for the well-being of my daughter.

After about three years of separation, my family was due to arrive in the United States on April 2, 1999. It was the day we would reunite again after all the time, the turmoil, the grudge, the doubts, and the confusion. My friend Siendou Ouattara, who had offered to accompany me to the Kansas City International Airport, was excited for me. He could never imagine how much I appreciated him being there with me. With him around, it would be much easier to break the ice with Chantal. I was extremely nervous, for I was about to cohabitate again with the woman I had known and loved, but a woman I was not sure to have known at all. I knew it would be a challenge. An instant change of heart and forgiveness was impossible for me. I would have to look for strength deep within to even look her in the eye. Simply picking up where we had left off was not possible. Every second that went by was a second I fought inside myself, blasting myself for being so soft, but praising myself the minute after for being so forgiving. I was going through an excruciating struggle. All that we had endured together urged me to forgive her mistake, but the human being that I was, was often bitter and grouchy about what she had done. That was something no one rehearsed in life, but it was one I would have to live through.

The plane had landed before our arrival and my friend and I rushed to the luggage claim to see my daughter and her mother, whom we spotted through the crowd, majestically dressed. My heart pounded as we got closer. I asked myself if I was still that man who always would shelter Chantal, who always would stand by her. This was not the time to think about it because my daughter was finally here, only a few yards from me. At last she saw me and became very excited.

"Welcome, girls!" I said.

They fell into my arms. It was a great relief to hold them tight again. My daughter was not the little girl I had left behind three years earlier.

"How are you, girl?" I asked Mylène.

"I am fine," she answered, displaying a beautiful smile.

"Do you know me?"

"Yes… you are Papa Joe."

Her mother held my hand, and didn't seem ready to let go of it. Amazingly, I was holding hers tighter than I would have ever imagined. Was it a sign that time had healed my wound? Was I healed by the power of her smile? Was I healed at all? I was sure her beauty alone was not going to be able to corrupt me; it had to be something much stronger and deeper.

Time had tamed my heart. Love once again had the last word. I was definitely healed, most probably by time, certainly—surprisingly—by Chantal. She had scrambled through the deep swamp of my fears and tears for the lost key to my heart. She earned her crown

Chantal's healing smile in Manhattan, Kansas

back, and seldom did I even look back. Life was worth enjoying to its fullest again. I was able to see a beautiful world through my wife's eyes again. How could I resist her smile? I was relieved to have her in my daughter's life. We attended parent/teacher conferences as a couple at Lee Elementary School in Manhattan Kansas, not just as a father and a mother. She was my wife.

A few months after our reunion, and after falling in love again, I had a scary dream one night. The dream was so vivid that I woke up soaked in my own sweat: *My wife had some kind of disease, and was trying to pass it on to me through a syringe filled with her blood, with the help of someone whose face I could not see. I vehemently fought, struggling to free myself from the grip of the evil person, while my wife lied down, lifeless after a short while. As I tried to defend myself, an extremely tall person, dressed in an all-white gown, emerged from behind a vertical layer of thick cloud, and said in a deep, echoing voice: "Don't worry, you are fine." When the syringe was about to pierce my forceps,* I jumped up and realized I was in bed. I was extremely troubled, but relieved it was only a dream.

I never ignored the voice from my rare gift. Through my years, it had shown me some wonderful and untold revelations, helping me be safe and out of trouble. Regardless, I just couldn't make any sense of that dream, even after confronting my wife.

"I don't know what this means," I whispered.

"Please, don't worry... I am fine, and so are you. You must have been very tired going to bed," my wife said, wiping the sweat off my face.

In the following weeks, I was troubled by yet several other dreams, the most perplexing of which involved my late father: *I found a scummy bottle floating at the shore of a troubled ocean, and braved the turbulent waters to pick it up. As I struggled to decode the enclosed message, my father appeared and, in perfect English, explained the anagram from Chantal's whole name, Ch**AN**tal **G**. Cyri**EL**. Before saying his farewell to me, he wrote down "ANGEL," and told me: "Don't worry, Son... she is an angel... she is your angel."* My father left me totally unable to get the true sense of his visit and the message left behind. At the very least, I thought he was shielding us, and came over to remind me of what a wonderful woman I had in my life.

My wife was not Chantal anymore, she was *Angel. (pic page 180)*

Because what lied ahead of us was still cloudy, we made the decision to establish a second residence in Chicago. I knew Angel would, without any doubt, be able to make some money from odd jobs, which would help us afford her education. After my graduation, we would all live in the Windy City, which had a lot more opportunities for us than Manhattan, Kansas, the "Little Apple."

After arriving in Chicago, I discovered that my wife had talked

With Angel and Mylène

to Father Ernest since coming to the United States. I decided to discuss the situation with her, in an attempt to save what we had managed to keep together—us.

"Chantal, can we talk?" I asked.

"Sure. Now?"

"Yes... Why call Father Ernest?"

"Joe, I told you he is my priest, and nothing more. Do you think he is my boyfriend?"

"Why are you going through so much to keep him around? Did you continue to see him after I left Cameroon?"

"No! Now I am done with this conversation. I am going to have whomever I want as a friend... You are free to think what you want."

She stood up and left the living room, leaving me baffled, hurt, and already regretful. I should not have brought her back in my life.

After that conversation, our relationship deteriorated. My lingering lack of trust in her explained my personal responsibility. On her side was lack of respect and her refusal to take advice. We made the decision to split in 2000.

Immediately thereafter, and partly out of revenge, we both started new relationships. Each day that passed was a day Chantal and I were pulled back to one another. We had made a monumental mistake. We didn't belong apart. We belonged together. We both realized it and came back together. We understood more than ever just how inseparable we were. Through that time, I had not consummated any relationship with anybody, as Chantal never stopped being my wife. She assured me of the same thing. We were back where we belonged—together, and decided to have Mylène's little brother or sister.

Angel was several months into the pregnancy, and preparing for the arrival of the newborn was exciting. Choosing a name was difficult. We wanted it to be an easy one for everyone. We had heard countless mispronunciations of "Mylène," now just *Milly* for everyone's convenience. Our son would not go through the butchering of his name.

One day in July, Angel felt a little dizzy and regularly gasped for breath. It was not surprising at all because she was about seven months pregnant. She was on the couch in the living room, watching TV. Coming back from Milly's room where I had been setting up her karaoke machine, I looked at Angel and felt worried. Since that morning, she had been insisting on having a conversation with me, and the time finally came for me to sit and listen.

"Hey, Chan, I am sorry it took this long."

"Joe, I have so much to say that I don't even know where to start."

"Really? Just start from the beginning," I joked.

"It is not a laughing matter, Joe," she said, being very serious.

"I am sorry..."

Her silence over the few following seconds seemed too long for me, and I wished I could just get in that brain of hers to uncover what she wanted to tell me, without waiting any longer. her usual beaming smile was grim, and her body language betrayed her discomfort.

"Joe, you are a witch."

"What did you just say?" I asked, shocked.

"You are a true witch."

"Why do you say such a thing?"

"I am going to start by saying how sorry I am," she continued, almost tearing up.

"What is it that you have to feel sorry about?" I asked, eager to understand.

"Joe, I lied to you, and I want you to know the truth now," she let out as if she were painfully peeling the words out of her pale skin.

At that moment, I didn't know what to do, other than hope to survive her next words.

"I lied to you about Father Ernest, and I die each time I look you in the eye. I have died over and over again."

As I battled to comprehend what I just heard, she continued, "Joe, I had a sexual relationship with that priest, and I am sorry. I had to lie... I did not want to lose you."

The whole world crumbled onto my shoulders.

"Oh, my God..."

"I am truly sorry, Joe. There were others," she launched.

She listed several men, some of whom I knew very well. One man was one too many! One being a priest was definitely over the top, totally against everything she believed. Once again, I found myself unable to give a straight answer to the question, "*Who is my wife?*"

I wanted to wring her neck. I hoped no one told me I should hug and comfort her, because I had no intention of doing so.

Remembering the start of the talk, I lifted my head and asked, "How does this make me a 'witch'?"

"...Do you remember the dream you had right after we arrived?" she asked.

"Of course, I do."

"There was some truth to it," she continued.

"What do you mean?" I questioned, puzzled.

"Before coming to the US, I went to the University Hospital Center in Yaoundé, and your colleague Yvette Deloko tested me."

"What are you talking about?"

"I was tested three times, and for all three I was found to be HIV-positive."

"No! No! No! This is not happening… No!" I screamed, visibly shaking.

Before I had a chance to say more, she added, "But the results were probably wrong."

"Stop it! Oh, my God… How long ago did all this happen?" I asked, attempting hard to keep my composure.

"In 1999."

"And you just tell me now. Why?"

She had been infected from unprotected sex with one or some of her partners, including Father Ernest—probably. My thoughts turned from disbelief to despair. I could be HIV-positive. She was my wife, and we understandably never used condoms. I knew deep inside that the noose had probably tightened around my neck. That was certainly the end for me. I was HIV-positive—definitely. And what about our children?

"Again, I love you… Had I told you, I would have lost you."

"Please do not use the word "*love*" now. Have you imagined that I would be infected too? Have you thought about Milly?"

"I am sorry, Joe"

"Easy to say! I just can't believe this, Angel. I have truly loved you, way more than you can ever imagine. For the three years I was alone here, I had not had a relationship with any woman. I have given you all my heart, and have found it almost impossible to take it back. My love was solid and true."

"I know, Joe. And I am very sorry about everything."

"Being sorry is not going to help."

I stopped talking, and the silence in the living room became chilling. Through the door, I heard Milly merrily singing, unaware of the apocalyptic atmosphere in her home.

Angel started having difficulty breathing and grew weaker by the minute. I thought it was her manipulative plan to get me to feel sorry for her, and to stop pounding her with questions. If it was the case, it certainly worked. I became worried about her and the baby she was carrying, and decided to take her to the Emergency Room.

Jackson Park Hospital was not far from our 7459 South Bennett Avenue apartment. The room was packed. Having noticed Angel's abnormal breathing, a nurse approached us.

"Hi, what is going on here?" she asked.

"She is hardly breathing as you can see; she is about seven month pregnant," I explained.

"Please come over here… Quickly fill out these forms, and we will take care of you."

"What forms are these?" Angel asked, flipping through the stack.

"These are for insurance, these for power of attorney in case you become incapacitated, and these give the hospital authorization to perform these tests on you," the nurse courteously explained.

"I am not signing these ones," Angel said in French, pointing the test forms.

"Why not? We have nothing to lose. It's probably just for formalities," I tried to convince.

"No, no, and no! I am not signing!"

"I don't understand at all," I said, visibly irritated.

"I don't need the tests or the power of attorney… I will be fine."

She handed the stack of papers back to the nurse, who certainly failed to notice the unsigned forms. She was hooked up to an oxygen mask after some x-rays, which tremendously alleviated her symptoms, to my relief.

After a few days, Angel completely lost control of her bladder and her anal sphincter. Every five to ten minutes, I held her up and supported her to the portable toilet that was brought in for convenience. Then she got moved to a single room, where I was allowed most of the time. Despite all of my efforts, the beddings were filthy, and the smell in the room, unbearable. Something was critically wrong.

The medical team assigned to her was doing *everything* it could—within the limits of Angel's will—to diagnose her deteriorating condition. The battle between her rights and her health became very frustrating; I unsuccessfully attempted to have her tested for all the diseases she had refused to sign the forms for, including HIV/AIDS. I believed her patient's rights must have never been in the way of her well-being. It did not make any sense to me at all.

On July 24, 2001, a few days after her admission in the hospital, we were in her room remembering the good moments we had had and the bright side of life. I managed to steal a few smiles out of her, which fertilized a seed of hope inside me. My worries over her had erased all other concerns and even the grudge I held. All I wanted and prayed for was her immediate and total recovery. Nothing else was important at that point.

It was about 7:30 p.m., and Angel's breathing worsened, despite the 100% oxygen mask over her mouth and nose. In a blink of an eye, she started to convulse and suffocate. I hit the red emergency button over her headboard. After storming in, the medical team made a quick decision for a C-section. As they pushed her down to the surgery room on a stretcher, she managed to wave goodbye and to blow a little kiss.

More than one whole hour passed, and I was still without any news from the surgery room, in front of which I alternately stood and sat. It had been too long, and I was losing it.

The door opened, and a nurse drove an incubator out, with a tiny baby inside. My heartbeat skyrocketed, and I jumped off my seat and stepped forward to meet them.

"Mr. Fotso, here is your son... You can insert your hand through this opening and touch him for a moment before I take him upstairs," he said.

"Hey, little guy... Hey, Chris... I am Daddy, okay? I will soon come up to see you," I reassured, gently caressing his cheek and touching his tiny fingers.

As the nurse took him away, I was left wondering where my Angel was. What was going on? When was she coming out? At what time was I going to see her again and tell her how handsome our son was? I was excited about my son, but at the same time, extremely worried about him and his mother. He was two months premature and tiny. I hoped no health issues lingered. I walked back and forth in the main hallway to escape from my confused thoughts. Then Dr. Wang came out of the surgery room.

"How is she?" I rushed to ask.

Dr. Wang hesitated a bit, leaving the impression of wanting to choose the right words.

"Mr. Fotso, she will be coming out in a few minutes. But I want you to know that she is not the same. Her lungs have collapsed, and she has lost the ability to breathe on her own. She is sedated, and is being assisted by a ventilator. She will not be up until tomorrow morning. It's important that you know before we bring her out."

"Is she going to be alright, Dr. Wang?" I asked.

"I truly want to say, "*Yes*," but I can't at this moment. To be straightforward with you, she has a 20-30% chance of survival. We will need to pray, Mr. Fotso. Pray a lot."

"Please, I want her back," I pleaded.

"We will do everything possible to save her. Please go home and try having a good night. Your son is in good hands, and we will do everything to help his mom."

He returned in the surgery room, and came right back out, followed by a swarm of nurses and aides surrounding the stretcher on which Angel laid motionless. Several little hoses were inserted in her mouth and nose, and one of the nurses was manually operating a small air pump. Angel passed by without noticing me, without waving at me like she did on her way in.

She was taken into the Intensive Care Unit, where I was not allowed. After my little talk with Dr. Wang, I was in disbelief, and thought he did not know what he was talking about. But after seeing Angel, I had the feeling *I* was dead wrong. Maybe he was right about the 20-30% prognosis. From that moment on, my duty and responsibility became to pray, pray my heart out for Angel to earn a place within that range.

I was allowed to go upstairs and bottle-feed my son, Chris, and I cherished the hour I spent with him. The only other thing that could be as soothing and comforting would be being with Milly. She was aware that she was having a baby brother, nothing more. On my way to the family friend's home where she was staying, I was unsure about what to tell her besides the birth of her little brother. Should I admit that her mom was not doing well and might pass away? How could I?

"Hi, Daddy. How is mommy?" Milly asked.

"Guess what, you have a baby brother. His name is Chris."

"Really? Yay!" she exclaimed, almost climbing on me. "How is he?"

"Just like you. But Mommy is not well yet, girl."

"What's wrong? Is she going to be well soon?" she questioned.

"The doctors said they are working hard to make her well, okay? Tomorrow I will go see her, and when Chris gets stronger, I will take you over there to meet him."

Looking at her, I could tell she was happy, but clearly missing her mother. Seldom had they been apart that long. I knew she was silently dying inside.

The next morning, Milly and I were among the very first visitors to the hospital. I wanted to see Angel and I hoped the night had brought some improvement. I wanted to see her like she was before, with no artifices inserted throughout her body. I wanted her to wave at me as I arrived in the ICU, and invite me to sit by her. I wanted her to hold Chris and feel what I felt the day before. I wanted her to be more than just his mother, but his mom.

After leaving Milly in the small waiting room, I opened the ICU door, and a young nurse came straight to me as if she had been waiting for me.

"Good morning, Mr. Fotso," she said.

"Good morning... How is she doing today?"

"She should be waking up in a few minutes... has she ever had an IV or blood transfusion before?"

"No... this is the first time," I ascertained.

"She has actually woken up, Mr. Fotso... I will pull the curtains and leave you guys alone for a moment. Please let me know if she needs anything."

"Thanks a lot."

Obviously, Angel was not like I wanted her to be. But at least she exhibited a sign of life, which was enough to replant a sprout of hope in my being.

"Hi, my Angel," I greeted, forcing a smile out.

I wanted to stay hopeful. I wanted to remain strong for her. But it was hard. With the tubes inserted down her lungs, she was voiceless. A ventilator was breathing for her, and I could tell she was not aware of her surroundings. Her eyes opened and revealed two red balls, highly vascularized. She tilted her head toward me. I guessed she was seeing me because she was not blinking at all. Putting my hand on hers, I asked her to squeeze it, and I felt the warm and shallow pressure she put on my finger.

"You are doing better, Angel. They are taking good care of you, okay?"

She managed to answer with a little nod. At the same time, the nurse returned.

"Mr. Fotso, I need to talk to you. Would you please come over?" she asked, almost whispering.

"Sure, I will be right there..."

The nurse informed me that Angel's medical team was waiting to meet with me in an adjacent conference room. Before I got there, Dr. Mendi, one of Angel's physicians, pulled me in a little office.

"Good morning, Mr. Fotso. I need to talk to you before the meeting. Do you need a cup of coffee or something?" she asked, inviting me to have a seat.

"No, thank you." I bluntly answered, tormented by not knowing why I was in there.

"First, Mr. Fotso, I want you to know that we are doing

everything to save Angel, okay?"

"I understand that, Madam."

"How are you, Mr. Fotso?" she surprisingly asked.

"Not so well, Madam. You know that."

"No… I mean, have you had any health issues in the past?"

"Not really, Doctor; the only health issue I have had in a very long time was when I broke my leg playing soccer last year."

"Oh, really? How was your recovery?"

"Eight weeks on crutches, and I was back to playing again."

She almost looked at me like she did not believe anything I said.

"Mr. Fotso, I know it is not easy, but you have to be very strong. We are here for your wife and you… I have to tell you that Chantal has AIDS, and is terminally ill."

"Excuse me?"

"I am sorry, Mr. Fotso. She is suffering from full-blown AIDS."

That four-letter word brought another to my mind: H-E-L-L. I instantly understood I was doomed. All odds were against me. Time stopped, and the world started spinning around me.

"Chris has tested negative; but he is on AZT right now to make sure he is completely cleared. Though he will have to be tested over the next two years, chances are that he will be fine."

Finally a piece of good news came my way.

"Chantal's CD4 count is extremely low," Dr. Mendi continued. "No matter what happens, we want you to be around for the two beautiful kids you have, okay?"

"How can I be around? How can I?" I desperately asked.

"We will make sure you are taken care of, Mr. Fotso. First you will have to be tested. Would you let us test you?"

What was the point not letting them? Whether or not I was tested, my fate was sealed. My life was over. My journey on earth would soon be coming to an abrupt stop. At best, life was never going to be the same. It had changed for worse.

"You can test me, Dr. Mendi."

"Great! I am glad you made that decision, Mr. Fotso. It is important that we find out in what stage you are, to better take care of you… After the meeting, an aide will draw your blood."

We arrived at the conference room, which was already packed with doctors and nurses. Milly joined me and was asked to have a seat in a distant corner, while I sat across the table from Dr. Wang.

"How are you, Mr. Fotso?" I heard.

"I am dying," I replied, bursting in tears.

That was the very first time my daughter had ever seen me in tears. Despite my state of mind, I knew I had to protect her. That was not how she was going to learn the excruciating truth about her mom. I would inform her myself, only when the moment was right.

"Would you please take my daughter somewhere else?" I asked, soaked in tears.

Milly was taken away as the team started to brief me about Angel's overall condition. They talked and I listened, but I was not so sure I understood a single word. I was subconsciously saying my farewell to the world. I was asking myself how Milly and Chris would make it alone in life, how my aged mother and mother-in-law would take it when they learned that their son and daughter, and the hopes we carried, were no more. I did not want Angel to die, and I did not want to die. But even if I didn't die, that terrible disease would devour the rest of my life, because I was sick, because I was HIV positive, or because I had AIDS. I was already looking at the world with the eyes of a ghost, as if I was already dead.

After the meeting, I went back in the ICU and found Angel a little more energetic, able to communicate by writing on little pieces of paper.

"How is the baby?" she asked.

"Very handsome. He looks just like you. Because of the possibility of infections, he cannot come in here… When you get better, you will go see him. You remember the name, Chris Hendrix?" I said, standing by her bed.

She grimaced a smile and gave me a thumbs-up. Then she tried to talk, but was harshly reminded not to by the pain from the tubes in her esophagus.

"They are doing everything to get you back on your feet." I continued.

"I don't understand. What do they say I am suffering from? Please don't hide anything," she wrote.

After a moment of hesitation, I decided not to ignore her plea, and to share the truth with her. I thought it was important for her to know why she was lying there, completely incapacitated. It would be better for her and for me.

"You are suffering from AIDS, Angel," I let out.

She started crying, and it was as if I saw some steam from the two tears emerging from the corners of her eyes and running down. I knew she felt exactly what I felt a moment before in the little office, and even more. I knew she realized "that was it." Despite the urge, I avoided joining her. I was there to support her. I had to be strong for her. I was not going to break her heart by tearing up.

"How is Chris?" she asked.

"He is negative."

After giving me another thumbs-up, she continued, "What about Milly, how is she?"

"She is fine. She will come see you soon. She asked me to tell you that she loves you."

"Tell her I love her, too."

A nurse came in and took me away to have my blood drawn. In the many labeled collection tubes filled with my red fluid, my naked eyes could see generations of AIDS virus diving in and out. The prognosis was obvious: I was sero-positive at best. I was about to become a statistic.

Three days passed, and Angel's health continued to deteriorate. She was not responding to any medications. Her handwriting got sloppier as she became weaker. She could really be going away—forever. My perpetual belief was that "miracles happen," and so I endlessly implored for one last one. If Angel recovered, I would be the happiest man on earth. If she didn't, I didn't know how I would survive without her. Despite what we had been through, she was my *every-thing*, and I would be like an empty shell without her. But why was I even thinking about death when she was holding tight to dear life? We were still a family of four, and that was it.

That morning, I was almost ready to head to the hospital. Saying goodbye to Milly was painful, more so because she always had a little message for her mom. As I approached her for a goodbye hug, she appeared very reserved and sad, as if she was hit overnight by what I knew and was hiding from her. She lifted her head and asked, "Daddy, are you going to the hospital?

"Yes, it's time to go see Mommy and Chris now. I will give them a big hug for you."

"Okay, Daddy… But first, can we pray?

"Absolutely!" I answered, a little bit surprised and pleased by her request.

She stood up, held my right hand, and closed her eyes. Then her mouth opened, letting out a heartbreaking plea.

> *"Oh, God, my mother is very sick, and I don't want her to die… I don't want to lose my mom… My baby brother and I need her… Please God or whoever is out there or up there, save my mom… Please. I will forever be thankful to you."*

She let go of my hand, and I furtively hugged her and turned away because I did not want her to see my steamy tears. I opened the door, ready to escape outside, but heard her calling me. I discreetly wiped my tears and got back to her.

"Would you please give this to Mommy?" she asked.

She handed me a little spiral-bound notebook, in which she had written a letter to her mom. It was not intended for me, and so I did not attempt to read it. My heart had been broken enough since the crack of dawn.

Unable to keep my mind off death possibly knocking at my door too, I tried engraving my beautiful daughter's image in my memory because every moment with her had become priceless. When the moment came, I wanted her and her brother to be what I remembered last.

Angel was communicating less effectively that day. I gave her the notebook, and she started reading what her daughter had written. As she neared the end of the note, tears fell from her red eyes. She then took a pen from the adjacent table-on-wheels and wrote back to Milly, at the bottom of the same page.

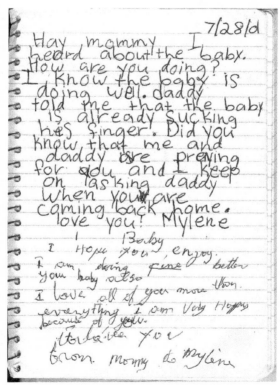

Mom and daughter communication

Chapter 19

Until The Last Minute

(2001)

More than four days passed after my blood was sampled for testing, and I still had not heard from Jackson Park Hospital. Not knowing was nerve-racking—at best. Expecting the worst with no hope, I spent a lot of time trying to figure out how my premature newborn son and my seven-year-old daughter would make it when the virus I was hosting decided to take my life. I did not have any life insurance, and with a pre-existing medical condition, no insurance company would cover me. So when my time came to die, I would only hope and pray that my children didn't live the life I lived when I was about my daughter's age. I had big dreams for them, and now all I could tell them was not to cry when my bell rang. I would pass my father's farewell speech on: "*My wish for you is that you catch a panther or a lion; and you will.*" I would tell them that God blessed them, and that Bandjoun's God would always protect them from all harm; that my ancestors would always sweep their paths and clear them of any pines. I broke down each time I practiced those heart-breaking words. But I brainstormed only in the middle of nights, when I had nothing other than the sometimes-soothing and always-scary ambient darkness around me—scary because I did not want to be taken away from my family; scary because I was powerless.

I constantly envisioned everything I had relentlessly fought for my whole life going straight down the drain. I had lived through unthinkable adversities in my childhood and found my way to a shaky adulthood. I had dodged bullets before leaving my whole family behind for a faraway country, the United States, in search of a better life and freedom. I had always thought of education as my trail to lions and panthers, but how could I even think about going back to my educational endeavor with my dying wife nailed down to her hospital bed? In a longer term, how would I study, work, and care for my tiny son and my daughter at the same time? As it seemed impossible, I started settling for what I had for sure, my determination to remain strong for my two kids.

I didn't lose all hope for Angel. No! Milly and I prayed for a miracle. On that morning, only a few days after my son's birth, the miracle I hoped for was for her to open her eyes and notice me holding her hand. I wanted her to realize that as promised on August 19, 1993, our wedding day, I was standing by her in sickness.

My cell phone rang, and it was the hospital calling. Because some devastating news was about to be shared, I knew I would remember that minute for the few months or years I had left to live. I held my breath, flipped my Samsung phone open, and placed it on my right ear. My hands were shaking, and my body temperature soared. On the other end of the line was a nurse:

"Mr. Fotso?" she asked.

"Yes, this is he." I answered, shivering.

"I am calling from Jackson Park on behalf of Dr. Wang. He would like to talk to you one-on-one, at your earliest convenience."

"Do you, by any chance, know why he wants to talk to me one-on-one?" I inquired, emphasizing *one-on-one*.

"We cannot discuss anything on the phone. You will meet with Dr. Wang when you get here, okay, Mr. Fotso?"

"Okay… Thank you."

This was it! They wanted to make sure that I was seated before they gave the bad news, which seemed to be written over the empathetic tone of the nurse's voice. After rushing to the car, I sped to the hospital to get it over with. The earlier the better!

I hurried down the hallways to get to Dr. Wang's office.

"Come in, Mr. Fotso… Have a seat, please."

"Thank you, Doctor."

"Take a deep breath, Mr. Fotso… Are you ready?" he said.

"Okay… Go ahead." I replied after a very long, loud, and deep sigh.

"My friend, your results are in," Dr. Wang calmly continued. "I do not know how, but your tests are negative… It means that you do not currently have antibodies in your system, but you may still be carrying the virus itself. You will need to be tested again about six months after your last intercourse with your wife, and regularly thereafter for the next two years. But I can give you my educated guess now: you will be just fine… cases like yours are extremely rare, almost impossible."

After his first two sentences, I stopped listening. I had never thought of that scenario, because it was, indeed, impossible. But reality was there, carrying a little torch through the darkest days of my life. I became very hopeful, because I was saved. In retrospect, I had been so "sick" that I could then just declare it: I was healed.

"How did you beat the odds, Mr. Fotso?" Dr. Wang questioned, making me realize that he was still talking.

"I don't know… I have no idea!" I answered, incredulous.

"Well… I am glad it turned out this way. Your children need you. Be very strong, okay? It is called *life*. Things happen, and they happen for a reason."

"Thank you, Dr. Wang."

"Oh, don't thank me. Thank the man upstairs… Good luck."

"Thank you."

As I stepped outside, the lights seemed a little brighter than a few minutes before. I might be around for Chris and Milly. Thank God, even if it was still a little early to declare *victory*. Thank God, anyway, for the newfound hope.

With the hospital feeding my premature son continuously, he caught up quite well. His mom, however, deepened into a vegetative state, completely held up by machines, from feeding to breathing. Her vital signs became erratic. The end was near, and I said goodbye each time I held her hand. When I met her eleven years earlier, I would never have imagined those poignant moments. We were full of love and life. But now, I was powerlessly watching her slip away, day after day.

Time to take Milly to her mom came. We had to start saying goodbye. It was the last thing I wanted to be doing, but sadly the only thing I had to do. Having left Milly in the waiting room of the ICU, I pulled the curtains as usual, and gave Angel a hug. If she could listen to my thoughts now, she would notice a little change in the words she was used to hearing from my silence by her bedside. That day, I was not going to let my teary silence talk to her. That day, I didn't want her to dig deep in my soul to get my comforting words. I wanted to talk to her. I wanted her to hear me, and I hoped she was still alert enough to understand what I believed would probably be my last words to her. If not, I hoped and prayed that her guardian angels seeded my voice in her vanishing soul. Holding her hand, my chapped lips spoke a promise to the love of my life:

"Sweetheart, I know how much you are suffering; you are in a lot of pain... I would give up the world right now for you to get better, stand up, smile again, and hug the kids; but it's not that easy. I am powerless. But I will give up the world any time for Chris and Milly. That's my promise to you... I am glad I had you in my life... Listen, sweetheart: Milly is here today. She is finally ready to come in, and I brought her to see you and say goodbye; I will take her back to Manhattan tonight..."

The room was silent. I hoped to see her blink, wink, or exhibit any sign of life. The sign never came. I wiped my tears and stepped out of the curtains.

The nurse insisted Milly should stay just long enough to say goodbye to her beloved mom. She had no idea this was the last time she would ever talk to her mother. I knew it, and wished I didn't. Even though I struggled for not telling her the whole truth, I believed I had to protect her. She was seven years old. I would let it sink in as slowly as possible.

We pulled the curtains, and I could tell how shocked my little girl was. I had prepared her by describing how Angel looked, but nothing would have ever prepared her enough for the traumatizing reality. The tears bursting out of her little eyes shattered my soul, and brought about a series of questions that I had asked myself on so many occasions: "*Why does this innocent little girl have to endure this? Why didn't 'somebody' listen to her prayer? How will she go through life without her best friend, her mom?*" Those tears were—more than anything else—the true measure of how big of a loss it was going to be.

Milly stepped closer to her mother and started talking to her in a shaky but resolute tone, "Hi, Mommy... I just came by to see you before I go... I have seen Chris and he is doing better... He eats a lot... Mommy, get better soon. I want you to come back home. I am going to go back to school, study hard, and make you proud. I love you, Mommy... Bye, Mommy..."

The moment was surreal, and I was glad it had not lasted longer. I wanted to cry my eyes out, but I had the obligation not to. I had to remain strong for my daughter. Any weakness that she saw in me would certainly affect her negatively. So I had to smile while crying inward.

"Goodbye, my love... Please, wait for me... I will be back soon." I whispered, as we stepped out of the curtains.

I left Milly to the care of my supervisor's family, the Smiths, in Manhattan, Kansas. She would stay there while I took care of her mom and her brother. The Smith children, Katie and Robbie, as well as the mom, Kathy, were everything she needed in those circumstances. They were good friends and I was so relieved and grateful for their help. I knew my daughter was safe.

Having driven for many hours on I-55 N, I was around Springfield, IL, on my way back to Chicago, driving on the edge of the speed limits, eager to be back at the hospital, where Angel was waiting for me. There was absolutely nowhere else I would rather be at that moment.

My cell phone rang and I picked it up. I knew it was my

daughter calling as promised.

"Mr. Fotso, this is Dr. Mendi from Jackson Park... When you are getting back here?"

The call wiped my *feet* off the road. After tripping over my tongue for a few seconds, I finally became able to articulate my question.

"What's going on?"

"She is not doing well. You should get here as soon as possible... Where are you right now?

"Oh, my God... I am just passing Springfield; so I should be there in about four hours."

"Okay... We are all expecting you, Mr. Fotso. Have a safe trip."

I started driving like a maniac. Angel needed me, and I would rather die trying to get to her, than respecting what I then considered "stupid" speed limits, just to avoid "stupid" speeding tickets. I had the impression of hearing her urge me to hurry, and I took it as a call for a last wish. It was my duty to grant her just that. It was certainly the least thing I could offer her at the twilight of her existence.

After driving at speeds exceeding 90 mph most of the way, I arrived in Chicago in no time. Someone had to be up there blindfolding all the cops on the highway, protecting me, and sweeping my path.

I ran into the hospital, where I had become a well-known face, and rushed upstairs to the ICU. To my surprise, Angel's curtains were pulled open, and she was not in her bed. One thing and one thing only came in my mind, "*She is gone!*" I was not able to get back to her in time, and I already felt like a failure.

I carefully inspected all beds and, after confirming Angel's absence from the room, I turned around and proceeded to find Dr. Mendi. As I started walking toward the main door, I saw one room I had not checked. Although it was the last place I wanted to step in, I had no choice. It was the end-of-life room.

As I tiptoed in, I realized who was lying on the only bed of the little room. It was my Angel, whose physical appearance had drastically changed in just a few days. I stepped closer to her, and my shaky legs gave up on me, not able to continue supporting my sunken body. I dropped on the floor, my back against the wall. Angel appeared as peaceful as I had ever seen her since the beginning of the ordeal. She seemed to be taking a nap, but I knew she was not. Around me, the room seemed to be spinning, shattering my sanity in tiny pieces.

"*So, this is it, Angel...*" I thought. I stared at her, reliving all of our moments together in just a few seconds. What a life it had been!

Dr. Mendi walked in and was surprised to see me in the room.

"Mr. Fotso, I did not know that you were already here. How did you make it here so fast?" she asked, certainly trying to divert my focus.

"I don't know... But I am here."

"I did not want you to come in here alone, and I am sorry for that... As you can see, the end is near. The last few days were very rough. We have attempted everything possible, but it wasn't meant to be, Mr. Fotso... Please be strong."

"Thank you, Madam... It just wasn't meant to be." I robotically answered.

"I would like to ask you a very difficult question," Dr. Mendi continued. "At this stage, we do not believe anything will really help... Do you want us to keep on trying to resuscitate her, or would you like us to pull off her life-support?"

"Please, don't!" I instantly replied, regaining my senses. "I believe in miracles *now*. I am most probably HIV-free, and that's a miracle. One more can happen. Please, try until the last minute. I am not going to decide when that will be. I don't have that power..."

"We will, Mr. Fotso... But we just want you to be prepared, okay? I am very sorry... I am now going to step out and give you a few moments with Chantal," she said, rubbing my shoulder.

Left alone with the woman of my life, I realized it was all real. Not that I had decided not to believe in miracles anymore, but I intuitively knew that none would be happening in that room. I stood up, and approached Angel. As I stepped forward, that room did not seem to be a hospice, but a sanctuary—a sanctuary of love and endurance... a sanctuary of hurting and healing... a sanctuary of life. That was the sacred place where I was saying "so long" to my love. That was the moment for a goodbye to my children's mom, and probably the last day I was seeing my Angel alive. So I had to talk to her one last time—maybe.

"Angel, I am here with you as promised... You are in too much pain for me to keep holding on to you; but I am not giving up. We have tried, and couldn't; but we did not fail... Please understand why I am letting you go now: I have to. I do not want you to suffer anymore. You will be just fine in Heaven. That's where you belong. Please, go and don't worry anymore. Always remember how much we, Chris, Milly and I, love you. Please, protect us from up there. Please, remember us. We will forever keep you alive. So long, Angel... Farewell my love... Goodbye... I love you, sweetheart. I will carry your torch."

After a visit upstairs to give Chris a hug, I walked home, understandably seeing the world and life in a whole different way.

As I went to bed that night, I was as lonely as I had ever been. All that time, despite her physical absence, Angel had been there with me. Suddenly, she was missing. I didn't seem to feel her, no matter what I did.

The darkness in my room materialized what I was going through, which could be described with that same four-letter word, H-E-L-L. In the abyss of my pain, I decided to listen to some tunes from André Marie Tala. His soothing lyrics had cheered me up through the most difficult moments of my life. Once again, he had the right words for me, slipping my being deeper in a sleeping mood. My crushing solitude paired up with that darkness, however, to continue torturing my body and mind.

Before long Angel appeared to me, as beautiful as she had ever been. Standing on an evergreen landscape, she was dressed in a long crystal-white outfit covering her from the neck down, dragging a fading white cloud as she moved, and displaying her most beautiful smile. Not surprised by her presence, I was simply glad that she was there with me:

"Hi, Angel; how are you?" I asked, excited.

"I am doing fine, Joe," she answered, with her trademark smile. *"You are not suffering anymore... I am glad that you are here."*

"No, I am just fine now. Don't worry anymore, Joe. I am fine, okay? I am not in pain any longer... I am healed and I want to let you know that. I love you."

"Thank you, Angel. I love you too," I added, as I opened my eyes without having realized that I had ever closed them.

Seeing and talking to Angel again and knowing that she was *healed* allowed me to be at peace with myself. It didn't matter that it was only a dream.

About an hour went by since the dream-like visit, and it was about 6 a.m. on August 18. I still had two hours before the hospital's doors opened. As I debated between taking my covers off and keeping them on, my cell phone rang.

"Hello?" I picked up.

"Mr. Fotso, this is Dr. Mendi again... I just wanted to let you know that the moment we talked about yesterday is here. Will you be able to come over?"

"Yes!"

I dropped the phone and stormed out of our apartment, only a few blocks away from the hospital. I wished I could fly and get there instantly, but I couldn't. I had to endure the huge pain of that short distance.

Dr. Mendi was standing at the hospice doorstep. As I entered, I was struck by the loud silence. There were no more revolving sounds from life-support equipment. All had stopped, although still attached to Angel.

"Mr. Fotso, we are going to leave you alone," I heard.

Angel's eyes were open, and she seemed very much alive. I gave her one last hug and a kiss on the cheek, realizing just how warm she was. Holding her hand, I said a few words:

"Angel, thank you for saying goodbye. You are in the best of hands now... Goodbye, sweetheart."

I then closed her eyelids in a single hand movement, and covered her with a white sheet, which was just down to her waist.

Shambling out of the room, I found Dr. Mendi waiting in the general area of the ICU.

"I would like to discuss what's going to happen next. Would you prefer I wait?" she asked.

"No, please. Go ahead."

"In an hour or so, she will be transferred to the morgue and then to a funeral home of your choice... Where would you like her buried?"

"I have to bring her back home where she belongs, as required by our tradition," I answered.

"Okay, Mr. Fotso. We will have a few forms for you to fill out and sign, and all will be set... Again, I am so sorry."

"That's okay, Madam. It is life, after all."

I sat in the waiting room and held my head in my hands. Only then did I realize, looking down, that I was barefoot, with wounds on my toes. I was also still in my boxers. Thinking back, it came to me that after the call, I ran instead of driving. That was why I was wet—from my sweat. But I did not regret my subconscious decision. Who knew what would have happened had I stepped in that car, behind that steering wheel?

Despite all the confusion, I began to ask myself how I was going to inform my daughter. How would I inform my mother-in-law of the death of her beautiful daughter? How would I inform my sister-in-law Anne of the loss of her sister and best friend? How was I ever going to be able to explain to Chris? He never had a chance to see his mom, and she never was fortunate enough to hold him in her arms. The hospital was reluctant to bring him in the ICU to meet his mom, as he was very fragile and prone to infections. But had I really understood that things were going to end like they just did, I would have done everything to give my son and his mom that ultimate present. I did not, and I was already slapping myself, even though I didn't know whether or not I would have succeeded.

Chapter 20

The Call Before
the Trip

With Angel lying lifeless at the Gatling's Chapel on South Halsted Street, my focus shifted to Chris, still in hospital care. At the same time, I constantly thought about how to tell Milly. She had already started school at Lee Elementary in Manhattan, Kansas, while I was in Chicago taking care of her brother and her mother's funeral details. After a few days, I felt ready to give her a call. I would have liked to face her in person and hold her tight as I informed her about the loss of her mom. But it was not possible. I couldn't wait much longer before telling her the truth. She had the absolute right to know, to hurt, and to start mourning. Encouraged by the hospital psychologist who stated that Milly did not fully understand death yet, I gave her a call.

"Hey, girl, how are you?" I asked, after she was handed the phone by Mrs. Smith.

"Hi, Daddy. I am fine."

"Great!"

"Daddy... How are Mommy and Chris?"

"Chris is doing fine. He is growing up fast... You want to see him?"

"Yes, I want to. Are you going to bring him here soon?"

"Of course. I promise."

"Daddy, what about Mommy?"

"...Girl, you know when people get very sick?"

"Yes..." she answered, dragging this monosyllabic word as long as she could.

"When they get that sick, they end up going to Heaven... and Mommy got very sick."

"Daddy, are you telling me Mommy is dead?" Milly asked, slowly pronouncing *dead*—almost spelling it—and catching me off guard.

"Yes, Girl. Mommy is dead. I am very sorry..."

"Noo!"

Her voice unleashed the deep pain she had been housing for some time, and I realized the mistake I had just made. I would have given up the world at that moment to be by her side, to hug her as tightly as possible. I wanted to be there but I wasn't.

"Girl, remember: Mommy loved you more than anything in the world, okay?"

"Okay, Daddy."

"Be very strong... I am now taking care of her and will soon take her back to Africa."

"When you are going, and where is Chris staying?"

"I don't know yet. I will figure it out and keep you posted, okay?

"Okay, Daddy. I love you."

"I love you too, Girl."

"Okay... Bye, Daddy."

"Bye, sweetheart." I said as I hung up, tearing up and already slapping myself for not being with my daughter when she felt empty, crushed and needed me the most.

About ten days after Angel's passing, Jackson Park Hospital informed me that it was time to take Chris home. Deep inside, I was scared to death but I did not let it show. How was I going to afford caring for that tiny baby, as broke and fragile as I was? Life had prepared me for a lot, but certainly not for this abominable situation.

Fortunately, my peace of mind came from three people, whom I liked to think of as Chris's guardian angels: Gwen Davenport, Sharon Hilton, and Jacqueline Durham, all living in the Chicago area. They were very compassionate family friends who offered to take care of my boy as a team while I was gone, and thereafter if needed. They became, each in her own way, my son's mothers. I would go to Africa with little worries.

Africa was not a cab ride away. The journey would cost a lot of money, and I had none. Fortunately, my sad situation allowed me to experience America's big heart and its ability to come together in times of need. My supervisor, Dr. Smith, set up fundraising in Manhattan for Angel's final trip, which helped alleviate my financial burden, enabling me to take her back home. After arranging for Angel to follow me some days later in a cargo plane, I traveled alone to Cameroon on September 5, 2001, and anxiously waited for her. The days passed slowly, as I was alone in all places I used to be with her.

But, of course, the day Angel arrived had to come. As the sun set behind the distant mountains of Yaoundé, the magnificence of the gigantic red star was not enough to subdue the sadness of my thoughts. I wished I could stop the time. I wished what was to come never had to be. I wished it were June 09, 1990 all over again, when I first blessed my eyes on that beautiful girl named Chantal. But it wasn't. It was the evening of September 8, and I had to go to Nsimalen International Airport where Air France Freight flight # 055 would land around 6:00 p.m. with Angel's body. In 1990, I had met her full of life in that same city. Only eleven years later, I was about to meet her again; but this time, there would be no soothing smile to make me the happiest man alive. There would be dead silence.

Members of both families had met at my sister-in-law Anne's house. Siblings, neighbors, and strangers took turns praying at the memorial board we had set in front of the house with Angel's pictures. Tears were profuse, and smiles, extremely scarce.

Clamped in a few run-down cars, we started our forty-five-minute drive to the airport. As much as I wanted the drive to never end, each mile brought me closer to my reality. I was not dreaming, but I wished I were.

Because of the heavy traffic and the deleterious conditions of the roads, we arrived late at the airport. Seeing the huge, immobile aircraft numbed all of my senses. I knew what was inside. Because of the special circumstances, we were allowed behind security lines, in an open shed in the back of the airport's main building. Waiting was long and excruciating, as the freight was emptied onto motorized luggage carriers. After an hour, I thought Angel had *missed* her flight. How was that possible? I had made all arrangements prior to leaving the US.

After another hour during which relatively small packages were carried out from the airplane, a big, rectangular one emerged. I knew my Angel was in that ugly, wooden crate. My heart broke. As tears erupted from my tired eyes, I slid down on the dusty concrete floor, with my sweaty back against one of the structural columns of the building. It suddenly seemed like Angel had died all over again. I thought I had already accepted Angel's death and said *goodbye* to her. I just had no idea how wrong I was.

After bribing airport officials for Angel's body, she was driven to us. I identified her as everyone else cried loudly. Then her coffin was loaded into a hearse, a black Mercedes that was rented to make sure her last trip to the village was in the best vehicle available. We then hit the road. It would take six hours to get to Bandjoun, our final destination; we would arrive around four o'clock in the morning.

Reaching my family compound, I found hundreds of people waiting for us. As soon as the hearse stopped, my half-brother, Jacques, opened the door, revealing the white-and-gold casket inside. All around me, those who knew her and those who never did cried their eyes out. As for me, I was no longer able to cry visibly. My tears were internal. Nobody but me could see or feel them. Angel was carried into the family house for an overnight viewing in the living room. I spent the following twelve hours standing by her, *crying* in everything I did and everything I was. I was numb and could not feel physical pain. When my body got to the point of collapsing, my mind took over and gave me the impression of floating, of being alone with Angel in a world where pain did not exist. Every now and then, I gently touched her right arm and her cheek, as if I wanted to wake her up. But I was forced to realize, yet again, that she was gone, never to come back.

Around 10 a.m., a religious ceremony started. As the priest said his prayers and blessings, I knew everybody had the same pressing question, "How did she die?" There had been rumors that I had traded her life in the United States for my Ph.D., and I felt the obligation to put them to rest, to tell that sea of caring people the truth. So when I was asked to speak to the tearful audience, I seized the occasion. I opened my mouth with one thing in mind: Angel's dignity.

"Dear parents, brothers and sisters, friends, ladies and gentlemen, I would like to thank you for all of your prayers and support... I am very grateful to have you here on this sad day for a farewell to my twin soul. Many of you knew and loved Chantal for what she was: caring, carefree, compassionate... I loved her also for who she was: a wonderful wife and mother."

The tears I thought had completely dried up began to trickle down my cheeks as I spoke. Four or five hundred eyes beamed at me without blinking, and four or five hundred ears raised to hear what I was saying. After a slow, deep breath, I took a few steps forward to be close to Angel. Absolute silence reigned.

"Chantal was everything to me," I continued. "So with her passing, I lost everything."

Then, putting my right hand on the coffin, I added, "She was very sick... She suffered from a cancer that was not diagnosed until it was too late... The disease was in its final stage."

A very brief rumbling erupted from the crowd, and everyone refocused on me as if they expected more. I continued, "We tried everything humanly possible to save her life, but couldn't. It was meant for her to go now—unfortunately. Goodbye, my Angel. May you rest in peace... Again, thank you!"

As soon as I ended my speech, the audience began mumbling with each other, louder and longer. I didn't care what was being said. I—like I did in the United States—had lied.

The time to take Angel to her final resting place came and, as the coffin was carried, I had to come back to the cruel reality that my Angel was in that horribly beautiful white-and-gold box and about to be put away.

> *"My Angel, you meant everything to me; you still do. You may be far away but you've never been deeper in my heart. I loved you then, I love you now and I always will. Please protect us: Chris, Mylène, and Joe. The candle will keep on burning… May your soul rest in peace.*
> *Your loving spouse, Joe."*

I did not have to say more as we put her six feet under. I had said it all and I hoped it had not gotten into death's ears. Letting her go was the only way to go. So long, Angel!

Childhood friends, cousins, and nephews carrying Angel to her resting place

Chapter 21

The Turning Point

It had been two long days since Angel's burial, and I was coming to accept that I would never see her again. I called Milly to inform her of everything that had happened since our arrival in Africa. Though she was hurt to numbness, she wouldn't let me hear it in her voice. She laughed and smiled, but I felt sorrow hidden in her confused laughs and her caring smiles. I knew she was asking herself where we would go from there. She was holding back. Probably because she knew I was hurt and would probably never heal, and she did not want to add to it. Even at her young age, she cared.

It was about 10 p.m. in Cameroon and 3 p.m. EST in the United States. We had started a ritual dance, an all-night traditional tribute to Angel. As my initiation to the dance steps started, a drunken neighbor, Charles, insistently pulled me aside and declared:

"The US was attacked by terrorists who took the Twin Towers down... Your country is in a state of shock and emergency."

There was no doubt in my mind that Charles was very drunk, certainly out of his mind, and hallucinating. After politely getting rid of him, I returned to the dance queue, where I vowed to stay until the break of dawn.

I left Bandjoun and returned to Yaoundé, where I had a room at the Meumi Hotel. After turning my little TV on, I realized that the United States had, indeed, been attacked. Thousands of innocent people were probably gone. It was still too early for any official statistics. But that tragedy instantly helped put my personal loss in perspective. Angel was one, and they were talking about thousands of lives. May they all rest in peace.

Back in the US, I retrieved my family. Seeing Chris and Milly again was healing. They were all I had now. They were my strength. We would hold onto one another.

After careful consideration, I left Chris in Chicago, to be close to the Core Center clinic on West Harrison Street, where he had a special connection with Pam Haerr, his nurse. The separation was crushing, but I knew he was in good hands—the hands of his three guardian angels.

Once a month I made the trip from Manhattan, Kansas to Chicago to take my son for HIV testing. During my visits, the psychologist repeatedly suggested I tried anti-depressants, but I always refused. Only time would help me. Only my children's smiles would heal me; nothing else.

After a few months of driving back and forth between the two states, I became extremely exhausted and felt disheartened each time I thought of hitting the road again. Chris's absence from our home amplified the crushing void left around me by the loss of his mom and made it almost impossible for me to endure much longer.

Missing him more each day, I became afraid that the special bond created between us when I first touched him in his rolling incubator would break. But I had to keep it strong. So, encouraged by the confirmation of his HIV-negative status, I made the decision to reunite with him once and for all. I brought Chris from Chicago to live with Milly and me. I was Dad, one that had to assume all the responsibilities of Mom.

I enrolled him at the Kansas State University Child Development Center, his home away from home, and established a routine. Between getting my kids up and ready for the day, driving them to and from school and daycare, cooking for them, changing diapers, braiding my daughter's hair, and continuing my education

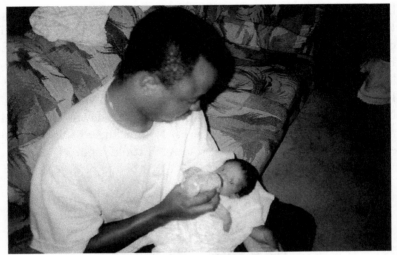

Feeding Chris his bottle of milk

and work, I had a lot to think about. My brain had adapted to Angel's death in a very strange way. My right cerebral hemisphere seemed reserved for her exclusively, as there was absolutely nothing I did without seeing or hearing her—like in a short film—smiling, calling me, hugging and kissing me, tearing up on her hospital bed, dying, dead and buried. I could not stop that frantic succession of happy and sad images from parading in my mind. I just dealt with them by containing my struggle deep inside, never opening up to anyone, and making constant efforts to focus on the positive side of life and my dreams. Though only the other half of my brain—the left hemisphere—was left to cope with everything else, I managed to stay focused and was more than ever determined to continue my education, my path to lions and panthers. Quitting was not an option. Succeeding was my only option.

We became one big, happy, unconventional family of three, or so people thought. The silent struggle continued to consume me from within, little by little. Although I appeared to be emerging from my tragedy, no one around me could imagine what a heavy toll my new life took on me. Going days without any sleep was not unusual, as I was up three to five times a night to feed Chris. Despair and pain grew in every inch of my body, and every day I battled to stay alive. Even playing soccer brought me no comfort. Time seemed powerless, and my kids' smiles, ineffective. Not scared of death anymore, I would have felt ready to take it on if it wasn't for Milly and Chris. No one knew it. Everyone only saw my after-dawn smiles and never my after-twilight fears and tears. No one knew I was about to explode; I didn't know how much longer I could hold.

My after-dawn smile, with grown Chris and Milly

On my fifth straight sleepless night, I hoped to finally catch some sleep. To increase my chances, I overfed Chris. Lying in my bed, I closed my eyes. After tossing and turning for some time, I had a sudden impression of looking straight at a movie screen that had instantly unrolled in the darkness of my room. *Angel was back, with the same magnificent smile and the same beauty. She was calling me to join her, but was so far up that I didn't know how to reach the hand she was waving. I dropped everything and abandoned everyone to get to her. Somehow, I started to levitate slowly. Passing huge masses of cold cloud, the shrinking distance between her and me revived my being. I was getting closer to happiness and fullness. I was soon to get there—again.*

As I reached her, she held my hand and without saying anything, she pointed far down. I didn't want to take my eyes off her, but she kept insisting for me to see something. I had no choice but to follow her eyes and look down. Extremely dazed by what I saw, I heard, "You wanted to be here with me, and you are now, Joe. But look... You see that?" Angel said.

"Yes, I see," I answered, shaken.

"Those children are Milly and Chris," she continued. "Is that what you want for them?"

"No... never!"

"Joe, they need you. You are everything they've got."

Milly was turning the contents of a dumpster upside down to find some food for her brother. What they had on seemed to be the very first piece of clothing from the dawn of time—just like mine, decades prior.

Having woken up, I was shivering. After a glance at the kids to make sure they were safe, I grasped that my dream was a warning, a clear wake-up call. That was what would happen to my kids if I didn't reverse the course of my declining life, my hidden torpor, and my dulled feelings. It seemed as if I had just seen the eight year-old boy I used to in a mirror. There was no way I would let my children take that path. That was my turning point.

I immediately vowed total happiness and fullness in my dullness and emptiness.

Several additional blood tests, including the ones for immigration and life insurance, confirmed my excellent state of health. I was miraculously sero-negative and healthy, just like Chris. Bandjoun's God and my father's ancestors had swept all danger from my way. Two years crawled by, and I did not have to be tested for HIV anymore.

I adjusted to the new routine in our lives. I got used to being lonely and nothing suggested that I would break that cycle any time soon. My sunken heart continued to be insensitive to all women, no matter how beautiful. In general, I found trust to be an issue, despite all efforts.

Nonetheless, I had some indications that my tunnel was not endless. The first beam of light was a very good family friend of Cameroonian descent, Linette, to whom Milly and Chris got attached as she helped care for Chris every now and then. She was a beautiful, respectful, down-to-earth, and compassionate girl for whom I gradually developed a new sense of trust. Unfortunately, unforeseen circumstances made any future with Linette impossible. However, I knew my heart was cracked for the first time in a very long time. We marched on without her, but the restoration of my human feelings had started.

After my wake-up call from *above*, I worked as hard as I humanly could under my circumstances, juggling my personal life, my courses, my lab work, my thesis, and my teaching responsibilities. I had to ensure that my kids did not have a childhood similar to mine. I had to follow the way to my dreams. As it became harder to make ends meet, I began searching for a regular job. Attending the Pittsburgh Conference (Pittcon) in Orlando in March 2003 provided me with the perfect opportunity. I dropped my resume in a box set up by a bio-pharmaceutical company based in Tarrytown, NY, and earned an interview, upon which I was offered the position, pending successful completion of my Ph.D. program. The job offer was galvanizing, as the starting salary was about three times my student wage. I was more than ready for it!

On June 5, 2003, almost two years from the fatidic day my life irreversibly changed, and after many years of hard work at Kansas State University, I was allowed to defend my Ph.D. dissertation. Still with only half of my brain functioning normally, I stood in front of my thesis committee and a conference room packed to maximum capacity. But first, I stood in front of my nine-year old daughter and my son, who was about to enter his "terrible twos." To me, they were more than just themselves. They represented my Angel, their mom.

"Good morning everyone," I started my presentation. "I would like to thank you for being here today either to grade me or to support me. I would also like to express my gratitude to all of you for your prayers following the recent tragic loss in my family. My wife is not here today, but she fought hard to see this day come. I want to thank her also... I have dedicated my thesis to her and to our kids Chris and Milly that you know well. Again, thank you... That said, today I will be presenting the work I conducted for my Ph.D. research, titled *Structure Elucidation and Toxicological Characterization of new FUSARIUM Mycotoxins...*"

My voice was trembling, and I hoped no one noticed. I was not nervous but on the verge of tears, as I kept picturing Angel sitting in the front row and silently encouraging me. Of course she was not, and I faced that cruel reality once more and marched on. After a little over two hours—from oral defense to deliberation—my thesis committee announced that I had successfully defended my Ph.D. work and for the second time, I had earned the right to be called Doctor Fotso. I was then ready for real life, ready to see my dream of working as a pharmaceutical scientist become reality, ready to make more money and pay off some of the debts I had accumulated as I struggled to afford life in the United States.

Chapter 22

The Reunion

(2006)

After graduating from Kansas State University in June 2003, I moved to New York to take my first job in a pharmaceutical company, which I considered the panther's tail. I was nervous stepping into the corporate world for the first time in my life. My qualifications could not prevent my uneasiness. I had no idea where I was taking my children, as I knew absolutely nobody in New York. I doubted I would find a daycare that would take good care of my two-year-old son, like the Kansas State Child Development Center had. But once in New York, the Small Miracles Daycare became Chris's new home away from home, which allowed me to have some peace of mind and focus on my work and my career. After my kids, my job was my only other priority. Things had to work for me. So I compensated for my uneasiness by working smarter, harder, and longer. I wanted to ascertain my skills and advance my career.

Four months after starting my job, in December 2003, I went back to Kansas to formally graduate. Going back not only gave me a great sense of accomplishment, but also brought back vivid images of my past I had been struggling to repress. My brain was still compartmentalized and I was fighting each day to cure it from within. In the late morning of December 12—graduation day—sitting in my hotel, I took a few minutes to go over my doctoral thesis' dedication page, which I had written for the people I held close to my heart.

I wish to dedicate this effort to my late wife Chantal Fotso, who did not live long enough to see this day. Her spirit of love, endurance, and compassion holds me up and will continue to do so forever. She was a lovely spouse and a wonderful mother. May her soul rest in peace!

To our children Milly and Chris, for their innocent smiles and the happiness they bring into our home.

I then stepped out of my hotel and headed to the campus. Soon after my arrival, I found my seat in the McCain Auditorium and patiently waited for the moment I seemed to have waited for all of my life. When it finally came, hearing my name echoing in the large room and holding the purple folder with my degree almost felt surreal. I had succeeded, against all odds. As I walked on the stage amid cheers from an applauding audience, I thought, "*Thank you, America! I have done it!*" lifting my degree up at the same time. No one understood my gesture. I simply did it for Angel.

After getting back to New York and during our first winter in the Empire State, Milly and I devoted a lot of time to working on a DVD tribute to her mom, the *Fotso 5*. We considered ourselves a family of five: Milly, Chris, Angel the mom, Angel the angel, and me. I wanted my children to always remember their mom, and nothing could be more helpful than a video that would last through generations.

I was grateful to have landed my dream job, excited to be using the scientific skills and knowledge acquired through my unusually long education, relieved to be making substantially more money, and determined to make it. I became a workaholic. I knew "*there is no free lunch*" in America, and that I would not be an exception to this economic principle. I analyzed drugs in development and animal clinical samples using a multitude of techniques. I also contributed to ensuring patient safety by implementing an in-house toxicity testing program—Ames test, Comet assay, micronucleus assay— aimed at detecting potential genotoxic and carcinogenic chemicals at very early stage of development. To me, my job was a call to further the welfare of humanity, and I was extremely delighted to help answer it. My company's higher management noticed my hard work and dedication, and rewarded me in a way I never dreamed of at that stage of my career. In only two short years, I went from being a benchtop scientist to being the Head of the Analytical Research Department, and in another two years I was promoted to Associate Director. *I*, the desperate little boy from Cameroon, was making it.

I decided to take a family trip to Africa, which I had planned far ahead to benefit from airfare discounts and to offset some of the cost of that expensive journey. With the excitement of preparation, time passed by very fast, and our departure date arrived. The kids were bouncing around the room, bursting with raw energy. They were very excited and I was eager but slightly nervous about the sad *reunion*. As much as I wanted Milly to *reunite* with her best friend and mother, and for Chris to finally *meet* his mother, I was very nervous about their reactions. Although I could anticipate some of their questions, I couldn't imagine the emotions tied to them, nor the reactions of my own. I prayed secretly for continued strength. Throughout our loss, my children had yet to see my tears, and I was determined for them to continue seeing me strong, not vulnerable.

I also wanted that trip to be an educational and life-changing experience for the kids, as they would learn about my cultural roots. Milly still had faded memories of living in Africa; however, it would certainly be a culture shock for her four-year-old brother.

On July 6, 2006, we embarked on an exciting thirty-day vacation in Cameroon. As we waited to take off from John F. Kennedy International Airport in New York, I was reminiscing of my family whom I had not seen for about five years. I couldn't wait to arrive. Milly and Chris would get to know their immediate and extended family members, who were all impatient to finally meet them.

After an eight-hour flight to Paris, a two-hour layover, and another eight-hour flight to Cameroon, we started flying at low altitude as we prepared to land at the Douala International Airport. I recognized the characteristic landscape of the city, its quarters wide-awake with life. We were, indeed, in Cameroon and would be landing around 4:00 p.m.

We crossed the security line into my motherland, and cheers frantically welcomed us. Almost every member of my family, including my in-laws, and some close friends had made it to the airport. Their bright-colored traditional clothing jolted my memories, and in spite of the almost-five years that had passed, it took only a quick glance for me to recognize each of their faces. They ran to us with open arms, and surrounded us. Without knowing when he got there, I saw Chris on one of his aunts' shoulders, smiling and staring at me. Milly hugged everyone and responded to many questions and comments with cute smiles, giggles, or just by repeatedly saying, "*Oui,*" or "*Non.*" Although a few people were able to converse in broken English—typically in an effort to accommodate the kids or to impress—almost everybody spoke French, which Milly understood very well. She had, however, become an English-speaking individual or Anglophone as known there; so her spoken French was lacking.

As for me, I loved being there. This time, unlike my visit five years before, I was there with a smile on my face. My children had arrived at my birthplace, a world of rediscovery for Milly and of complete discovery for Chris. No one understood a word he said, and he had no clue of what people said to him. Even though some people could understand some English, his American accent was troubling. After the first day of frustrating miscommunication or lack of communication, he developed some sign language.

Chris also acquired some unusual friends—an indoor lizard he named Larry, and a very shy stray dog, Natasha. He was completely fascinated by Larry who came out mostly at night and hung out around the light bulb to prey on unsuspecting insects. His desire to pet Natasha grew by the day, but she was clearly not a pet, as she ran away at each attempt.

After five days in the city, we made the trip to Bandjoun as Chris fought some food poisoning caught from sharing an ice pop with a kid. At my family's compound, reality set in. Despite all the smiles and excitement of being there, I realized it was only a matter of time before I led Chris and Milly to Angel.

We woke up at sunrise, with numerous roosters singing loudly from all directions, and various birds continuously announcing their presence with a multitude of melodies.

We stepped outside and Milly paid a visit to the family pigs, while Chris became fascinated with live chickens, as it was the first time he ever saw any. Then time to take the kids to their mom came, time for the reunion I dreaded and looked forward to, at the same time.

"Would you guys come here?" I called.

"Where are we going, Daddy?" Milly asked.

"You probably know..."

"Oh, I do. Chris, leave those chickens alone and come here!" she called.

As Chris approached us, I saw Milly's facial expression change from joy to worry. She saw that I was holding the beautiful artificial red roses we had bought in New York, and she knew exactly where we were going. She was nervous and I tried to be strong for all of us.

As we started walking along the narrow grassy path that led to Angel's resting place, Chris and his cousin, Neph, followed us. The two hundred yards separating my kids from their mom seemed very short, yet it was an extremely long walk on that short distance. We emerged from higher weeds and I saw the peace tree we had planted on Angel's grave five years earlier. It had grown bigger, greener, and taller. I held Chris's hand, and Milly had Neph's hand as we all walked together silently. I wanted to joke a little bit, but couldn't.

"Here we are, guys... here is Mommy," I declared as we arrived at the site, fighting hard to hide my trembling voice and the tears about to gush from my eyes.

As Milly approached the grave, I lagged a little behind and

discreetly wiped my eyes. She was very emotional but did not make it obvious. She silently scanned the area. Chris looked puzzled and confirmed his confusion with a question.

"Where is she, Daddy?" he asked.

"In there, boy," I replied, not sure if I understood his question.

After looking bemused for a few more seconds, he added, "But Daddy, you told me Mommy was in Heaven... Heaven is up there, and not in *here*!"

For as long as he could possibly understand, he knew that his mom was deceased, although I didn't think he ever understood what it meant. After taking a few steps forward, he continued, "So when people die they go underground?"

"Yes, they do."

"So, then how do they rise up? There is no hole here. That means Mommy is still in here."

"That's true, Chris. Her spirit or soul goes up there to protect us, and her body stays down here to rest and to be closer to us."

He tenderly leaned on me, and I understood that I made a point. As I looked over at his sister, I realized that while I was talking to Chris, she was silently crying. Her lips were extremely dry and tears ran down her cheeks. Seeing this sank me, and I stepped over to hug her.

"It's okay, girl… It's okay." I comforted.

I felt her tiny body trembling in my arms. As I gently rubbed her back, I asked myself, "*Why her? Why Chris? Why at all?*" If my daughter's prayer had been heard five years before, she would most probably not be there tearing up. However, as much as I wanted to think that her prayer was never heard, I also believed it was answered in a lot of ways. Otherwise, Chris and I wouldn't possibly be healthy.

After a few minutes, we mutually let go of one another, without a word.

"Hey guys, let's remove the weeds around here. Let's clean it up," I recommended.

As little Neph held the roses, we meticulously cleaned the grave and the immediate surroundings. We then planted the flowers in between the branches of the peace tree, as I quietly said a few words:

"Hi Angel, I am here with Chris and Milly. They are grown now and are doing fine. They are what you wanted them to be, and more. Be very proud of them... We love you."

I could not imagine what the kids were thinking, but the few words they said as we left Angel summarized everything for me:

"We love you, Mom... We will be back tomorrow."

As we walked back to my mom's hut, I felt very bad. That should not have been the way Chris learned about death. Not that of the

Milly and Chris, after meeting their mom

woman who would have loved and nurtured him more than anyone in the world. Not that of the woman who carried him in her womb for seven months and who was getting ready to care for him for all of her life before it was taken away. Not that of his mother!

Chris spent the whole day chasing his chickens around and Milly continued to struggle with the French and Bamiléké languages.

After another good night of sleep, we decided to go to the grave again as promised. It was much easier this time around and we rushed to get there. But upon approaching, we realized Angel's roses were missing.

"Where are the flowers, Daddy?" Chris asked.

"Boy, Mommy came and got them in the night," I replied.

"Really?" he questioned, very excited. "Do you think she liked them?"

"Yes, she did, and she is very proud of the two of you."

My little boy seemed very happy and proud of himself. His mom had received his gift. As we talked, Milly and I exchanged glances. We knew Angel's roses were stolen and were most probably on the way to the local market for sale.

Over the next few weeks, the kids learned new survival skills and embraced some African culture. Chris inadvertently witnessed the slaughtering of his pet chicken, despite my strong recommendation to ensure the secrecy of the act. As a consequence, he cried for days and I was afraid he would never let go.

With all the exciting experiences, time passed very fast. Chris and Milly reunited with their mom as well as my culture. But they just couldn't wait to get back to the United States. They were already telling me how much they loved and missed our old car, my 1994 Mitsubishi Galant, which was named "The Joesmobile" by teasing friends. The unpleasant squeaky noise at start-up and the early-morning thick smoke would no longer be embarrassing. They had seen worse. Their wish came true on August 5. Our vacation had been a success and we were on our way back.

After about twenty excruciating hours, we landed at JFK International Airport. As the gigantic airplane's wheels touched the runway, Chris screamed, "New York, at last!"

The passengers laughed out loud, turning around to see *this* child. It was a sign of relief. He had lived through a lot over the previous four weeks. He had also made a unique connection with his mom. After experiencing misery firsthand, Milly understood and stopped questioning me each time I sent some money over to my relatives. I was their hope, their provider.

Chapter 23

Me, My Daughter, and Her

Before leaving Cameroon, I had remembered a beautiful little girl I knew growing up named Yva, and whom I used to tease about being my wife. I had not seen her for about eighteen years and felt a strange yearning to reconnect with her. I had obtained her contact information only after my return. Since then, we had been communicating regularly. Thus, we had already replaced the faded images of our younger selves with much more representative and current pictures.

Only four months passed and I had to go back to Cameroon for an urgent family matter that required my presence. As I landed at Douala International Airport, Yva was waiting for me. I was a little nervous, not sure whether or not beauty in photographs would be beauty in reality.

After clearing customs, I saw Yva, dressed in a colorful African skirt and shirt. The pictures had not lied. She was beautiful.

"Hi, Yva," I said, advancing toward her.

"Welcome back... How was the trip?"

"Wonderful... You are really beautiful."

"Thank you," she said. "You haven't changed much either."

"Well, are you ready to go? And where are you taking me?

"I have made a reservation in a nice little hotel in the Bonanjo quarter for you," she replied, helping me carry my luggage.

As she talked, I was not able to take my eyes off her. She was upbeat, not shy, and funny. It was obvious that I had feelings for her, and I knew then that love was knocking at my door, seeded in me by months of long-distance communication. The few days spent with her allowed me to let my guard down and demolished the walls raised around me by years of fear and lack of trust.

After taking care of the family matter that had brought me back to Cameroon in the first place, Yva and I took our relationship to a higher level, and she became the woman in my life.

After returning to New York and talking to Milly about her, I discovered that my daughter could not stand my relationship with Yva, even though they had never met. I did not understand why Milly disliked her so much. One was in America and the other far away in the depths of Africa. So, although I was very happy with Yva, Milly was very sad and spent weeks without saying a single word to me. It was perplexing to see Milly's natural kindness slip away. As much as I couldn't stand seeing her in tears, locked up in her room for endless hours, I was not ready to give up another big bite at life. But how could I let the little girl I loved so much continue to hurt that much? Allowing myself to hurt some more in my loneliness, giving up my personal life, were the only ways to heal her. We had gone through thick and thin together and she surely knew I would never let her down for anybody.

In retrospect, I had been where she was. Thus, I understood her. Milly had not let go of her mom yet, and probably never would. She most probably still had vivid memories of her mom, her best friend.

For over six years, she and her brother were my world, and she was desperately fighting to keep it that way. She thought I would love her less once a woman stepped in. She certainly had never imagined that with all the love I had for her mom, I would ever devote any attention to any other woman. So my daughter—just like a lot of other young women—was jealous and broken-hearted over her dad getting romantically involved with a woman other than her mom. She was losing her sense of normalcy. Things would never be

Milly glitters, showered by her mom's attention, care and love then, now a constantly teasing reminder of what would never be again

the same, indeed, but only for better—I hoped. I wanted to restore her cocoon. She had a void that needed to be filled. I knew it, and she did not. It was my responsibility and duty to make her aware of her true needs. Success was not guaranteed, but I had to try.

Just like me, my daughter was resilient. On many occasions, she told me Yva was not the one for me, not knowing that she was talking to a man already in love. In Milly's eyes, something was wrong with *"that woman"*. One day, after a passionate phone discussion with Yva while I was driving Milly to her school, the Anne M. Dorner Middle School in Ossining, NY, she reached out once more in an attempt to open my eyes and regain my heart.

"Daddy, she is strange. You guys argue a lot… Not normal!"

"Girl, when you are a couple, you don't always agree on everything; we are a couple, and this is one of those times for us. Don't worry, everything will be fine," I reassured.

"Okay… Just be careful about where you are heading," she said, before retreating into her capsule.

I knew my daughter was blessed with the same kind of natural gift I had, being able to see and sense what most couldn't. But I thought she was totally wrong this time. I knew exactly where I was going. I was about to write a new chapter in my life with a great woman, whom, by the way, Chris loved very much. Some extra love in the house would heal us all, starting with Milly, who would certainly blossom again.

Despite constantly *fighting* with my daughter, I decided to take a giant step forward. I traveled to Cameroon, where I officially introduced myself to Yva's family, and she to mine. Being with her gave me the needed reassurance that I was not making a mistake, and that Milly was wrong. All the pieces of my life seemed to have fallen in place. I touched love again, enjoyed companionship again, and felt complete again. We had not planned our wedding yet, but were sure it would not be very long before we tied the knot.

My visit ended and time to leave Cameroon arrived. Upon entering the restricted zone of the Douala International Airport, eight high-ranking members of the Cameroonian National Security Police appeared and surrounded me. Astonished, confused, and scared to death, I had no idea what the problem—my problem—was. I believed it was a huge mistake, and expected an apology from airport officials.

"Good evening, officers," I said, unmoved outwardly but mortified internally.

"Mr. Fotso… We have your papers here, and you shouldn't be on Cameroonian territory," one of them said.

"What do you mean?"

"Well… You are a political refugee, Mr. Fotso; and as such, you should not be here. You are arrested, sir."

"No! Look again, officers... That is a US Travel Document, not a Refugee Document," I pleaded.

"You are a political refugee, Mr. Fotso."

The officers moved a little closer each time I talked, as if they did not want me to escape. At that instant, I started thinking about my two kids back in New York, trying to imagine what they would become without me. I knew that once they had me incarcerated in the infamous *Nkondengui* Prison, I would never have a chance of being freed. It would be a one-way trip for me, a one-way trip to Hell—definitely. No good story had ever escaped from those feared premises.

"Sir, please look again. I am not a refugee," I implored.

I was either a refugee or a total stranger in Cameroon. In reality, I was none, but I quickly grasped that from now on, I was both. How could I accept being a stranger in my own country? Something was extremely wrong. For a few seconds, I thought about what might have brought this on me. In my fearful state of mind, I could only guess. I recalled the night in 1990 when I witnessed the gruesome rape of a pregnant college student by diabolic soldiers working for the Cameroonian government and its tyrannical president. But my gut instinct told me, "No, that's not it!" Then I thought of a satirical book I had written—*Soupirs et Soucis d'Afrique (Worries and Sighs of Africa)*—which was accepted for publication in 1997 by Les Editions La Bruyère in Paris. In it, I castigated the Machiavellian actions of African leaders, including President Biya—without ever naming him—and his corrupt government; that would be an excellent reason for me to get in deep trouble on Cameroonian territory. Though I had decided not to publish *Worries and Sighs of Africa* for safety reasons, I thought its contents might have leaked and the Cameroonian government became aware of it. This time, my gut instinct told me, "That might be it!"

"Wait here, Mr. Fotso," one of them, apparently the boss, said, taking six others with him.

With only one left, I had the chance to look around and see the crowd staring at me, certainly waiting to see me handcuffed and taken to jail. The policeman left to guard me seemed friendly, as he proceeded to talk to me:

"Mr. Fotso, I want to help you," he said.

"Please, do. I want out of here, back with my kids."

"If you have about one hundred dollars, pass them to me...."

After an attempt to lecture him on moral values, I gave up.

"Officer, I am not sure I have what you are asking for, but we can certainly work things out."

He then looked at me as if to tell me he did not eat words, a language I knew well from the years before my life in America. I was cornered. He took me to a secluded part of that floor where I emptied my pockets into his, and some of my important belongings from my carry-on luggage into a small adjacent office. He had no time to check what I gave him, as he was very nervous. Just the fact that I gave was probably enough.

After we emerged from the distant corner, he went away and came back only a few minutes later with all of my documents.

As I stepped in the plane, I was burning inside. I had almost lost my freedom and my children. Never again! I was ready to give up the country that had raised me, and let the one that I had embraced adopt me. I was ready for freedom, ready to be a son of the Land of the Free and the Home of the Brave. I had been waiting for some kind of switch, and there could be no better one than that incident. I filed for American citizenship shortly after my arrival.

Chapter 24

Not Again!

On the evening of January 13, 2007, I had been in my room for about an hour and half talking to Yva who, for some reason, seemed inconsolable.

"Yva, calm down," I repeated. "Can you tell me what's wrong?"

"I am just too lonely over here, and it's very hard on me," she finally replied.

"But we knew it was going to be some time before we could reunite. You are not alone... I am here with you."

"No, you are not. Where are you then? I can't see you."

"Please calm down, Yva. I love you, and I don't want to see you hurting that much."

"Then do something about it, Joe."

"What can I do?"

"Get me out of here. I just want to be with you."

"I know... but we both knew that we would have to wait... I need you to be strong."

She burst in a louder cry, which left me baffled. I was very confused and didn't know what to do, being thousands of miles away. Now with two very sad and angry women—Yva and Milly—on hand, I felt squeezed.

"Joe, there is something I want you to know."

"I am listening, Baby." I said, a little nervous.

Deep down, I was more apprehensive than I let it appear. My gut feelings were that she wanted to tell me she no longer wanted to be my wife. What else could it be?

"I want to ask you a question," she said.

"Okay, go ahead. I will tell you whatever you want to know," I replied.

"It is a 'What if' question… What if I told you that I have a sexual relationship with another man?"

"What?" I interjected, already furious, but maybe wrongfully so. "What do you mean?"

"I have been having sex with another man, Joe," she bluntly said.

"You are kidding, right?" I asked, in total denial, as she started crying loudly again.

"No… I am not," she whispered.

At that moment, I knew Yva had just hit me with the truth. A dark curtain of sadness instantly fell upon me. I felt as if a wall suddenly rose up between the woman I had learned to love and all the glitters her voice and her distant presence brought in my life. The room started to spin. My world was in shambles. I was enraged, but still lucid enough to want to make sense of it.

"Who is this man?"

"Joe, the problem is not even what I did, but who I did it with; and that's killing me."

"Who is it?"

"No, Joe… No…" she answered, still reluctant to fully disclose her secret. "I just want to kill myself. I cannot live with this."

"Don't say such a thing. It is not the end of the world. I want to support you, but I need to know the whole truth."

"Okay. I will tell you now: It's Igor Thomas."

"Who is Igor Thomas?"

"You don't remember him… Father Igor Thomas KUATE?"

"Oh… Wait a minute!" I exclaimed. "The priest?"

"…Yes."

"Oh, my God! How could you?" I shouted. "I told you my story, and warned you after you met him the day of his consecration. I asked you to stay away from him… Oh, my God. Not again!"

"It was never my intention to let it happen, Joe. I am sorry. If I could take it back, I would, in the blink of an eye. But I can't…"

"How could you do that to me?"

"I am sorry, Joe… very sorry. But I want you to know that I love you, and I have never loved any man as much. You have changed my life."

"I see… Obviously," I sarcastically said.

"I am relieved now that I have lifted this off my chest."

"Okay… How and when did all this happen? I want to understand."

"Do you remember the night of prayer we had at my sister's house for her son's healing before your trip here?" She asked.

"Yes, I do."

"I was the one who organized it… After the prayer, I went back home with the priest," she explained. "I went to bed with him with no intentions whatsoever, and as time went by he became very tense, constantly touching me. So I gave in. After that we just continued our relationship."

"But I called you several times that night, and you never told me the priest was home with you; you hid him, and now want me to believe your act was not premeditated? Give me a break! I am not dumb."

"I just cannot explain it. Please, forgive me, Joe."

Lightning had struck once again. I was challenged once more. I had forgiven Angel for cheating on me with Father Ernest, the other priest. I did it in the name of true love. I forgave because we were already united for better or for worse. I had to, also, for my daughter's sake. This time around, with Yva, I was not going to get there. It was too much for me to handle. I didn't think I had the strength to forgive and forget.

"Joe, this might be the last time I talk to you," Yva resurfaced.

"What do you mean?"

"The best thing for me is to die," she calmly said. "If I were dead, I would be in peace right now. I would not have you or anybody questioning or judging me."

"It's normal that I question you. If I don't now, when would I ever do so? As much as I don't want you to take your life over this, I have the right to know and I want to know."

"Listen: now you stop it! It is hard enough that I did it. But don't question my morals. Yes, I *fxxxed* the priest, and I enjoyed it! Now what? You wanted to know and now you got it. I can even give you a lot more graphic details. Are you happy?"

"Unbelievable!" I exclaimed, shocked by this new facet of her. "I should just hang up and turn the page right now... But I know you need some support, and I am here to offer just that before any decision."

"Joe, please forgive me... I did not mean to hurt you."

"Give me a break!"

"I mean it, Joe... I am ready to die. That is the only way I can have some peace."

The tone of her voice revealed desperation and lassitude, and I sensed that she had already given up on life. I believed she was, indeed, ready to *die* to have some peace in her *life*.

All of my senses instantly turned to my crushed heart in an attempt to know the verdict, as one was needed sooner rather than later. I heard a loud voice calling upon my being. Some would say it was God's voice, others, my conscience. For me, it was just indefinable. It was a pressing voice asking me to do what I humanely couldn't. It was not love calling. How could it be so deaf and blind? It was definitely not Milly's voice, because I knew what words she would be rubbing in my face: *"Didn't I tell you, Daddy? You have to listen to your own daughter."*

After a long moment, it came to me from deep inside that it was a call I had to answer, a call urging me to spare a life. It was a call to my heart and soul from Humanity. I believed Yva had to be a very strong and sincere woman to disclose something as secretive as her sexual relationship with Father Igor Thomas. She had no reason to tell me, but she did, and I commended her for it. She could have taken it to her grave.

"Yva, I am not going to let you take your life," I surprised myself saying. "It's on me to help you. I will not let you down, okay?"

"Thank you, Baby. I love you so much, Joe... Again, I am sorry."

"But I need one thing from you... Can you give me that priest's' phone number? I *need* to talk to him." I said, insistent.

"Does that mean you have not forgiven?"

"Can I have his number?"

"Okay... I don't have it, but you can get it in my Yahoo inbox... Log in and get it from one of the mails he sent me; but please do not read them."

I rushed on my laptop, logged into her account, and performed a name search, with her still on the phone.

"Are you in?" she asked.

"Yes, I am."

"Did you find it? ... Joe, you are not talking; that means you are reading those emails."

What I read was horrifying.

> *My Dear Yva,*
> *I am pleased to have a beautiful woman like you as best friend and confident. Making love to you is always wonderful. I never felt that good before. I also appreciate you introducing me to your boss, colleagues and family. Here is my phone number: (...). Please, do not share it with anybody...*
> *Igor Thomas*

> *Father,*
> *As much as I enjoyed the moment and look forward to the future, I want to warn you: our relationship must be very secret. Our lives would be destroyed if it were uncovered. I know God has His hand on us, and I pray every day in His name to preserve our relationship for as long as possible. May God bless us.*
> *Yva*

"Joe, delete those emails!" I heard again.

"Okay... I am deleting them. What are you hiding, insisting so much that I destroy everything?"

"Nothing; you have been hurt enough. That's all... You have the number?"

"Yes... Give me a few minutes. I am calling him right now."

My hands were trembling as I dialed the priest's number. Connection difficulties between the United States and Cameroon added frustration to my growing fury. After persisting for about fifteen minutes, I finally heard a ring and soon enough, my call was picked up.

"Father Igor Thomas Kuate?" I asked, as politely as I could under the horrible circumstances.

"Yes, this is he," he replied in a very calm voice, almost whispering.

"Well... This is Joe, Yva's fiancé."

"Ooh, Joe!" he exclaimed. "I am very pleased to hear from you. How are you?"

"*You* should know how I am doing!"

"Why are you talking to me like that? You don't even know me."

"I don't have to know you, do I?" I lashed out, out of control.

He was fortunate not to be standing in front of me at that moment. He was fortunate to be thousands of miles away, hiding behind his long white robe. I could not predict what would have happened. Certainly a clash, whose magnitude I could not tell.

"What is the problem? What did I do?" he continued to ask.

Hypocrite! I thought, as he formulated his questions.

"You do not know what you did, *Father*?" I sarcastically asked. "Well, let me tell you: you have destroyed a family by having sex with my fiancée. How could you?"

At that point, I was yelling and everybody probably heard me in my apartment building. Father Igor Thomas stopped interjecting. He certainly realized his secret was out.

"How could you?" I repeated. "What about God in all this? The God you preach every day!"

"You have to listen to my side of the story, too," he finally said.

"What side of the story? That you were raped by my fiancée?"

"No, I am not denying the fact, but I just want to say…"

"Shut up! You absolutely have nothing to say. Listen to me now; I will not repeat myself, and don't even think about hanging up on me, okay?"

"Okay, sir," he replied, in a trembling voice.

"I want you to stay away from us. Don't you ever dare get in touch with Yva or any other members of her family! Do you understand that?"

"Yes, sir."

"Now listen! From now till the end your days on earth, I want you to remember this: You are a demon; you are Evil itself, and you will burn in Hell… What do you preach every Sunday? The least I can say is that you are a visual rapist, who violates all girls and women that have given you their trust in the name of God. You are a shame for Humanity."

"Sir…" he tried to verbalize.

I hung up, disgusted and on the verge of throwing up. I was torn apart. Though my reason—which I began to picture as a miniaturized Milly—urged me to get out of that messy relationship, another voice was still there, tenaciously calling, louder and louder. It became very difficult to listen to. I was certain that the relationship between my fiancée and the priest was well thought about. Taking a moment to think about it, I believed I needed some earplugs to block that unreasonable voice. Even though I had none, I pretended I did for the time being.

After two more hours spent secluded in my room, I was finally sane enough to get out and check on my children. Milly looked at me as if she knew what had just happened.

"Gosh, Daddy… Are you okay?" she worried.

"Yes, I am," I answered, trying to appear as normal as possible.

"You look very tense. I hope everything is fine."

"Don't worry; I just need to clear my mind."

"Is it *that woman*?" she persisted.

"Ooh, no!" I lied bluntly to protect my pride.

"Okay then, relax, Maaaan… The way you look is frightening."

"Really? Sorry, girl… It's been a very long day. But don't worry, I am okay."

She returned to her room, leaving me some space to *relax*. Could I?

Chapter 25

The Eyes I Recalled

A few months went by and Yva reached out to me in many ways, touching my hurt and healing heart. Although we talked every now and then, resuming a more normal relationship was very difficult for me because trust had vanished—once again—leaving behind the crumbs of a friendship struggling to stick together.

However, little by little, we picked up the shattered pieces of our togetherness and a narrow path was slowly building again, bringing Yva closer each day. I was certain that her revelation was the worst thing that could ever happen to me with her. From there on, things could only get better. I hoped I was not wrong, and I prayed not to be making a monumental mistake by ignoring what could have been a wake-up call. I picked up the phone one morning knowing exactly what I was going to tell Yva, certainly what she had been expecting to hear from me.

"Yva, how are you?"

"Hanging in there... What about you?"

"Not too bad," I replied, keeping my focus on why I had called her. "You know, I have thought a lot about us."

"Really? Just like me, all the time."

"Yes, I have... But I need you to assure me that what happened recently would never happen again with any other man."

"Joe, I told you I made a mistake, and I truly regret it each minute of my life. Please take my word for it. That would never happen again... I swear."

"Okay, I understand and forgive you. Let's focus on building a strong foundation to a great life ahead."

"Thank you, Baby. You have been alone for too long, and I want to be there with you and for you. I want to make you happy."

"Wonderful… I will talk you tomorrow. I need to go now. Have a nice day."

"You too, I love you."

"Me too," I struggled to say.

After a few months of waiting in line for my citizenship application to go through, the day finally came, the day I officially became a free man. On September 19, 2007, I became an American citizen. I could never even begin to put a value on that day. Life took a new, wonderful turn.

Just became a US Citizen, on September 19, 2007

I took the sad events with Yva as a challenge to our love, a challenge I had to surmount. I believed in redemption, in second chances in life. My forgiveness provided Yva with hers. As I flew to Cameroon on December 5, 2007 to marry her, there was no more doubt in my mind. I had answered the *call* from the tenacious voice within me, and on December 15, we would tie the knot. I had for-given, and I was sure Lady Humanity would be sitting in the front row of the chapel, applauding me and cheering us.

December 15, 2007 came and went with all the trouble I believed was inherent to all wedding ceremonies. Yva and I officially became a couple—Mr. and Mrs. Fotso.

With Yva, Mrs. Fotso, on Honeymoon

After a three-day honeymoon in the coastal city of Kribi, we toured various other cities to personally express our gratitude to all those who participated or contributed to the success of our big event. After Yaoundé in the Center Region, as well as Bandjoun and Bafoussam in the West, we were in a bus back to Douala, the main coastal city of the country.

Looking a little back however, I had experienced more than just a few things right before, during, and after our wedding, which made me wonder if Milly had not been right after all. Though stress certainly was a contributing factor, certain facts still did not add up. One incident occurred during the traditional marriage, when I was supposed to bring ceremonial dowry—goat, palm oil, liquor, and money—to Yva's family. After I gave her dad an envelope containing about $100, she came out of the room where she was being kept, unveiling her face—thus disrespecting the Bamiléké culture—and shouted, "Joe, you and your family are a disgrace. How can you be so broke? You are covering me with shame! I can't believe you gave only 50,000 francs to my dad? It's an insult!"

As she spoke, she became the absolute center of attention. The audience kept quiet and listened to every word she yelled, at the same time looking at me—the envied or admired man from America—and expecting some kind of reaction. I was shocked by her insults and disrespect toward my family and me right before the day I would say "I do," right before the day I would commit to live and die by her side, and to always stand by her. I realized she was emotionally and physically uncontrollable. Only days before our wedding, it came to me that I might not have known my soon-to-be partner for life well or at all.

I was in an unthinkable situation, and only guessed what most people would say or think: "Why don't you dump her right there?" Or "If I were you, I would never have gotten this far with her in the first place." Or "The warning signs were all over the place, and you should have listened to your own daughter."

The love I had for her put a rosy spin on the dilemma I had over calling it off. I believed true love had the power to lift mountains, and I knew I would be able to provide Yva with the support she needed to be a better person. That was my commitment to her and my promise to myself.

Still on our gratitude tour, we would not arrive in Douala until about 9 p.m. on December 20. My college friend, Piné, had invited us for a reunion after more than a decade without hearing from one another. It was about 8 p.m., and we were already two hours late. I felt bad for having Piné's family wait for that long, and most certainly for the hour ahead.

The bus crossed the bridge on the Wouri River, the horrible roads not helping us, as going in and out of potholes was extremely time-consuming. In Douala, we would first go to our hotel room and take quick showers before honoring the rendezvous.

As we stepped down from the bus, Yva decided to swing by her parents' house to get some traditional potion for the stomachache she had been complaining about for the past thirty minutes.

"Please, be quick." I said. "If you take too long, I will go leave. When you get back, you can come over at Piné's when you feel better, or just lie down and take a break. In that case, I will make sure I don't overstay."

"No problem," she replied.

Reuniting with Piné and remembering the past felt great, though it would have been better with Yva's presence. Luckily, she called and was on her way. We eagerly waited for her to get there for the party to really kick off.

Yva arrived in the neighborhood and we went to the main road to get her. We would all be together, like we should have been in the first place. We knew she was waiting in a cab, but didn't seem to spot her easily in the midst of the traffic jam. I followed a flashing headlight signal from a parked yellow cab and saw my wife on the backseat.

"Hey, honey, here... let's go." I said, after opening the cab's door.

She looked at me with the same eyes I had seen in my early childhood—my *mom's*—and lashed out: "Joseph, get in this car now! I order you to get in here right now!"

"What's the matter, Yva?"

"What are you doing here? Get in here, and let's go!"

At that moment, I realized how serious the situation was. Piné also grasped there was trouble in my paradise, came closer, and tried to calm her down.

"Madam, we are very pleased to have you here; my family has been preparing for your visit…"

"You better shut up and get out of here! I am talking to my husband. Who are you?"

She was furious and I could almost see blood bursting out her enraged eyeballs. Some capillaries were protuberant on her neck as she gesticulated vehemently. It came to me at that moment that I had never known her. I just thought I did. It also came to me that I was wrong and Milly was right—all along. I should have listened to my own daughter. I knew that if I stepped in that cab, I would be putting my whole body and soul in my lunatic wife's hands. I was in deep trouble, and I needed out.

"Piné, let's go," I turned around and said, extremely tormented.

As we began distancing ourselves from the spot where a few people had started to gather, the cab proceeded to follow us. We did not rush. She was very welcome to come. She would just be ignored. She was definitely a mistake for me. I should never have gotten that far with her in the first place, because the warning signs were all over the place. They were written in bold font in her characteristic short temper, erratic moods, lack of respect, and materialistic nature. I had hoped to help her later by seeking some counseling for her, so I ignored all the signs, and was already suffering the horrific consequences of my decisions.

After a few minutes, we lost the cab and continued our short walk home alone, without Yva behind us. Sitting at the dining table, we started eating, as we no longer expected her. Just as we were all coping to regain our composure, the gate's bell rang, and Piné went out to see who it was.

"It is me," he heard.

He unlocked the gate, and my wife knocked him down, storming in.

"Where is he?" she roared.

"Please, calm down," Piné's wife, Marlyse, implored.

After insulting every single person present, she turned to me, grabbed my fork and knife, and pitched them in the far left corner of the living room. Then, surprising everyone, after shattering my wine glass on a wall, she grabbed me by my shirt and started pulling me. I was furious and just about to lose it, feeling the urge to grab the hand gripping my clothes and break it in a swift movement.

As I stood in front of her, held by her disrespectfully, I saw rage in her eyes. I did not see love, but hatred. What in the world had I done to that woman? She pulled me outside and, in the process, ripped my shirt, and bit Piné as he attempted to peel her off me.

"Stop it now!" I ordered.

"You are my husband, and you are coming with me!"

"Forget about that husband stuff, okay? You must be dreaming," I said.

"You haven't seen anything yet."

"Ooh... Let me tell you right now, it is over, and you can take this with you."

I took my rings off my fingers and threw them at her. From then on, I was a single man again, only five days after my wedding. That piece of paper was as meaningless and worthless as my horse bone. I had forgiven her for disrespecting my family. I had forgiven her infidelity with the priest. I had carried her through a number of deal-breakers. But there was absolutely no way I was going to let physical violence in. My kids would be traumatized for life. My wife was probably schizophrenic, and I was lucky to find it out in time enough to prevent further damage.

After I returned to the US, Milly expectedly repeated everything I knew she would say after I informed her of the disaster. She was ecstatic and relieved—understandably.

However, understanding that Yva was a human in need of professional help and treatment, I lent a hand through her brother Salvador and her sisters. It killed me to see her consumed by incontrollable impulses. Treatment was available, and she could get some if she wanted. But apparently, she did not want to be called "crazy," and never made the first step. I let it be. I tried to help, but could not. I wanted to help her be a better person for herself and someone else—just not me.

I filed for divorce in the Westchester Supreme Court, which was granted on July 11, 2008, deciding not to *look* again. Being a bachelor for the rest of my life seemed to be my only option.

Chapter 26

The Lie

(2008)

Having reached a point where I could not tell half-stories any longer, I believed it was time for me come clean. I had not always been honest. In fact, I had lied repeatedly, each time I was asked about the cause of Angel's death. With each falsehood, I covered myself with shame. I would go home and spend sleepless nights, because I knew I had violated the trust people had in me.

Even before taking her back to Cameroon, I had chosen not to disclose the true cause of her death. I made up something to answer questions from curious or empathetic people. Then when I found myself surrounded by hundreds of people at her funeral, wanting to know what had happened, I told everyone Angel had passed from a cancer that spread to her vital organs, ending her life. The truth was my guarded secret, never to be revealed. AIDS was a stigmatizing disease—wrongfully so, and I did not want my family running the risk of being shunned by almost everybody. I did not want anybody to *isolate* Angel even if she was no more.

While I still believed I made the right decision then, I lost an ounce of my essence and my dignity each time I looked someone in the eye and said, *"Angel died from cancer."* I had thought nothing was on the line, that no one had anything to lose. But over the years, I learned the hard way that something important slowly vanished by my lie—trust in me, and my pride. On the other hand, had it turned out that Chris and I were sero-positive at best, I would have let the truth out much earlier. But because we were miraculously saved and free of the disease, I acted as though disclosing the truth did not matter at all.

One day, I would look all the people I had lied to through the years in the eye and express how sorry I am. I would apologize to those friends who had helped care for my kids all that time. They had showered my daughter and my son with what was missing in their lives—motherly love. They totally deserved to know the truth, the whole truth. Instead, I told them all *but* the truth. I really did not mean to be deceptive. I just meant to be protective. I wished they could understand and forgive me. *I am sorry.*

Most importantly, I realized I had an opportunity to open some minds. I had probably indirectly contributed to the widespread misconceptions of this devastating illness. I knew better. I owed the truth to the support and respect of the sick women, men, and children around the planet. I owed it to the AIDS prevention cause. My silence was a kind of failure to assist or lend a hand to human-kind in this endangered world. I hoped my truth would contribute to a wake-up call to some who needed to straighten certain aspects of their personal lives.

After many years of lies, I decided to start by having a straight talk with my fourteen-year-old daughter. She always insisted on knowing my income, and I always planned on telling her *every-thing* she didn't know only after her graduation from middle school. She successfully completed her academic year and was very excited about being a freshman at Ossining High School. I chose that time to open up to her.

One evening in September, I asked Milly to join me in my room. "Hey, girl, would you please come here? It's time to talk."

She came in and sat on my bed, staring at me as if to say, *"Just tell me how much!"* Even though I had prepared her to expect a lot more than only a discussion about my income, she had no idea of the magnitude of the conversation.

"I want you to know that there is a lot more to me, to us, than just how much money I make," I said, as the look on her face betrayed her nervousness. "But I promised, and I am going to tell you that now, before everything else."

"Ooh, Daddy... I don't really want to know anything else," she said, looking scared.

I was determined not to let her playful curiosity affect my motivation. That day, I considered her a grown woman, and she needed to be treated as such.

"Here, girl. This is what I make bi-weekly. With this calculator, you can easily find out what I make per year."

Her face brightened as she started doing the math. With the display of the result on the tiny screen, she exclaimed, "Daddy... Wow!"

"I am sharing that with you because I want you to make a lot more than that. Always aim higher, and keep up the good work in school, okay?"

"Okay, Daddy."

"Now, you also have to understand that since Mommy passed away in 2001, I have incurred a lot of debt. That's why the majority of my salary goes toward paying bills. I hope you understand now why I can't afford a lot of things for us. For instance, you don't seem to understand why I still drive the "Joesmobile" I bought ten years ago."

Milly listened earnestly, but still had no idea of what was to come.

"Let me ask you a question now: can you tell me what Mommy died from?"

"What kind of question is that?" she exclaimed, perplexed. "She died from cancer."

Hearing those words washed me with deep shame once more. For seven long years, I had lied to my own daughter.

"Girl, I don't want you to live a lie anymore... Mommy did not die from cancer."

She now looked at me as if her heart had stopped beating. She was motionless on the bed, and I guessed that a million ideas were crossing her mind.

"What?" she asked.

I opened the black briefcase where I kept my important documents and grabbed a protected piece of paper. Milly decided to lie down, as if her body muscles gave up on her all at once. Only her puzzled eyes followed my movements. As bad as I felt for her, I was determined to continue the important talk.

"Take this, girl. It is Mommy's death certificate. The cause of her death is on there."

"Where is it?"

"Here... Mommy died from AIDS." I let out for the first time.

"No!" she exclaimed.

I knew she was hurting very badly right then. I also knew she would be hurting a lot more in just a few minutes.

"I am sorry I lied to you all these years. I thought you were too young to understand. Also, it was my duty to protect you."

She started to sob. Profuse tears flew out of her eyes. I rearranged myself on the bed and hugged her. As I held her in my arms, I felt her trembling, and there was no doubt then that her heart was broken. For a moment, I thought about ending our straight-talk session. But it was not a good idea. If I stopped, I might never have found the strength to resume. I had to go on.

"There is more, girl."

"Oh, gosh! Noo."

"Please be strong, okay?... It is about how she caught the disease."

With those words, my daughter abruptly detached herself from me and sat back up on the bed. I knew she was guessing what I was about to tell her. I had never seen her cry so much. Nothing could stop her tears. She seemed to have a water fountain behind her red eyes. Even if I could have turned them off, I would not. Crying was important.

For about twenty minutes, I told her everything about the events that led to her mom's death, and she realized then just how much I had loved her mom.

The Lie

For many years, it had seemed vital for me to lie; but it became crucial now to tell the truth for everyone to hear, and I had started with my daughter.

Chapter 27

The Urge

The bride my mother had arranged for me—Gina—has not heard my shattering life story. She has no idea what made me who I am. What would she think if she knew everything? Would she still think I am a good man sent by God or would she think my heavy baggage is too much for her to lift, let alone carry for the rest of her life? Even if I decide to tell her everything, I cannot—I am out of time. The day has arrived, our wedding day. The early sunrise sends beams of bright light through the various holes in the east wall of my room. I must hurry and get ready, as I have to travel a bit to get to City Hall.

The minuscule front yard of the City Hall building is packed with people dressed in their best, very few of whom are here for me. Looking in the crowd, I spot a few family members and friends. Gina sees me and smiles, certainly ready to embrace her new life. She looks very different in her white skirt, blouse, and hat. The few steps she makes in my direction give me an additional opportunity to scrutinize her even more, in search of the one thing I will fall for. But with each step, my chance of finding it shrinks. I must suppress my feelings and emotions, and just follow the trail left behind by my ancestors.

Our turn has arrived. We are now sitting in separate chairs in the front row. As there is no chemistry between us, we exchange few words. I do not know how she feels, but she must be having the same doubts. Nonetheless, we will soon be spouses, united for life by the Mayor. We will soon tie the knot and from there on, I will no longer wrestle with the decision of whether or not to marry a teenage stranger, a young woman only about three years older than my own daughter.

Soon enough, the mayor announces, "We are gathered here today to unite Joseph and Gina... Please stand and come closer."

We each step forward and stand about five feet from him. After verifying that we have our rings, he continues, "Joseph, do you take Gina as your wife and do you swear to always love and support her, in sickness and in health?"

My throat is unusually dry as my nervousness spikes. "Yes, I do," I manage to say, fighting my urge to stop it right there, but sliding the ring onto her finger.

At this moment, I can't escape thinking about what Milly really has in her heart about all this. After I told her why I was heading to Africa, she never expressed any opinion. After the Yva experience, I guess she felt it was not worth challenging my decision. As for Chris, he was just happy to be able to have a sort-of mom in the house, and he never cared who it would be. Just a mom!

"Gina, do you take Joseph as your husband and do you swear to always love and support him, in sickness and in health?"

"Yes, I do," She answers, also sliding the ring onto my finger.

"Joseph and Gina, you are now husband and wife. You may kiss."

"*No, we may not!*" I immediately think, almost whispering as the audience applauds. To cover up, I spread my arms and give her a big hug while patting her on the back. This first "kiss" to my wife is not less and not more than a typical friendship hug.

Within the span of just a few minutes, I am a married man walking out of the ceremony room with a woman who was just a stranger to me not long ago, but is now my wife. I feel relieved, as it is one less thing in my life to worry about. I will now focus on making it work.

Immediately following the wedding, Gina and I strangely go

off in different directions. We will celebrate our union like almost no other newlyweds in the world—apart. She has returned to her parents'. On these special occasions, couples usually cannot wait to be alone and make love for the first time ever, or for the first time as husband and wife. I am numbed by the grip of my true existence—my adopted Western culture—and my strong morals, which would condemn the over forty-year-old man I am for being sexually intimate with the naïve eighteen-year-old I have just married. I won't. A successful life together would be, in itself, the ultimate celebration. I am just going to hang out with my friend Louis and a few family members.

Although I am excited to be with everyone I hold dear and still struggling to comprehend my marriage to Gina, I am also pondering a reunion with one person. In fact, I have been torn for years about the importance and the outcome of meeting Father Ernest, one of the Catholic priests that crumbled my world. I know that what *is done is done*, and meeting him could surely be a waste of time. However, a tiny voice deep inside has been prodding me—each time I consider forgiveness—to track Father Ernest down first and speak to him face to face.

After paying a visit to Angel's grave, I am burning inside; but it's not about her. She is resting in peace and has absolutely nothing to do with my uneasy feelings. That little voice is growing too loud to be ignored.

It's Sunday morning, and he is certainly preaching at this very moment, captivating more women as they listen to his guiding voice, the voice that enchanted my beloved wife. Just thinking about him is infuriating and I am becoming uncontrollable. If God had made me an *animal*, I am afraid I will prove Him right today. If He had made me an *angel*, I am most probably going to prove Him dead wrong. I am more than ready to treat that *man of God* with incivility.

But it isn't about revenge. It isn't just about receiving answers. I want to face that religious pervert and see if I can possibly find it in me to forgive him and let go. It's about my own understanding. Giving that tainted priest a chance at redemption will give me closure and peace.

I know about Father Ernest's transfer to the Saint-Paul Parish in Bafoussam, which is only a twenty-minute cab ride away. I must go. As the taxi drives me there, I cannot prevent my memory from wandering back to the excruciating words my wife had written to him so many years ago. Despite my efforts, I am unable to keep my imagination from envisioning that hideous preacher blaspheming his vow of celibacy to God, kissing my wife, and lifting his white gown to satisfy his carnal desires. I know I should contain myself, but an urge to crush him is taking over my reason. I am only human, and what's left of my humanity may not be enough to tame my rage.

Over the years, I have thought about and waited for the day I would finally get to meet that priest. I have stopped hearing the voice urging me to forgive. My angry side wants to send him straight to Hell. My insecure and jealous part keeps on questioning what he had to offer my wife that I could not, other than the institutionalized trust that he most certainly used and still uses to lure her and other women into his bed, undeterred by his laminated copy of the Ten Commandments probably hidden under his pillow, and a prominent statute of Jesus Christ above his headboard.

As I approach the century-old church, I hear hymns being enthusiastically sung. I am very nervous. It is the first time in years that I have set foot in a church. I could never find the strength or the courage to listen to any priest. My days were as dark as they could get with Angel's confession and her loss, and all preachers the same to me.

The singing has stopped. Other than a few sporadic coughs, nothing seems to be moving. I run up the few steps to the main wooden door, turn the knob, and pull the heavy frame as slowly as I can. I don't want to disrupt the peace of this moment. As cautious as I am, I am still noticed right away, and all heads turn. The chill I get from the unwarranted stares is numbing. Luckily, the priest starts preaching again, recapturing everyone's attention. I sit in the back row, and can't see him clearly in that big room; I am not even sure whether or not that man is who I am looking for, but I am hoping he is. The page is about to turn, for him and for me.

When Sunday mass ends, I sadly discover that the preacher is not the man I have been looking for. I thought I was close to confronting that Evil, but I am now back to square one! I don't have much time left in Africa, and I am afraid I will not be able to find the only man on my *Most Wanted List*.

Extremely disappointed, I ride to my sister Martine's home, which happens to be just two miles away. Fortunately, she knows where to find Father Ernest.

"He is at the Marie Reine des Apôtres Parish in Kamkop, Bafoussam," she says.

"Really? Is it far?"

"Not at all."

"Okay... Thanks a lot, Ma'a."

He is only a few miles away, but I know that the twenty minutes it will take to get there will be the longest twenty minutes of my life. Satisfying my urge has become the most important thing for me, and I won't rest until I stand in front of that priest, look him in the eye, and make my peace—in whatever form the moment will choose.

On this February 15, I wake up resolved to go to the Marie Reine Parish. It is a beautiful, blue-sky, sunny day. I'm going to meet the one man who cracked my love for my wife, and further shattered the sense of trust I had struggled to regain since my traumatic childhood.

I have asked my nephew—Dexter—to keep me company on my mission. He will also serve as photographer to immortalize the possible clash between his uncle and a man of God. But he has no idea why we are going through so much trouble, traveling along impractical roads, to get to the parish.

It's about 10 a.m. The Mass is over and the parishioners are outside. I am informed that *the* priest is in a meeting, which will last about an hour. Not a problem at all. I have waited eight long years to get here; I can certainly wait one little hour. To kill time, Dexter and I take pictures of the church and check the settings of the digital voice recorder I have brought because I want to be able to play the scene back and hear everything Ernest has to say. We wait under the increasingly hot sun, and no one knows what for.

After three and a half long hours, the meeting comes to an end, and I see a man dressed in a white gown walking down the hill. He notices me hurrying in his direction.

On February 15, 2009, after introducing myself to Father Ernest

"Good afternoon, Father Ernest." I say, interrupting his conversation with a parishioner.

"Yes," he answers, with an intrigued look on his face.

I know deep inside that he is asking, "*Who are you?*" So I don't waste any time before giving him an answer to his unspoken question.

"I am Mr. Fotso, late Chantal's husband."

"Chantal? Chantal… Chantal?" He tries to remember, even though I feel sure that he has.

"Yes, Chantal who passed away in 2001 in the United States," I sarcastically explain.

"Oh, yes… Chantal… yes… Chantal."

His body language abruptly changes as he speaks. He stops looking me in the eye and stares at the red, dusty ground.

"Yes, Chantal… I want to have a few minutes with you," I say, in a tone that indicates an order rather than a request.

"Sure; not a problem at all. Let's go down to the episcopal residence," he says.

We walk through the wooden fence to the front yard of the house. The priest is slightly in front of me, and I don't know what's

Following the priest to the Episcopal Residence

holding me back. I have noticed very young girls mopping his floor and doing his dishes, and I can't stop imagining what will or has already happened to them. At that young age, they have probably been sexually molested by their adored priest, or they most certainly will be soon. They are trapped.

The urge to tackle him and beat him up begins to overwhelm me. But I decide to try treating him with divine dignity even though he had treated my family with demoniac disrespect and inconsideration. I will try, and I wish to succeed.

Opening his office door, he invites me in. Surprisingly, I feel calm, although I am conscious that it might just be like the very last seconds before a thunderclap. I remember to turn my recorder on and sit down. He is avoiding my eyes; but I have some understandable interest in looking straight into his. That's why I'm here.

His metallic nameplate faces me, and every letter of it seems to echo very loud in the promiscuous room as I silently read: E-r-n-e-s-t M-b-u-b-i-a. The next few seconds are awkward. But it does not take long to break the uncomfortable silence.

"Like I told you, I am late Chantal's husband..." I calmly say.

I know his unstated question is, "*Why are you here?*" So without waiting to hear it, I tell him precisely why I'm seated in his office.

"I am here because I would like to understand certain things I heard... about the relationship that you had with my wife. I—"

He cuts me off. "A relationship?"

"Yes, a relationship. So I am here to listen to you and understand. I have tried to let go, but I have been tormented by that."

"Is that right?" he asks.

"Yes. I have to tell you that not only have I heard it from third parties, but also from Chantal's own mouth... She confessed to me before passing away."

"Her?"

"Yes. I also have to tell you that the day I left Cameroon in 1996, I inadvertently discovered a letter she had written to you, in which she was sexually explicit... She told me then that there was nothing to it. But three years later, she confessed, on her death bed..."

He is listening and I am reading shame in his eyes once again. Feeling bad for him is not an option; this is not the time for empathy.

"Help me turn the page," I continue. "I can't do so without having the opportunity to talk to you. I don't know if I could say that it is to pardon you, but it is at least to vent... So, that's why I am here."

A moment of loud silence follows. I wait for him to open his chapped lips and say something, anything. But he doesn't. He looks pale, and his forehead and the tip of his nose display a fine mist of cold sweat. I can only guess he doesn't know where to start. He is trembling, as indicated by the piece of paper he has purposelessly picked up. Finally, he gets out of his mutism and says, "Speaking of Chantal... She came to my church to invite me to bless her family home. After I went there and did that, she came back again for more prayers, to alleviate the problems the family was having. And that's it..."

"Nothing else?" I ask, enraged by this preacher's lies.

"No, wait..." he continues. "That is how I knew her... She was even going to go up north for her school exam... Then I went to Côte d'Ivoire, only after that did I come here."

What he is saying is totally irrelevant to what I have asked. He has uncomfortably talked about everything and substantially nothing. He is scraping for words and I am determined to listen.

"I knew her. She had even come to see me when her mom was sick, and we all prayed together... Later on, after a trip to Côte d'Ivoire, I learned about her death... So when I came back, I went to her grave with one of her sisters-in-law and I prayed."

With those last words, I instantly picture that priest over Angel's grave, with his rosary beads in his transgressed hands, reminiscing about the X-rated good times he had on top of my wife, at the expense of my family. I picture him whispering, "*Oh God! Oh God!*" as he fulfilled his demonic desire. I just can't help it! At this moment, I wish I could stand on his wooden desk and smack his sweaty face with his heavy nameplate. But this isn't the time, the place, or the purpose of my visit.

"So I do not understand what her motive was, saying things like that; but I praise you for taking this time to come here for answers," he continues.

"Let me tell you: I have never hoped that I would get here for you to tell me, "*Oh, by the way, I had a sexual relationship with your wife.*" I am not hoping for that… I came here because if I don't forgive, God will not. God will go through me to forgive… About the letter, it's true," I continue. "When I saw it, I called her sister Anne and when she got in the room, she never had a chance to read it."

As I tell him about the fate of the letter, he grows smaller and smaller. He is definitely a long way from being the same powerful man that was venerated by a swarm of men and women earlier that morning. He is subdued. He is only a human being now—just like me—but one with a rotten soul—unlike me. Nothing else.

"I have no reason, whatsoever, to lie." I proceed. "Chantal is at peace where she is, and it's not my intention to destroy anyone. I am a peaceful man, but this has been troubling me. How can I go church with my kids if priests can do this? I cannot trust any."

If I continue for too long, my animal instinct can instantly wake up and prompt my human side to seek revenge violently, to make him pay. I have started to give up. He will not confess.

"…I have no reason to put words into the mouth of a person that is no longer with us. I have no reason to build up lies. Like I told you, God's pardon will go through me… Well, I am done. That was the purpose of my visit. That's it… We are all humans, and we make mistakes. Human dignity would want us to recognize them. I am not forcing you to say things, but that's just what I think."

"I don't understand why she had said things like that. To what avail? Was it to hurt you?"

"No!" I vehemently reply. "The letter was never intended to hurt me. She was writing about all the good times you guys had had, saying how much she wanted to hear your voice every night at bedtime. In retrospect, you used to call a little too often. But I thought it was a true relationship between a priest and a believer. I understood everything with that letter. I took that woman back with me only because I loved her so much…"

"I understand your pain," he manages to say. "I understand

your reaction, and I thank you for taking this initiative."

"All that I have to say now is that I am going to leave the relationship you had with my wife between your God and you. And once again, I know God's pardon will go through me."

To his relief, I stand up, signaling to him that it's time for me to go. I will let his conscience—if he ever had one—judge him each time he goes to bed and each time he shamelessly stands in front of little boys and girls, women and men, to preach. I believe I have achieved my goal at this point.

I discretely turn my recorder off; but as I take the first step, I realize I am not done. Not just yet. I have more to say.

"Father Ernest, can you swear, with your hand on this bible, that you have never had a sexual relationship with my wife?" I bluntly ask.

That straight question visibly shakes him and, for a moment, he struggles to find an answer.

"*Father*," I sarcastically call him, "please be careful about what you are about to say. I think you are already in big trouble with God, and you don't need to make it any worse... Before you say anything, look at me... I want you to imagine this: you are now looking into God's eyes, and His ears are ready to engrave what you say onto the judgment book."

We are both standing by the door, looking into each other's eyes. His mind is obviously very preoccupied with the gravity of the question he is facing. He has lied to me. Should he lie to God, too?

"Can you swear now in the name of God that you never had sex with my wife?" I ask, ready to hear and accept his answer, and forgive him.

After an extremely long thirty-second wait, I understand what his shameful silence and his scorned eyes tell me, "*No, I absolutely cannot swear; because I had sex with your wife.*"

"I thought so, Father. You are exactly what I have been thinking, a sexual predator that just happens to have the right tools—a long white gown and the trust and respect of your followers." I conclude, with my hand on the door knob.

"By the way," I turn around and say, "Angel did not die of cancer. She died of AIDS. Are you the one who infected her or were you using condoms? Think about it, *Father*."

With my final words, I see panic on his sweaty face, and he deserves to panic.

As we get outside, I feel the need to immortalize that moment.

"I would like to take a picture with you here."

"No problem, Mr. Joseph."

We stand close for the pose, and I can feel him burning. He has become very small, and none of the little boys and girls that were waiting to meet him can ever imagine what we have just talked about.

"Remember what I said, okay?"

"Sure, Mr. Joseph."

Knowing I have given him a life sentence within the jail of his

With Father Ernest, after the face-to-face meeting

dirty conscience, I go down the few steps leading to the front yard and depart with my nephew. I have my closure. I can now go to bed

269

The Urge

and sleep; and I don't really care if Ernest doesn't. I gave him numerous chances to ask for and receive forgiveness, but he decided not to grab them. He did not appear repentant. Should he be forgiven? Should I forgive him? Even if I do, his soul will wander restlessly in and around the Celestial Fire— hopefully.

We exit the now-empty premises of the parish, and start our long walk toward the main road. Looking around, it's hard for me to believe that a few hours ago this place was full of believers. It now seems like a ghost town with only two *ghosts*—my nephew and me—and the crying soul of a despicable human being, the priest, Father Ernest.

The layer of dust on the street is probably an inch deep, very characteristic of the dry season. Despite all the caution I have taken not to get my outfit dirty, a fine coating of red particles has gradually covered my shoes and pants. As we round the corner mid-hill, I look back and notice a human being exiting the church grounds. It's one of the girls I saw earlier in the Episcopal residence doing the priest's chores, slowly walking uphill. I slow down to let her catch up with us. The closer she gets the more frequently I turn back, a little more inquisitive with each step. The main question in my mind is, "*What was she still doing at the residence when everyone else was gone?* Obviously there had to be a last one to leave, but why her?"

As she approaches clutching a tiny paperback Bible, she keeps her head down with no intention—it seems to me—to ever look up. Her tiny face is damp with sweat. She wears a knee-high gray skirt, a light pink top, and a white scarf on her head.

"Hello, young lady. How are you?" I intrude.

"Fine, sir. Thank you," she hesitantly answers.

"What's your name? Mine is Joe."

"My name is Nikasoh," she replies, shyly shaking the hand I have extended to her.

"You must be very tired from all the work at the Church," I purposely say, walking alongside her. "Why were you still there, being the last one to leave?" I continue, without even knowing whether or not she really is the last one.

"Father Ernest had asked me to stay and wait for him," she innocently declares.

Her statement raises all of my red flags instantly, and I know I am about to step where Father Ernest would never want me.

"Do you know why?" I ask. "By the way, don't be afraid, okay? I am a friend." I try to reassure but to deceive at the same time, hoping she opens up to me.

"I stay sometimes to pray with him."

"Just with him?

"Yes."

"*Oh, no!*" I yell inwardly. With her answer, I know I am close to possibly uncovering another dirty secret, one dirtier than the one Father Ernest, my wife, and God shared for years.

"Listen to me. I just had a meeting with him. So I know everything. I just want to confirm. Hold on to your Bible, and tell me the truth. When was the last time Father Ernest touched you?"

A heavy silence follows my question, and I start to think I might have gone too far, far enough to confuse that naive little girl who might be no more than twelve or thirteen years old, just as young as my own daughter.

"Last Saturday evening," she answers.

At those words, my heart drops.

"Where was that?"

"In his room… I don't want to, but I have to." Her straight answers lead me to believe she is probably reaching out for help.

"Wow! What a monster!"

"But he helps me too. I don't even know why I am telling you."

"Don't worry, Nikasoh. You are telling me because you are a wonderful girl with a bright future ahead."

I stop and watch powerlessly as she disappears in the labyrinth of the neighborhood. Nothing and nobody will ever be able to erase that girl's image from my memory. What can I do? How can I help? I have no answers to my burning, silent questions. I choke thinking of the incredible ordeal that little girl is suffering at the hands of her own priest. I came to that church in search of some answers from Father Ernest, about his sinful sexual relationship with my wife. However, it has become clear to me that my story was just one fraction of the dark truth behind Father Ernest's white robe. How many little girls has he raped and how many more will he continue to rape? How many more innocent lives will he shatter? Will he ever stop? I wish The Holy Spirit could instantly beam Its light on that priest and his devilish lifestyle for the world to know. It will only be a tiny portion of all the abuse cases the Vatican has heard of over the years from across continents, but it will be one more—sadly. Unfortunately, I have to go. I wish I could stay, but my time has quickly come to an end. I have to tame my rage and go.

After a rough, sleepless night, I have awakened still dazed by horrible images of a little girl being sexually molested by a trusted man of God. Although this vision has kidnapped my brain, there is another inner call battling for my attention. I am feeling the pressing need to meet my "mother"—Mama Marie. I have not seen her for over thirty years and have no idea of her life after divorcing Tino, my "father." But it should certainly take little effort to locate her in her tiny village.

From my tortured youth until now, I never even attempted to contain my rage over what she put me through as a child. Instead, I constantly fed my fury with my undying grudge. Each time I thought of her, of her steely eyes or her hard breathing, I had the impression of pain just as if I was living my childhood all over again. Thus for years, I felt tormented and kept my emotions boxed up inside me. I was never able to grow out of them. But over the past few years, I have been asking myself so many questions. What was she really thinking? What were the reasons behind her careless actions? Had she ever considered me her son? Had she ever imagined that I would eventually grow up and become *a man*? With all those questions, my feelings toward my "mom"—Mama Marie—began to soften, increasingly leading her into a place where I had always thought I would allow even "Evil" before her if at all, a remote place in my heart. It's true that she had failed to be what she should have been—loving or even just fair mother. My tears should have been the lantern showing her God's inviting hands. My sniffling should have been a wake-up call to the love and care, dormant right under her unrepentant skin. Above all, using my bare hands to clean up my fecal deposit should have been a summons to her disoriented conscience and essence, an order to stop asphyxiating my aspiration and right to a fair life. Nevertheless, I have gradually overcome my anger and fury, and I need to turn them into something positive.

Having gotten the name and address of someone who knows exactly where to find Mama Marie, I hire a mototaxi to take me there, around the Petroleum Reserves in Bafoussam. The closer I get to my destination the higher my emotions. Am I going to recognize her after all this time? Will she recognize me? Will I be able to look into her intimidating eyes? Will I still be terrified by her presence? What will I really feel?

As these questions fill my mind, the motocab stops. We have arrived at my informant's place.

"Here is the *Force de Dieu Temple*, where Mr. Jonas lives," the driver explains, pointing an imposing traditional building.

"Thank you." I say, after paying him.

As the cab drives away, ascending the dusty hill, I knock at Mr. Jonas' door. "Good morning, Mr. Jonas." I politely greet.

"Hello..." he answers.

"I am Tino's son, and I would like you to help me meet my mom," I surprisingly declare without any second thought.

"Marie?" he asks.

"Yes. I really would like to meet her today. My time is very limited."

"Marie... Let me tell you: I don't think it's possible. She is very unstable, by the nature of what she does for living."

"What does she do?" I ask, intrigued.

"She is a nomadic laborer, working on people's farms for money. She might be here today, and twenty kilometers away tomorrow."

"So, there is nothing we can do to find her?"

"No. With what she does, she comes to us. We cannot go to

her. In fact, you are just one day late. She was around yesterday, and might not be around until sometime next week. So, if you had a week on hand, I am sure you could possibly meet her."

"How is she now?

"She is very tired... very tired. But she has to work."

"Unfortunately for me, I have less than a week left. So, I won't be able to meet her... But if you see her, would you please tell her that her son, Fotso, came looking for her? Please tell her I will be back some day."

"I surely will."

As I reach the road, I am very sad and disappointed. I was hoping to see my "mom" again. I wanted to be able to hold her in my arms and feel her heart. I wanted to give her what she had never given me—a hug. I wanted to tell her, "*It's okay,*" because I knew that her cruelty was rooted in her pain. But I couldn't. Not this time. Even without having seen her in more than three decades, even after all she had done to me, I vow to get her out of the infernal life she is living. As a son, I don't want to fail. It has become my duty and my responsibility to watch over her. I will be back someday. I have forgiven.

Over the years, my reflections have brought me to believe that Mama Marie never really understood the power of a hug for a child, maybe because she didn't have one of her own. Additionally, through what I have learned from my education and my life in the United States, I realize she could be suffering from some undiagnosed mental illness that blinded her conscience and obscured her heart all those years. But most of all, even if she truly hated me with all of her sanity, I will not show her how wrong she was not to love me by not loving her back, by hating her and rejecting her like she did to me. I hope to understand the *why* of her actions one day; but before then, she is forgiven. Some of her actions made me who I am today—resilient. When I get a chance to meet her, I will approach her with open arms and love. Just like with "father" Tino, *an eye for an eye* is never going to be on the menu of my reunion with her, whenever it comes.

Back in Yaoundé, I find myself still dragging Nikasoh's image with me everywhere I go. Realizing I am paralyzed by my thoughts of her, I start searching for a way to possibly help her and probably others. There is not much time left before my return to the United

With father Tino, in front of his tiny barbershop

States. If I do not act soon, I will turn my back on her, and leave for my faraway world. Then she will slip back in the normalcy of her life of abuse, in full view of a blind congregation. I decide to attempt to rescue her by disclosing to Father Ernest that this secret too has been unveiled. As I am already very far from Bafoussam, I decide to write him a letter:

Mr. Ernest,
You are probably surprised to hear from me. I did
not intend to ever speak to you again, but I am now
forced to. I know you are raping a little girl, Nikasoh.
Sadly, she most probably is only one of many.
These are her or their unspoken words: Stop it!
Stop hurting her! Stop hurting them!
Joe Fotso

Feeling a little better and hoping my words produce the intended results, I start focusing on the rest of my agenda. There are still a few people I have not seen yet, including my "father" and Sita Fidèle. Each time Sita saw me in the past, she was always moved to tears, not believing that I, *Skirty Fotso*, was really the grown man standing in front of her. When we looked into one another's eyes, there was never a doubt about what we saw and felt: my rough past, the raw thrill of having survived, and the wonderful chills that only a son and his mom would have, reuniting for the first time in many years. I believe our emotions were beyond what we could ever put in words. We always ended up just enjoying the moments, like there was never that past, but a present that we were grateful to be living, and a future we were hungry to embrace. I am eager to reunite with her again, and it won't be long before I do. I have decided to make this day hers.

I walk down the same path I used to walk after a hard day of banana sales. Though it has been a long time, a lot of old faces are familiar. I don't dare introduce myself, as they would probably never believe it is me. I step on each bump of the dusty road, just like I used to, going downhill.

After rounding the corner and crossing the little wooden bridge, I move toward the tiny courtyard that used to serve as our hangout spot, our soccer field, our dance floor, and our boxing ring. I then run up the little hill to Sita's house and find Jo'o, one of her sons, napping on the couch. After looking around for a moment, I wake him up. "Hey, brother... up!" I say, gently shaking him by the shoulder.

He opens his eyes and sits up.

"Is that you?" he asks, incredulous, as no one expected me.

"Yes, Jo'o. How are you?" I question.

"Big brother, I don't know," he replies, standing up.

"You haven't changed, have you?" I joke around. "Where is my mom?"

"Who?" He sits back down. "Where have you been?"

"What do you mean?"

"She passed away."

"Noo! You are kidding, right?"

He shakes his head, and I know it's no joke. Sita, one of the most important people in my life, is no more. My mom is forever gone, and I will never experience her affectionate look again. Another huge void has opened around me. A feeling that I know too well invades my being, leaving me unable to think straight.

After crying tears of extreme sadness, I hurry to wipe my face, as I stand in front of her picture hung on a wall in the living room. I remember she never liked seeing my tears. She always wanted me as happy as she could make me, just like the other kids. Even though it's extremely difficult to keep a smile on my face like she always wanted, I am trying hard not to disappoint her. She deserves it from me, and I will honor her by being the best son I can be, saying "*Thank you!*" with a smile. I know she's gone to meet her daughter Bébé, who passed away just about a year ago. I am extremely hurt by Sita's death, but I am healed by my memories of the life she lived, the life she gave me, and the loving and compassionate person she was.

"She passed away last September, after a brief illness. Mom knew she was going to die, and she wanted to say goodbye to you. We tried but could not get in touch with you… Sita cried every day, calling your name. In the end, she left a message for you. She said she couldn't see the full man that you will become, but that she knew you would become one. That she was very proud of you, and that you should never forget your family…"

Sita Fidèle (Essombè Moussongo Epalè), 1945 - September 20, 2008
Rest in Peace

"Wow... I will not, Sita." I promise.

Jo'o informs me of where she was buried, and my next mission instantly becomes to go on a pilgrimage to her final resting place. I need to get as close to her as possible, before going as far as I will soon be going in just a few days. Her resting place is about 250 miles away, deep in the Bessoungkang village, in the Littoral Region. It takes Jo'o and me a little more than half a day to arrive there, and we head straight to Sita.

As we approach the cemetery, I really cannot define my feelings. A part of me is very sad and almost shaky, but the other part is actually excited, as if Sita will emerge from six feet under and hug me.

The graveyard finally comes to sight and I instantly start guessing which one of all these rectangular blocks is my mom's. I am not sure whether or not I will be able to contain my sadness, but I am not letting it show. I am zooming in on gravestones to locate *Sita Fidèle.*

"Here is Mom." Jo'o says, pointing at a little mount of soil, covered with flowers.

My heart sinks. It's very hard for me to imagine her down there, but I know she really is. I spend time remembering how that woman helped rescue a part of my childhood. I am profoundly sad, and all the tears in the world will never say it all.

After a few days, still hurt for having lost Sita, furious about Nikasoh's misfortune, disappointed for having missed Mama Marie, but proud of my face-to-face meeting with Father Ernest, my focus

Farewell to Sita Fidèle

shifts yet again. I have one more answer to seek. Since the tender age of nine, I have often thought of the day Erodiis, a teenager I looked up to, raped me. I have gone to bed so many times thinking about that horrible experience, trying to understand why, only to wake up with nightmares. As a child and into my teenage years, I clearly blamed myself for allowing it to happen. There was no doubt in my mind that it was my fault. Had I not followed him for his bananas, he would never have molested me. I would have just gone home to endure my punishment. As an adult, I now understand there is no justification—whatsoever—for that unforgivable act, the raping of a child. Erodiis irreversibly stole my innocence, and caused me to lose any trust for any teens or adults.

Tonight as I lie in bed thinking, I make the decision to find Erodiis. We both are adults now and I want to look him in the eye and ask him, *"Why? Why me? Why at all?"* I will demand to know how many other little boys he raped. I want to remind him of how he violently secured me to the ground by my neck. Then, I want to understand if I had escaped with my life, because had I not been able to fight back, it could have been an easy crime for him. Only he, God, and I share that secret.

I must seek answers. After seriously thinking about the horrific incident and the emotional pain that I endured over the years, I am resolved not to stop until I get some answers. Recollecting how Erodiis lured me infuriates me. It makes me want to find him and cut his penis and balls off. He knew exactly what he wanted, and he had it all planned. Abusing the innocence of a child, his plot was carried out with ease. I was too young. As a father now, I understand that rape is one of the worst things to ever happen to a child. I always keep an eye on my young son and sometimes I am afraid I may be sheltering him a little more than I should. I need to protect him from what happened to me decades ago. Looking back, I have often tried to understand what twist of fate pushed me into harm's way. I believe Mama Marie, unknowingly and unwillingly, had played a central role in the misfortune of my childhood. Had I had a loving or doting mother or father early on in my life, I would certainly not have been where I was on that day and at that time. I would certainly never have been raped.

I release the daydream of my past, along with my furious imagination, and fall fast asleep. Tomorrow, I hope, will bring me some long overdue answers.

Noise from shouting merchants and the beeping of loud car horns from impatient drivers has awakened me earlier than I hoped. My second-floor room at the Meumi Hotel, which is adjacent to the Nkol-Eton market, is very poorly insulated and provides very little isolation from exterior noise.

After about an hour, the time to begin my day arrives. My agenda has but one focus, which is to find Erodiis and have a man-to-man talk with him. I just can't fathom the idea of a moment alone—just the two of us—like on the day he stole my innocence. Because I still remember my fear, pain, and anger then, I have no idea what my raw emotions will bring upon him today. I am afraid to guess, but I think I will want to hold his big neck down like he held my tiny one that day, and watch him beg me for a gasp of air. I will then let go of his neck, but only to grab it back again a few seconds later, a little tighter than before as he wheezes.

As I step in the bathroom and find my toothbrush, a realization occurs to me: I am in Cameroon and not in the Unites States where personal rights are protected. With that, I also realize that I am about to discuss one of the most incendiary subjects in the world, the raping of a child.

My thoughts deepen and a dreadful story resurfaces in my mind, one that I remember as if it happened yesterday. After a young man was caught raping a little girl in the early 1990s, four automobile tires were securely draped over his body and set on fire. Desperately crying for mercy, he was burnt alive among applause from a merciless crowd of onlookers.

That was a rapist's fate then, and likely now. As my imagination populates images of Erodiis being lynched by an unforgiving crowd, my conscience urges me to take a firm step back and reconsider my intentions.

I understand he is now a married man with four young children. How can I be the reason for his public slaughter? Can I ever find sleep again if his kids are orphans? I should not punish his innocent family for a sin that he committed three decades ago. But how can I? The pain often seems as vivid as if he had just molested me. Despite all of my efforts, I find myself contemplating the possibility of forgiving the man who raped me and took away my sense of trust.

After thinking it over, I decide to let it go.

Chapter 28

Back Home

Prior to my return trip to the United States, I have made an impromptu visit to Bandjoun for a final farewell to my family, including my new wife, Gina. In fact, this trip has given me the opportunity to see her again for the first time since our wedding. She will continue to live with her parents after my departure, and while I file a petition for her entry into the United States. We should be separated only for about six months. In the meantime, we will do our best to keep in touch and allow our feelings to kindle and possibly deepen.

Although still confused by my new marital status, I am comforted by my Mom who does not miss her goodbye ritual. She blesses me with fresh branches of a peace tree—as usual.

I am now ready to return to hunting panthers and lions, eager to get back to my kids.

On February 19, 2009, as I board Air France Flight # 941L that is about to take me back to the United States, I am overwhelmed by emotions. Once again, I am leaving my mom, sisters, brothers, and friends. I am conscious that I will not see them again for about five years. The feelings I must bear for abandoning them seem to override all possible benefits of being away, so far away. However, I know I must go. I must not give up. I must not forget that I am going to pursue my American Dream. After all, my success will help make everyone I am currently walking away from better off. I must not stop.

Over the years, each of my visits has always left me with at least one thing that I will remember for the rest of my life. This time, for the first time, I found my mom walking with a cane, moving as slowly as I have ever seen her, and exhibiting frequent signs of memory loss. Age has taken a toll on her and at this point, only God knows whether or not I will ever see her alive again. After I discreetly wipe my tears, I incline my seat and cover myself with the light gray blanket offered by a flight attendant. I do not want to cry again. I do not want to spend my time being negative. As I close my eyes, I wish to only reopen them at JFK International Airport in New York.

The loud and shaky landing of the aircraft jolts me back to reality once again. I am now a married man. As I impatiently stand and reach up to retrieve my belongings in the overhead compartment, I am overpowered by the raw truth behind my own thoughts. I feel as if the exhausted passengers furtively looking at me are eyeing what seems to be engraved on my fatigued forehead:

"This over forty-year-old man has just married an eighteen-year-old girl he does not love."

The words are true, and I feel ashamed and awkward. My only hope now is that time nurtures my feelings toward my wife and that love ultimately blossoms and prevails.

I left Africa yesterday with tears in my eyes, only a few days after my arranged marriage. I felt cowardly to have walked away from my family again. Seeing my mom alive again appears uncertain. Hundreds of times during this trip, I have replayed images of her jovially blessing me and painfully saying goodbye, praying for these films of her not to be the last. I can never forget the sadness on her face as I walked away and gradually disappeared behind the banana trees of the east corner of her hut. I will always remember her trying to conceal her gloom during those last moments of seeing her son for the last time in years to come, or for the last time ever. No one on this flight can ever imagine all the mixed emotions I have just lived through during the eighteen-hour trip. Absolutely no one.

Today, February 20th, 2009, I have just landed in New York. I am here, in the Home of the Brave, to hunt lions and panthers, pieces of my American Dream. As I drag my burgundy canvas luggage through the aisle of the emptying aircraft, I am smiling to the flight attendants. This is where I now belong, on the Land of the Free. With each of my steps hereon, I am resolutely following the trail that will lead me to my prey.

Having reunited with my children and recovered from the exhausting trip, my daily routine has begun. My workload keeps me very busy and prevents me from overthinking. The few weeks that have elapsed so far have not changed my feelings for Gina, but I am still determined to make it work. My daily struggle might just be a sign that our marriage will never be one built out of love, but one of convenience. I must now understand that love is not for me anymore, and move on with what my inherent tradition and my mom have planned.

Although we now communicate a little better, the lack of chemistry between Gina and me is obvious. I have not found the courage or the immorality to ask her anything of a romantic nature, and I doubt I ever will. However, I hope that with some patience, we can get to be a normal couple, as she matures and we get to know one another better.

To allow myself a little more time to make peace with my bewildered feelings, I decide to wait a few more months before filing the USCIS petition for my wife. I want her to seem less of a stranger to me than the day we wed, before we live under the same roof and share the same little space.

As I get to work early today, I am eager to tackle the backlog that has piled up since my return from Africa. It will likely be a typical nine- or ten-hour workday. I will devote my few breaks to thinking about my fate with my wife. Thinking about her often can possibly seed some love in our marriage. All I will have to do then is to fortify it with my determination to have it, despite the high probability of never finding it.

I take a deep breath as I enter the building. At the end of the long hallway, an employee I have never seen before comes through the door that leads to my department. As we come closer, she looks straight up, almost avoiding any eye contact with me. I cannot help but look straight at her.

During the hours and days that follow, I have not been able to resist the temptation to go back to the front of the building and find out who the lady is. Today, an undefined force has propelled me into the main hallway. I am absolutely resolved to find the mysterious employee who seems to have vanished as quickly as she appeared in my sight and thoughts. As I approach the point where she made a sharp left turn a few days ago, I discreetly start scanning all the nearby offices and cubicles. Looking straight ahead, I cautiously sneak side-glances; I don't want to make it obvious that I am looking for someone. Maybe when I see her, I will understand why I am looking for her.

As I round another corner, I spot her seated in her cubicle and facing away. It only takes a fraction of a second for me to take in her physical appearance. With her blond hair down to her neck, she is wearing a long-sleeved blue-green sweater with black-and-white stripes, and a pair of black pants.

I proceed to pass by without disturbing her, but she hears my furtive footsteps and turns around. As she looks up, our eyes meet. She smiles at me, and then returns to her work. She is beautiful and I am charmed by the dimples on her cheeks. She certainly has no idea of what she has just done. The explanation I was looking for lies in the glitter of her bright eyes and the indescribable appeal of her beautiful smile. I instantly understand that my intuition has guided me here to glance into those eyes and experience the effect of that smile.

Over the course of the following days, something inside me pushes me toward her, always wanting me to lay eyes on her, even from a distance. When I do, the thrill that runs through me from head to toe always brightens my day. The feeling that follows is as priceless as it is confusing and scary. I think I have finally found love—at first sight. I don't even know her name, but I strongly believe she embodies what I had been looking for before marrying the woman my mother chose for me. Nonetheless, I am a married man, and I am a man of my word. No matter how unconvinced I was when I said, *"I do,"* I said it; and that's all that matters now. Am I allowed to fall in love with another woman? I shouldn't and I won't. If it is truly love that I am feeling for this stranger, I will have no other choice than to fight it until I conquer my heart back.

A week goes by, and I am on my way home from work. I have stopped in the parking lot to have a discussion with a colleague. A few minutes into the talk, the lady, whose name I have learned is Bree, appears and is coming straight at us. Although I say hello to her, we are still complete strangers to one another. I am, indeed, in love with her, and she has no idea whatsoever. Over these few days, in an attempt to keep my word to my family, I have secretly fought my attraction to her, but I find it impossible to resist. My inner struggle has only grown bigger. On the one hand, there is my loyalty to my mom and my word to the little girl I am married to, still thousands of miles away. But on the other hand, I am now only a few feet from the beautiful woman I love. Do I keep my dignity by upholding my commitment to my mom and the teenager she chose for me? Or do I keep my dignity by being loyal to myself, and not to them? At this moment, my heart pounds, making it very difficult to keep my equanimity. As she gets closer and I look into her beautiful eyes, I take a stand. I will keep my dignity by following my heart. I am no longer going to follow the road chosen by my mom. I will follow mine, the one my heart has paved for me.

Following my heart has led me straight to an emotional cul-de-sac, and I am forced to realize that Bree will never be mine. I believe Destiny sent her my way to open my eyes to the mistake

I made by marrying my eighteen-year-old wife. It is evident that I must free Gina and myself. On this day, March 12, 2010, I have filed for divorce at the Guilford County District Court Division in North Carolina and I hope it does not take too long to be granted.

Chapter 29

Audacious Love

By now you know how resilient I am; so don't be surprised to hear that I still have not given up on love. I just never quit. By nature, I need to love and be loved. My heart is resilient and audacious, and there is absolutely nothing I can do about it. After sailing in so many troubled waters, I have faith that my heart will one day capsize on the graceful shore of an evergreen island, away from all worries, fears, and tears, anchored to some harmony, joy, respect, and peace.

Chapter 30

The Back Mirror

E ven if it might have seemed like it at times, I have never let any situation drag me down. I have always found strength where many people would give up. It was that simple expression in French, the one I wrote on my windowsill, that kept me focused back then, and that still drives me these days, and always will:

LES AUTRES, POURQUOI PAS NOUS!? (*"Others, Why Not Us!?"*)

I was a fourteen-year-old boy, determined to make *it*, resolute to break out of the misery cycle that I saw around me. I now believe that line was left out of my destiny book, and that I managed to write it back. Each time it seemed impossible, I kept looking for that cracked door to force open. I absolutely refused to accept my fate, which would have left me lying down in the ruin of my dreams. I was on a crusade against poverty and misery, a crusade against my destiny. Once a year since 1997, when I arrived in the United States, I make sure my family enjoys the rare dishes the little boy I used to be expected in vain year after year: rice and tomato soup with fish, fried chicken, mixed spicy plantain and pork, and lots of soda and beer.

The lack of hugs and love just made me a loving and caring person later on, as I know how sad it is to be without. Ever since Mrs. Justine opened my eyes to love, I have never closed them. I would have liked her and her son Henry to know that I have survived and now have a family of my own. My kids are precious, and my love for them is as solid as a diamond.

I currently own at least one hundred and fifty pairs of shoes, mostly for the satisfaction of looking at them and feeling proud, as I certainly don't need that many. Each time I see a shoe, I automatically see myself decades ago, digging into grubby dumpsters for discarded sandals. I see myself stealing my own friend's shoes. This image of *that* depraved little boy just makes me want to buy more, and more, and more, just because I now can. Surprisingly as time passes, looking at all these belongings brings a feeling of guilt and sadness. I have started giving some away, for I have to give back. I have to add to my satisfaction of owning the joy of giving, sharing, and helping. It is a process I have started, and which shall never stop.

After growing up without toys, I have always wanted to have a house full of toys. I have never really lost my grip on my little toy car from Henry. In an attempt to fill the void left behind by that car and to make my daughter feel my childhood excitement, the very first toy I bought her was a yellow Mustang convertible with a remote control. Even now, I continue to buy remote control cars for Chris, whom I have spoiled with all kinds of toys. I have always wanted him to *have everything I wanted to have and be everything I wanted to be*, everything I was not fortunate enough to have or be—and more.

The recurrent anger and hunger in my childhood made me want to be a happy man in my adult life, well able to afford any food. I am often told that I seem happy, with a permanent big smile on my face. To me, I have already seen it all, and there is absolutely nothing more to be mad or sad about.

Epilogue

You have *seen* me grow up, and I am sure that in many instances you have wondered about a few decisions I have made. For instance, why did I take my wife back after having the black-on-white proof of what she had been up to with Father Ernest Mbubia, the Catholic priest? Only my pure and genuine love for her drove me to making that decision. Angel was the woman of my dreams, the one I had vowed to stand by unconditionally. And I did. My feelings for her may have bent a few times, but they never broke. They rose up and grew greener and stronger each time my heart started to limp. One had to know her to fully understand. I have opened up not because I want to demote her from the pedestal where she stood; certainly not because I want anyone to feel sorry for me either, but because I want everyone to see how complex loving someone can be. My sole intention is to show what a great woman Angel was, with her human complexity. She changed my life in all senses, and I am glad she is living through the two wonderful children—Milly and Chris—she left behind. They are the burning flames of my torch. I am now a happy single father of these two amazing kids.

Determined to find true love once again, I never gave up hope.

Along the way, a lot of people have carried me through those moments when some important pieces were missing from our life puzzle. I have only introduced some of them, not because I wanted to leave any out, but because I subconsciously left some of the best for last. In the past years, for instance, my kids and I have had the chance to be involved in my daughter's soccer team in Ossining, New York, and every girl of the Flash Team showered Chris with unforgettable attention and love. Flash became like a family to us, something we couldn't do without. I sometimes felt like Chris had sixteen sisters and fifteen moms. I want to express my gratitude to every one of them for contributing, perhaps unknowingly, to the social stability of my son and my family.

Flash Soccer Team, 2008: Standing up, left to right: *Frank Redzeposki (Assistant Coach), Juliana, Kendra, Briana, Camille, Katie, Olivia, Petra, Ani, and Armand Paganelli (Head Coach);* Down, left to right: *Milly, Jackie, Sarah, Liz, Emma, Victoria, Megan, and Estefania*

One of the greatest acquaintances in our lives in the United States has been Armand Paganelli, Head Coach of the Flash Soccer Team in New York. He is a kind, compassionate person with a big heart. Being around him and his family, including his wife Janice, his kids Nick, Chris, Olivia, and Gillian, as well as his brothers and sisters, has made me a better person. With Armand, life means love—and vice-versa. Around his family, love becomes a contagious disease, the only ailment I am ecstatic and grateful for having caught. My kids and I are grateful to have the Paganelli family in our lives.

During my difficult times as a grownup, I have rejected what I would call conventional therapy, only because I knew what was best for me. I prescribed myself a soccer regimen: two hours per dose (game), two to four times per week, rain or shine. It kept me focused, in shape, healthy, sane, and out of trouble. Soccer has always been what my body needs to lift my spirit. One of the last teams I played with was a group of deprived children in Africa, growing up like I did, but without abuse. Playing with this wonderful group of kids, a few of whom I am currently mentoring, was uplifting both for them and for me.

With little teammates in Bandjoun (Gloryland), Cameroon

I also would like to express my appreciation to Dr. Esaïe Deffo Tamboue; his help allowed the United States to rescue me from the social, professional, financial, and political turbulences of my adulthood in Cameroon.

I was very fortunate and humbled for finally having the life-time opportunity to meet the legendary Cameroonian singer, André Marie Tala, whose lyrics have carried me through the saddest and happiest moments of my existence. He is now one of my mentors in life.

In the end, if there were a few things to take home from my life, they would definitely be resilience, hope, love, and forgiveness.

No matter how deep in a swamp I have been, I always kept in mind that it could have been a lot worse, and that the end of that dark tunnel was soon to come. When I appeared crushed, I always refused to lie down where I stumbled, in the rubble of my dreams. Instead, I dreamed through those ruins, because I believed there always was a way out. It was up to me to find *it*, which I did time and time again, helped by a mighty hand, be it God's, my ancestors', my father's, my Angel's later on, or a combination of all. I held on to hope dearly. It was and still is my life jacket. I would drown if I lose it.

Having struggled so much for love has earned me the right to ascertain that no one should ever grow up or live without some. I have gone through crushing periods of emptiness when I felt as if I was not loved at all or not loved enough. I have learned from those dreadful moments, and I am now tenacious in love. I continue to fight, pray, and hope for my hidden love to be revealed. I am certain my day is close.

Finally, I have experienced the power of forgiveness. It's seldom easy to forgive, but it is always wonderful when one does. It's dignifying and fulfilling. After an abominable childhood, I have found the strength to forgive my adoptive parents. Today, I am still struggling about how to forgive Erodiis, the boy who raped me decades ago, and the two Catholic priests whose immoral acts changed my life and shook the roots of my faith and beliefs. How do I forgive someone who pinned my tiny neck down, suffocating me and sexually molested me as I desperately attempted to scream, gasping for air? How do I forgive those priests, Father Ernest Mbubia and Father Igor Thomas Kuate, whom my wife and my fiancée, in an unusual twist of fate, respectively cheated on me with—time and time again? How can I forgive Father Ernest Mbubia for molesting the little Nikasoh? How can I forgive that diabolic man of God despite the likelihood that at least one more of the little girls I saw mopping his floor was his toy? How can I?

My biological father has been a driving force in my existence.

I was him, proudly.

I will take the first copy of this book—*HURT*—to his grave, and whisper, "*Hi, Father. I just wanted to let you know that no one has taken what's mine. Look at what I have brought home, one of the*

My sister, feeding our ancestors' skulls with palm oil and salt

panthers. But the hunt is not over yet; I am out now to get a lion. I know you are sweeping my way, and I will not falter. I am you... proudly. Thank you, Father." Then, I will ceremonially *feed* him some palm oil and salt before getting back to the lion's trail.

My whole life has been shaped by the countless misfortunes I have endured. Without them, I would, without a doubt, never have had enough strength to be who I am and where I am today. Each strike from the electric cord and each of the tears dripping down on my dusty cheeks were a wakeup call to my determination and my focus, which I have never lost. With each wave of hunger, I became more resilient. Losing every single one of my toenails many times as I grew up barefoot only infused in me the drive to make it, to never give up. Each time I put my hand in my *father's* moneybag, the shame gave me a million reasons to be more than just a thief. Today, I stand tall and strong, and I aspire to stand even taller and stronger. I have endured everything for a reason, and I know I have a purpose in life that I have yet to serve. My son and I escaped the tight grip of AIDS for a reason.

Just like in the 1980's, President Paul Biya of Cameroon is still in power with no intention of ever letting go of it. Through decades, he has established himself as one of the many presidents in Africa who would only lose to death, creating and maintaining an atmosphere of intimidation and fear around him and throughout the country. In 1992, he won a close presidential election by only 40% of the votes against 36% for John Fru Ndi, but won the next election in 1997 by a landslide (93%), despite the country's socio-economic situation going from bad to worse in five years. Through his on-going over-thirty years of careless reign, he has contributed to the dilapidation of Cameroon's wealth and brought the whole country to its knees. As I now feel safe with my country—the United States—I must decry it!

We currently reside in the Chicago, Illinois area, where I am a manager in one of the world's leading pharmaceutical companies. I continue to meet wonderful people, to enjoy my new life environment and my passion for soccer and writing. I have started writing a sequel to my life story, as my journey on earth continues to be sometimes exciting, often challenging, and always full of shocking anecdotes to share, and lessons to be learned.

I also would like to express my sincere gratitude to the United States of America for rescuing me. It took away my fears, wiped my tears, and rewarded all the efforts I made through my long crusade against destiny. Every time I stand to salute the flag of my country with my right palm on my heart, I feel great pride. With the Star-Spangled Banner echoing in my grateful ears, I am moved to tears. I know *I* belong. I know *I* am! I know *I* made it. No one took what's mine. Thank you for the opportunity, the hope, and the freedom. May God bless the United States of America.

I want to thank you—you, the readers—for bearing with me through my life in words. I am honored and extremely humbled that you listened to what the little boy I once was had to say, and what the grown man I now am has to share. Thanks for being that ear I longed for all those years. In part because you have listened and supported me through my journey, I am healed.

CPSIA information can be obtained
at www.ICGtesting.com
Printed in the USA
LVHW04s2302010518
575645LV00001B/43/P